Robert E. Howard

ALSO BY LEON NIELSEN
AND FROM McFARLAND

*Arkham House Books:
A Collector's Guide* (2004)

Robert E. Howard

A Collector's Descriptive Bibliography of American and British Hardcover, Paperback, Magazine, Special and Amateur Editions, with a Biography

LEON NIELSEN

with a foreword by Damon C. Sasser

McFarland & Company, Inc., Publishers
Jefferson, North Carolina, and London

> The present work is a reprint of the illustrated case bound edition of *Robert E. Howard: A Collector's Descriptive Bibliography of American and British Hardcover, Paperback, Magazine, Special and Amateur Editions, with a Biography,* first published in 2007 by McFarland.

LIBRARY OF CONGRESS CATALOGUING-IN-PUBLICATION DATA

Nielsen, Leon.
    Robert E. Howard : a collector's descriptive bibliography of American and British hardcover, paperback, magazine, special and amateur editions, with a biography / Leon Nielsen ; with a foreword by Damon C. Sasser.
       p.   cm.
    Includes bibliographical references and index.

    ISBN 978-0-7864-6109-7
    softcover : 50# alkaline paper ∞

    1. Howard, Robert Ervin, 1906–1936—Bibliography. 2. Fantasy fiction, American—Bibliography. 3. Howard, Robert Ervin, 1906–1936. 4. Authors, American—20th century—Biography. I. Title.
Z8419.5.N54   2011
[PS3515.O842]
016.81352—dc22   2006033193

British Library cataloguing data are available

© 2007 Leon Nielsen. All rights reserved

No part of this book may be reproduced or transmitted in any form or by any means, electronic or mechanical, including photocopying or recording, or by any information storage and retrieval system, without permission in writing from the publisher.

On the cover: Robert E. Howard in 1934; art from *The Hour of the Dragon* (both images © Glenn Lord)

Manufactured in the United States of America

McFarland & Company, Inc., Publishers
  Box 611, Jefferson, North Carolina 28640
    www.mcfarlandpub.com

To Glenn Lord,
who preserved the literary legacy of Robert E. Howard,
made his writings available to new generations
and kept the torch burning in the darkness—
this work is gratefully dedicated.

Acknowledgments

In the preparation of the manuscript for this book, I want to express my appreciation first and foremost to Glenn Lord, the author of the Robert E. Howard bio-bibliography *The Last Celt* (Donald M. Grant Publishers, Inc., 1976). The book is out of print, but copies may be obtained from antiquarian booksellers. Glenn Lord, a devoted Howard admirer, collector and former agent of the heirs to Howard's literary work, has done more than anyone else to keep the works of Robert E. Howard alive and accessible to the public. Without the dedicated and unflagging effort of Glenn Lord to preserve and perpetuate Howard's works, this book would not have been a viable undertaking.

I would also like to acknowledge the invaluable information I found on Robert E. Howard dedicated Internet Web sites. These include, but are not limited to www.rehupa.com (this site has a number of related links and forums), www.rehoward.com, www.gentzel.com, www.howardworks.com, www.robert-e-howard.org, www.thecimmerian.com, www.barbariankeep.com, www.wanderingstarbooks.com and www.rehtwogunraconteur.com.

The Web sites provided a considerable amount of detailed information and are well worth visiting by anyone who wants to know more about Robert E. Howard, the man, the writer, his work and literary legacy.

A special acknowledgment of gratitude goes to Glenn Lord and Rusty Burke, recognized Robert E. Howard scholars, for reviewing the manuscript, answering questions, providing suggestions and corrections, and adding new information, which greatly enhanced the quality and usefulness of the finished work. Glenn Lord graciously gave permission to reprint material from his book *The Last Celt* and from other texts copyrighted by him, and offered sound advice on the bio-bibliographical compilation.

I am indebted to Damon C. Sasser, for taking time out of his busy schedule to look over the manuscript and write the foreword. With his profound knowledge of Robert E. Howard, Damon Sasser was a leading candidate for the task of penning the foreword. Furthermore his comments, additions and corrections to the manuscript added immeasurably to the completeness of the book's title description chapter.

My sincere appreciation goes to Jim Baen of Baen Publishing Enterprises, John Betancourt of Wildside Press, April Derleth of Arkham House Publishers, Inc., Jo Fletcher of Victor Gollancz, The Penguin Group (USA) Inc., and the University of Nebraska Press, who gave permission to reprint book covers as indicated in the text. I also wanted to express my gratitude to Jack Baum, Barbara Baum and Terry Baum Rogers of Robert E. Howard Properties, LLC., for their cooperation, encouragement, comments and thoughtful personal regards.

This is not the work of a single author. Much of the information provided herein was obtained from the sources listed in the reference bibliography at the end of the book. Every author listed has in some way added to the sum total of the present work. While this book would not have been possible without the references, assistance and encouragement provided by the aforementioned individuals and literary sources, any errors or omissions in the text are the sole responsibility of the author.

Contents

Acknowledgments	vii
Foreword by Damon C. Sasser	1
Introduction	5
1. Robert E. Howard: A Brief Biography	11
2. The Robert E. Howard Legacy	36
3. A Robert E. Howard Cast of Characters	80
4. Collecting Robert E. Howard	105
A. *Identification, Condition, Grading*	105
B. *Values, Buying and Selling*	124
5. A Robert E. Howard Bibliography	134
A. *Books*	135
B. *Mass Market Paperbacks*	168
C. *Magazines*	200
D. *Special Publications*	211
E. *Amateur Press Journals*	227
6. Most Collectible Titles	247
7. A Representative Robert E. Howard Collection	253
8. Reference Bibliography	260
Index to Poems and Prose Poems	263
Index to Story Titles	268
Index to Book Titles	275

Trumpets die in the loud parade,
The gray mist drinks the spears,
Banners of glory sink and fade
In the dust of a thousand years.
Singers of pride the silence stills,
The ghost of empire goes,
But a song still lives in the ancient hills,
And the scent of a vanished rose.
Ride with us on a dim, lost road
To the dawn of a distant day,
When swords were bare for a guerdon rare—
The Flower of Black Cathay.

—From *Red Blades of Black Cathay* by
Robert Ervin Howard
(1906–1936)

Foreword
by Damon C. Sasser

I was very flattered and honored when Leon Nielsen contacted me about writing the foreword for his new bio-bibliography of Robert E. Howard. While several other bibliographies have popped up in the past 30 years, it has been way too long since a comprehensive volume was published. The one and only other was *The Last Celt* by Glenn Lord, published in 1976, and it was a benchmark event in Howardom. Long anticipated and much appreciated by the legion of Howard fans, no one other than Glenn could have written and compiled such a magnificent book. Leon certainly had big shoes to fill and he has proved to be equal to the task.

My first exposure to Howard came in 1972 when a bookstore clerk suggested I read Lancer Books' *Conan the Conqueror*. Shortly after that I picked up issue # 17 of Marvel's *Conan the Barbarian* comic book and I was hopelessly hooked. More than three decades later I'm still collecting Howard and am always on the look-out for tools that make collecting easier and more enjoyable. The present work certainly fills the bill.

We all know what we like in the way of Howard material and collectors come in all shapes and sizes. For some collectors first editions are a must have. Some of those collectors are satisfied with only those editions, while others collect every edition published. Some just collect the "Big Four" (Conan of Cimmeria, Solomon Kane, Kull and Bran Mak Morn), while others go for it all. Still others stick with a particular genre (fight stories, westerns, historical fiction, etc.). No matter what type of collector you are, you'll find this volume helpful and very user friendly.

Of course, everyone has his favorite Howard characters and I'm no different. In addition to Conan and Solomon Kane, I particularly enjoy the Turlogh O'Brien, Cormac Fitzgeoffrey and Francis X. Gordon ("El Borak") stories. Howard's imagination and writing style could take one just about anywhere in the world and indeed beyond. In addition to being great reading, it's downright fun to scour out various Howard editions or that one rare story you've always wanted to read.

Having said all that, this volume is an excellent tool for both the beginner and long time collectors. Within these pages you will find a well organized guide with a wealth of Howard material, which is cross-referenced for easy reading. This book is a virtual database of knowledge, containing valuable information on all aspects of collecting Howard, including how to grade, buy and sell Howard material. From the first page of the brief biography of Howard through the last page of the reference bibliography, this collector's guide is a treasure trove to the Howard collector. Everything Howard is catalogued here, including the Holy Grail of Howard books, the Jenkins 1937 edition of *A Gent from Bear Creek*.

So how did we get where we are today with this new collector's guide? Everyone knows Howard was born in 1906 and lived just thirty short years. While he was alive, the majority of Howard's stories first appeared in the pulps from 1925 to 1936, with the remaining unpublished yarns being published posthumously. From the late 1930s to the early 1960s Howard appeared in print sporadically (first in pulp reprints, and later in three Arkham House anthologies and Gnome Press's Conan editions). Then, in the late 1960s, the Lancer Conan paperbacks appeared and were a precursor to a new age of Howard publishing.

Under the guidance of literary agent Glenn Lord, a boom in Howard material materialized in the 1970s. Hardcover books, paperbacks, comics, fanzines, and limited edition booklets were published at a breakneck pace. In the early eighties, this publishing frenzy tapered off, but the interest was still there, albeit carried on by a few small publishers who regularly published some of Howard's more obscure and unpublished fiction (a lot of this material were juvenalia and fragments). After a long drought, a set of eight paperbacks collecting some of Howard's best stories were published in the mid-1990s by Baen Publishing Enterprises. Yet a new age in Howard publishing was born in 1998 when Wandering Star began publishing a string of deluxe hardcover books, the first being *The Savage Tales of Solomon Kane*. Wildside Press, Del Rey Books, and Bison Books followed and soon new fan publications emerged and old ones were revived. Howard fans rejoiced at their newfound fortune—stories long out of print were back and with fully restored texts to boot!

Today interest is still on the rise and fans are enjoying a resurgence in publishing coinciding with the centennial of Howard's birth in 2006. While this new "boom" pales in comparison to the publishing frenzy of the 1970s, it is welcome nonetheless. Renewed interest means new readers, who will propel a demand that more Howard material be published.

Some fans take collecting a step further and visit Howard's home town, hoping to get closer to the man and writer. A stalwart, die-hard group of fans led by members of the Robert E. Howard United Press Association

(REHupa) gathers each June in Howard's home town of Cross Plains, Texas, to celebrate his life and writings. Located in the center of Texas, Cross Plains has a population of just over a thousand and looks pretty much as it did during Howard's lifetime. For nearly 20 years this group has met the second weekend in June (to coincide with the date of Howard's death). The two-day event brings people of all ages and backgrounds together for discussion panels, guest speakers, a banquet, and tours of the Cross Plains area, culminating in a sunset barbeque dinner.

The 2006 Howard Days was the centennial of Howard's birth with an expanded schedule of events. Anyone interested in getting on the mailing list for the yearly event can write Project Pride, P.O. Box 534, Cross Plains, Texas 76443. Tours of the Howard house are available at no charge year-round.

The centerpiece of this annual gathering is the house, owned, fully restored and cared for by Project Pride (a local nonprofit organization). Adjacent to the house is an outdoor pavilion used by Howard fans to congregate, swap tales and listen and participate in discussion panels. The small white frame house has been restored and furnished to reflect the Depression era in which Howard lived. Just behind the master bedroom is a tiny room about the size of an average walk-in closet in which Howard slept and worked for half of his life. The room is actually a porch that was converted to a second bedroom for Howard. It is hard to imagine how a big man like Howard could comfortably write in such a small space, even more so when you consider the fantastic worlds and adventures born in such cramped quarters.

Howard's tormented last days were spent in this house, standing by helplessly as his beloved mother slipped away. Scholars and casual readers alike ruminate on what led to that fateful event on the morning of June 11, 1936. Certainly his mother's impending demise played into it. However, despite all the essays and arguments, there is no simple answer. Howard took the real reasons for his suicide to his grave. He wrote these poetic last words shortly before he walked out of the house and to his car where he ended his life with a bullet:

> All fled, all done
> So lift me on the pyre
> The feast is over
> And the lamps expire.

The lamps never expired. Each of the stories written by Howard is a bright flame burning and as long as we keep reading and collecting those wonderful tales, those flames will burn eternal.

Damon C. Sasser is a lifelong Robert E. Howard fan and collector. A native of Texas, Mr. Sasser is the editor and publisher of two Howard magazines, REH: Two-Gun Raconteur *and* The Chronicler of Cross Plains.

Introduction

My first encounter with the writings of Robert Ervin Howard happened on a rainy evening in the spring of 1976 in Calgary, Alberta, Canada. I was making a few purchases in a Super S drugstore on the south side of the city, when I noticed two paperbacks on a book display rack near the checkout counter. More than the titles or the name of the author, of whom I knew little, it was the cover art by Jeff Jones that caught my eyes. The books were titled *The Book of Robert E. Howard* (Zebra Books, 1976) and *The Second Book of Robert E. Howard* (Zebra Books, 1976).

I recognized the author's name as that of a late pulp writer on whose characters the 1970 Marvel comic book series *Conan the Barbarian* and the 1971 Marvel fantasy magazine *Savage Tales* were loosely based. The cover art showed Nordic warriors and perhaps because I was born and raised in Denmark, with a keen appreciation of my Viking heritage, I picked up one of the paperbacks and skimmed through its pages. After reading a couple of paragraphs of storyline and poetry, I realized that I had chanced upon the work of an exceptional writer with a unique talent for powerful, descriptive storytelling, an intensely compelling writing style and an inexhaustible imagination.

I bought the books and read them cover to cover. As with most anthologies, I found that not all of the stories or poems were equally well plotted or composed, but after turning the last page of the second volume, I wanted to read more of the works by this remarkable storyteller. The front matter of *The Book of Robert E. Howard* included a brief biographical sketch of Howard's short life and tragic death written by Glenn Lord, the editor of the books. These few pages gave me a glimpse into the life of an exceptional and prolific young writer, who turned out page after page of heroic adventures, westerns, horror, boxing and fantasy stories from a small room in a frame house in the little central Texas town of Cross Plains. In the process, some of his best known works gave momentum to a unique, emerging trend in fantasy literature, the sword and sorcery genre.

With the Zebra books as a starting point, followed by the Ace Books reprint of the Lancer Books Conan mixture of original text, revisions and

The Book of Robert E. Howard. Zebra Books 1976. Cover art by Jeff Jones. © 1976 Glenn Lord.

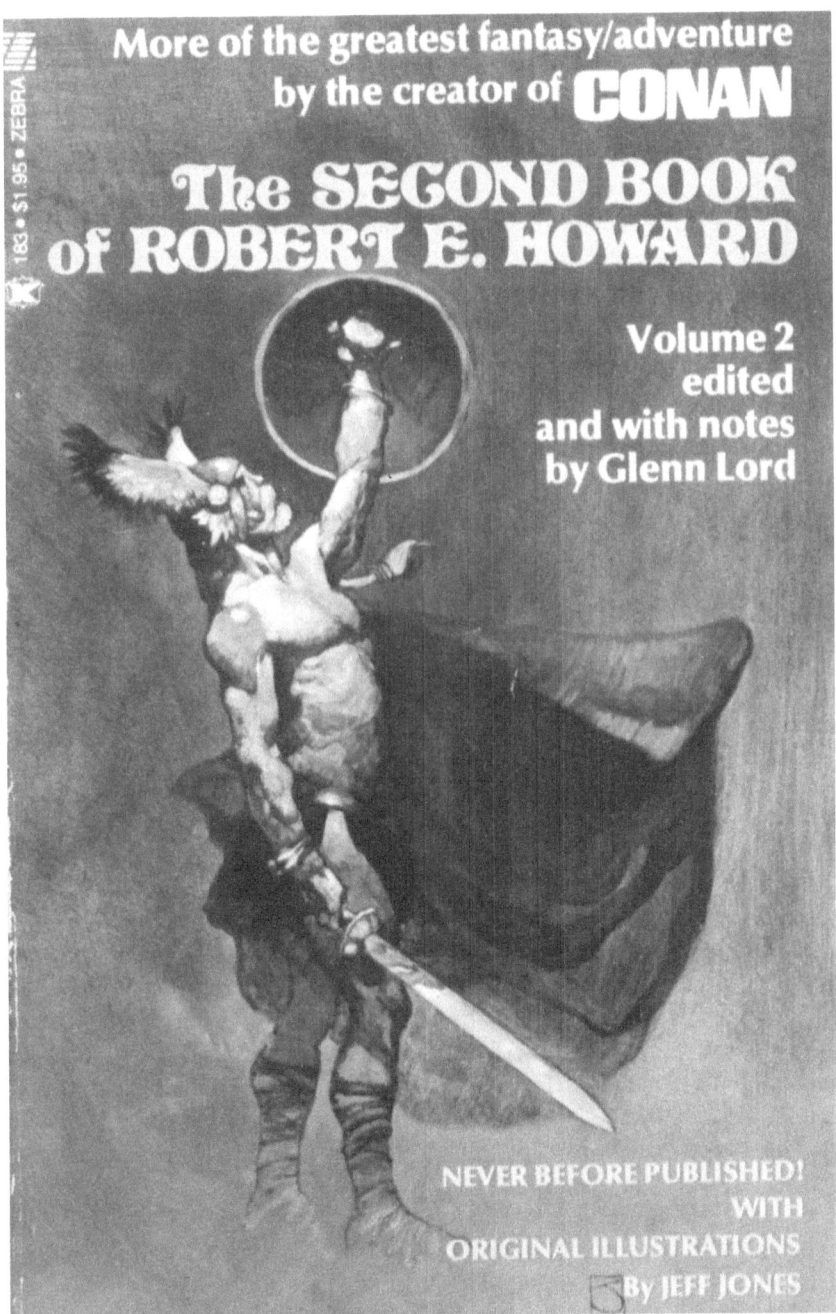

The Second Book of Robert E. Howard. Zebra Books 1976. Cover art by Jeff Jones.
© 1976 Glenn Lord.

pastiches and the Berkley corrected editions, my Robert E. Howard paperback library grew. Following a career change in the 1980s, I moved to the United States and discovered the hardcover editions by Arkham House, Gnome Press, Donald M. Grant, and Fax Collector's Editions. This opened a new realm of collecting potential and I acquired the six volume Conan series by Gnome Press, followed by several Grant and Fax volumes. Since then I have continued to build my Howard collection.

In the 70 years after his death, volumes have been written and much speculation has been articulated both favorably and unfavorably about Robert E. Howard, the man, his life and his works. I have by choice abstained from expressing my personal views or perceptions of Robert E. Howard, nor have I engaged in any literary criticism of his writings. These matters, I believe, are best reserved for the proper scholarly media. In the preparation of the text I have followed the narrow path of the bio-bibliographer and purposely left out opinions and speculations. With this said, I have included some personal observations on specific items or bibliographical topics which may be helpful to the collector.

This book evolved primarily from my personal interest in Howard's writing and the experience gained from collecting, buying and selling his works for better than 25 years. The principal motivation was the perceived need for a portable, concise and current source of information. Accordingly I compiled the book mainly to be a useful, ready reference for collectors, readers, antiquarian booksellers, and libraries. It was not intended to be a scholarly dissertation or a criticism of Robert E. Howard's literary work.

The table of contents is traditionally organized. The opening chapter on Robert E. Howard's life is followed by a chapter on Howard's literary legacy and a chapter that highlights some of his best known characters. This is succeeded by a chapter on points of book collecting, identification, grading, buying, selling and associated topics. The latter was included for the purpose of information and to standardize the terminology used to identify and describe collectible books and magazines. Although more comprehensive volumes have been written on these matters, the comments herein, brief as they are, may provide a measure of guidance for both new and seasoned collectors. For more detailed information on the life and works of Robert E. Howard, and book collecting in general, I recommend the titles listed in the reference bibliography.

The major part of the book consists of a bibliography of Robert E. Howard's work as it is generally known at the time of writing; however, new material is still being published. Included in the bibliography are books, mass market paperbacks, magazines, special publications and amateur press publications. Although Robert E. Howard's stories have been translated into many foreign languages, I have limited the bibliography to material published in the United States and the United Kingdom. Also omitted are fantasy and science fiction anthologies that reprint single Howard stories, comic books, and the multitude of pastiches, editions, revisions, corrections and posthumous collaborations which do not include original work. Few authors have been as imitated as Robert E. Howard, particularly his Conan, Bran Mak Morn, King Kull, Cormac Mac Art and Red Sonya characters. At least a dozen fantasy writers have tried their hand at rewriting or reinventing the works of Howard.

The book concludes with chapters on a personal selection of the most collectible titles, a representative Howard collection, a reference bibliography and three indexes which should make the text easier to navigate. For the sake of completeness, current catalog values have been added to each title; however, price guides are often outdated before they are published and the book trade is as volatile as any other collectible market. The values listed herein should always be considered in the light of their timeliness and the current demand for a specific title.

It would have been preferable to show images of the cover of each title listed in the text; however, since that would have required considerably more space, volume restrictions necessitated a reduction in illustrations to a much lesser number. Also it proved difficult to identify the copyright holders of many of the printings listed herein and subsequently obtain cover or jacket reprint permission. Regrettably there was little I could do to remedy this and I apologize for the lack of some relevant illustrative material. In all cases the cover and jacket art used herein is reproduced from original copies. All cover art and photographs shown are copyrighted by their respective owners. Many of the illustrations are used in accordance with the provisions of the fair use concept of the copyright law of the United States.

Every possible effort has been made to ensure the accuracy of Internet addresses provided as references in the text at the time of publication. However, I cannot assume responsibility for errors or changes in Internet addresses or Web site contents that may occur after publication.

During his brief, but intensively productive writing career, Robert E. Howard produced a gargantuan amount of material, some of which was lost and some that still has to be recovered. Many of his stories, poems, fragments and other writings have been published only in lesser known magazines, private printings and amateur press journals. Although I have attempted to cover the range of Howard's known works, it is inevitable that some pieces may have slipped through the cracks and will be missed or that some data are incomplete. There may also be and probably is disagreement among Howard scholars and collectors on which material should or should not be included in a bibliography. I apologize for and assume complete responsibility for any omissions, failings or errors. Perhaps I will have the opportunity to address such shortcomings in future printings.

1
Robert E. Howard: A Brief Biography

Introduction

When the July 1925 issue of the magazine *Weird Tales* appeared on the nation's newsstands, it included among stories by its more prominent contributors, such as H.P. Lovecraft, E. Hoffmann Price, Henry S. Whitehead and Seabury Quinn, a short tale by an unknown, young writer from Texas, Robert E. Howard. The title of the story was "Spear and Fang" and it recounted the rivalry between a Cro-Magnon and a Neanderthal. The following issue of *Weird Tales*, August 1925, carried another story by Howard, a short werewolf tale titled "In the Forest of Villefére." Its longer sequel, "Wolfshead," appeared as the cover story in the April 1926 issue. From these humble beginnings evolved a relationship between *Weird Tales* and Robert E. Howard that eventually would make him, together with H.P. Lovecraft and Clark Ashton Smith, one of the magazine's three most enduring contributors.

During his brief but prolific writing career, Robert E. Howard also contributed to other pulp magazines such as *Action Stories, Argosy, Cowboy Stories, Fight Stories, Oriental Stories, The Magic Carpet Magazine, Spicy-Adventure Stories, Strange Tales* and *Top Notch*, but it was the editor at *Weird Tales*, Farnsworth Wright, who gave Howard his start as a writer. Without that happening, we might never have known this exceptional storyteller and Conan of Cimmeria, Solomon Kane, Bran Mak Morn, King Kull of Atlantis and the many other unforgettable characters who inhabited Howard's fantastic worlds and would not have made their way into our hearts and memories. On the other hand, with his unique and considerable talent as a writer, it is possible that a more mature and accomplished Howard successfully may have turned his effort and attention to other markets, as many contemporary fantasy and adventure writers did, as the Depression took its toll and the popularity of the pulp magazines began to fade. We shall never known.

Wolfshead. Cover art by E.M. Stevenson. *Weird Tales*, April 1926. © 1976. Glenn Lord.

The Complete Action Stories. Wildside Press 2003. Jacket artist unknown. © 2001 Paul Herman.

Autobiographical Notes

Robert E. Howard did not write a proper autobiography. In 1928 he finished a semi-autobiographical novel titled *Post Oaks and Sand Roughs* (Donald M. Grant, 1990), which he tried unsuccessfully to get published at the time. The novel recounts four years (1924–1928) in the life of Steve Costigan (a familiar name in the Howard canon), a struggling young story writer, his passions, triumphs and discontents. The novel is a lightly disguised autobiography, in which Howard's hometowns Cross Plains and Brownwood becomes "Lost Plains" and "Redwood," and his real-life friends, acquaintances and writings may be identified without much effort. Glenn Lord, who wrote the introduction, has furthermore provided an identification index of names, places and literary works mentioned in the book. The last 20 pages are purely fictitious, but the remainder of the novel is close enough to be recognized for its autobiographical qualities.

Other sources of autobiographical information may be found in Howard's voluminous correspondence. In a letter to Farnsworth Wright, the editor of *Weird Tales*, Robert E. Howard wrote in the summer of 1931:

> In your last letter you asked me to give you some information about myself. Well—it's risky to get a writer talking about himself; ask him to give a brief resume of his accomplishments and he's very likely to inflict his whole biography and philosophy to you.
>
> I noticed that question about my being a professor, etc., in "The Eyrie" [the reader's letter column in *Weird Tales*]. Well, if it had not been for a scourge of cholera, I'd have been a Californian instead of a Texan. Cholera hit a band of '49ers on the Arkansas River and wiped out all but seven of the party of nineteen; others were so weakened by the disease they had to turn back, one of whom was William Benjamin Howard—whose grandson I have the honor to be.
>
> Well—my tale is soon told. I come of old pioneer American stock. By nationality I am predominantly Gaelic, in spite of my English name—some three-fourths Irish, while the rest is a mixture of English, Highland Scotch, and Danish. I was born in a little, fading ex-cowtown about forty-five miles west of Ft. Worth. Practically all my life has been spent in the country and small towns, outside a few brief sojourns in New Orleans and some of the Texas cities. I have only a high school education and not a particularly elaborate one at that.
>
> Like the average man, the tale of my life would merely be a dull narrative of drab monotony and toil, a grinding struggle against poverty. I have spent most of my time in the hard, barren, semi-waste lands of Western Texas, and since my childhood my memory holds a continuous grinding round of crop failures—sandstorms—drouths—floods—hot winds that withered the corn—hailstorms that ripped the grain to pieces—late blizzards that froze the fruit in the bud—plagues of grasshoppers and boll weevils that stripped the cotton. I remember year-long drouths that killed the very mesquite trees, when the

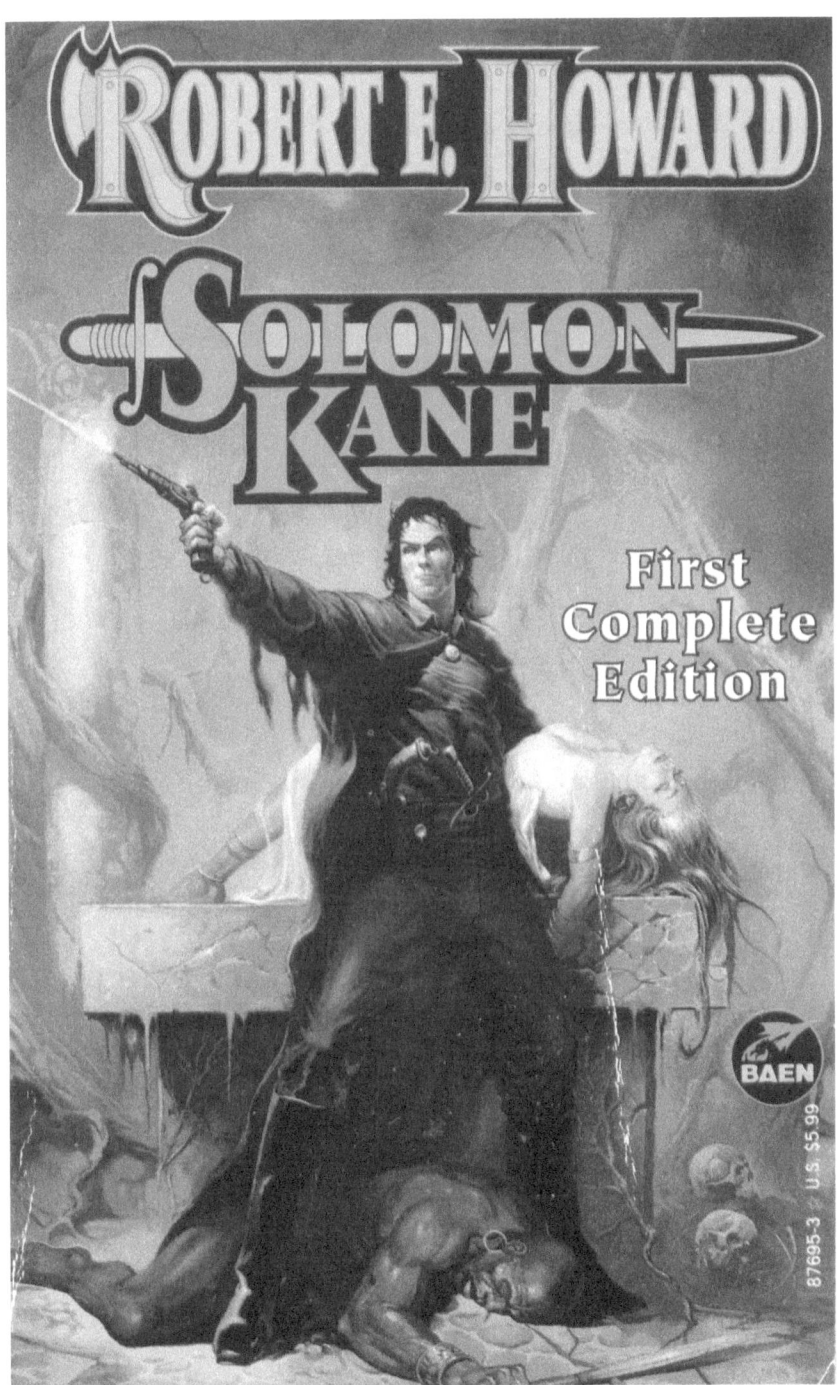

Solomon Kane. Baen Publishing Enterprises 1996. Cover art by Ken Kelly. © 1995 Baen Books.

Bran Mak Morn. Baen Publishing Enterprises 1996. Cover art by Ken Kelly. © 1996 Baen Books and Glenn Lord.

streams ran dry and the cattle ate cactus until their mouths and bellies were stuck full of spines, and then lay down and died when even the cactus was gone.

My boyhood was spent in the oil country—or rather oil came into the country when I was still a young boy, and remained. I'll say one thing about an oil boom; it will teach a kid that Life's a pretty rotten thing about as quick as anything I can think of.

I've worked at several jobs, but wasn't a success at any of them; I've picked cotton, helped brand a few yearlings, hauled a little garbage, worked in a grocery store, ditto a dry-goods store, worked in a law office, jerked soda, worked up in a gas office, tried to be a public stenographer, packed a surveyor's rod, worked up oil field news for some Texas and Oklahoma papers, etc., etc., and also etc.

I've always had a honing to make my living by writing, ever since I can remember, and while I haven't been a howling success in that line, at least I've managed for several years now to get by without grinding at some time clock-punching job. There's freedom in this game; that's the main reason I chose it. As [Robert W.] Service says:

"In belly-pinch I will pay the price
But God let me be free—
For once I know in the long ago
They made a slave of me."

Life's not worth living if somebody thinks he's in authority over you.

You gave me my start in the racket by buying my first story—"Spear and Fang." I was eighteen years old at the time. Pounding out a living at the writing game is no snap—but the average man's life is no snap, whatever he does. I'm merely one of a huge army, all of whom are bucking the line one way or another for meat in their bellies—which is the main basic principle and reason and eventual goal of Life. Every now and then one of us finds the going too hard and blows his brains out, but it's all in the game, I reckon.

And after all, even the bitterness of existence has certain compensations, slight though they may be. To be brought up in the lap of luxury, to live a life of idle pleasure—never to know the bite of the cold, the sting of heat, the pangs of hunger, and the agony of unceasing toil, the black bitterness of failure, the sordities of poverty, the blood, the grime, and the sweat—to live such a life is to miss the full grip of human realities. The best way a man can live is by hard slugging, and the best way he can die is with his boots on.

Well, I started to tell you something about myself, but there's so little to tell, I'm rather at a loss as to what to say. I've been working at the writing racket pretty regularly since the age of fifteen and hope eventually to get somewhere. It's a game I honestly love, and praises the readers have been kind enough to give me in "The Eyrie" have given me an immense amount of sincere pleasure.

I was lucky enough to discover early in life what I wanted to do, though I've done a great deal of wandering in bewildered circles, even so. And here and now, apart and aside from the subject, I want to make a prediction: that the Southwest is entering what I believe will prove to be a gigantic literary boom, and the next generation will see this section of the country fictionized, dramatized, and glorified generally. I believe the reading public is growing weary of the pseudo-psychological rot and ultra-sophisticated muck the writers of the present predominant school have been inflicting upon it, and is turning more and more to a cleaner, more wholesome phase of life, such as is exemplified by the epics of exploration, conquest, and settlement. And certainly the history of the Southwest is rich in drama. And I shall be glad to see my part of the country come into its own—my people had no hand in the very early conquest of the Southwest—they were all Southern slave holders who drifted West after being ruined by the Civil War—but they all had a part in the settlement and development. And so I feel linked to the country, not only by birth but by descent and tradition.

And there I believe is about all the information I can give about a very humdrum and commonplace life.

The Early Years

Robert Ervin Howard was born on January 22, 1906, in the small Texas town of Peaster, west of Fort Worth, the only child of Dr. Isaac Mordecai Howard and Hester Jane Ervin Howard. The family ancestry was predominantly Irish-Scottish and as an adult Robert came to identify strongly with the early Celtic people. As a country physician Robert's father was often away from home, and it was Mrs. Howard who became the main influence in the life of the young boy.

Dr. Howard appears to have been a restless man, a seeker of opportunities, and the family moved often in the early years of Robert's life. From 1906 when the Howards lived near Dark Valley Creek in the Palo Pinto Hills and to 1915, the family moved widely around the state of Texas, with brief stays in Oklahoma, Missouri and Louisiana, before settling in Cross Cut in Brown Country in central Texas in 1915. They would remain in this vicinity and finally move to Cross Plains in 1919, where they stayed until the deaths of Robert and Mrs. Howard in 1936.

After the Howards settled in Cross Plains, Robert attended high school there. By his own admission he hated school and would always remember his school days with dislike. It was not so much the curriculum that he resented as the indoor confinement and having to keep to the school's rigorous time schedule. Throughout his life it was no secret that Robert did not like anybody to have authority over him. He treasured personal freedom over all other human conditions. During his school vacations, that often lasted six or seven months, he found temporary work on the nearby farms and cotton plantations.

Since the Cross Plains High School went only to the tenth grade, he moved with his mother to the larger nearby community of Brownwood, where he completed the last grade required for college admission. He graduated in 1923.

Robert E. Howard. © 1976 Glenn Lord.

It was at Brownwood that he met Tevis Clyde Smith and Truett Vinson, who would become his lifelong friends. They also shared some of the same literary interests and encouraged his affinity for poetry and writing. During his year at Brownwood High School, Robert had four of his stories published in the high school paper. It was his first published work and most likely provided the motivation for further effort.

In early 1923, Tevis Clyde Smith published a small magazine titled

Dr. I.M. Howard. © 1976 Glenn Lord.

The All-Around Magazine. It was printed on a hand printer given to him by his parents. Volume one consisted of issue No. 1 and 2, a combined No. 3 and 4, and No. 5. In the three last issues can be found a serialized story, "Under the Great Tiger," by Howard and Smith. As far as it is known *The All-Around Magazine* ceased publication after the first 4-issue volume.

Robert E. Howard's interest in storytelling and later writing evolved at a very young age, and it has been suggested that his decision to become a writer was made at an early age. The catalyst for this choice may have been the many hours spent in the company of his mother while his father was away. Mrs. Howard was not of good health and suffered from a number of ailments, which kept her less ambulant and often bedridden after Robert's birth. During their time together, Mrs. Howard read volumes of fairy tales, adventure stories and poetry to the young boy. Robert listened attentively and when he was old enough to read became a voracious reader of historical fiction, adventure, mystery, horror and fantasy stories. Poetry, anthropology, biography, geography, and other equally diversified subjects also had his interest. He had an exceptional memory. It is claimed that he was able to memorize Cole-

Hester Jane Ervin Howard. © 1976 Glenn Lord.

ridge's "The Rime of the Ancient Mariner" after having read it only twice. At the age of nine or ten, he wrote his first story about the adventures of a young Danish Viking, "Boealf," and his battles with the Celts, Gaels and Saxons, before joining the entourage of King Canute the Great.

THE FIRST PULP MAGAZINE STORIES

At the age of 15, the year before he moved to Brownwood, Robert E. Howard began writing seriously. His stories at that time centered around

The Howard House in Cross Plains. © 1976 Glenn Lord.

two characters, Frank Gordon (who later became Francis Xavier Gordon) and Steve Allison. Allison was an old fashioned western gunfighter and Gordon was an American adventurer traveling in the Orient; the latter was most likely inspired by the novels of Talbot Mundy, Harold Lamb and Rider Haggard. None of the stories, which were targeted at magazines such as *Adventure* and *Argosy All-Story Weekly*, sold. In early 1923, the year of his high school graduation, *Weird Tales* appeared and Howard began to submit his stories to this publication.

In spite of the wishes of his parents, Robert did not seek college admission after he graduated from high school. He did eventually, at his father's urging, take some courses in stenography, typing and bookkeeping at the Howard Payne College in Brownwood between 1923 and 1927, during which time he continued writing. Although he was successful in selling some stories to *Weird Tales*, the money came slowly. The magazine paid on publication and not on acceptance and months would pass without any income from this source.

To make pocket money, Robert tried his hands at a number of odd jobs, including oil-field reporter, stenographer, private secretary, assistant to an oil geologist, and clerk in the local drugstore. The various jobs, tedious as they were, kept him busy and left little time for him to write. He finally made an agreement with his father that he would take a year off and focus entirely on writing. If he did not make it a success within that time, he would seek a job as a bookkeeper.

In the summer of 1927 in Austin, Howard was introduced to Harold Preece, who became a good friend. He also met Booth Mooney, the future editor of the literary circular *The Junto*, to which Howard, Preece, Tevis Clyde Smith and Truett Vinson contributed. On the same weekend that he met Harold Preece, Howard purchased a book of verse which included G.K. Chesterton's poem "The Ballad of the White Horse." The poem tells about King Alfred, who united the Celtic and Anglo-Saxon tribes of Britain in the fight against the Danish invaders of the ninth century. Howard was very excited about the poem and quoted long passages in letters to Tevis Clyde Smith. The poem inspired him to begin work on "The Ballad of King Geraint" about the early Celtic peoples' struggle against invading Angles, Danes and Saxons. It may be from Chesterton that Howard adopted the concept of mixing historical periods, as later used in his Hyborian Age stories, featuring his most famous creation, Conan of Cimmeria.

Robert E. Howard 1934. © 1976 Glenn Lord.

During the years 1927 to 1928, Robert focused all his energy on writing and turned out a considerable volume of material. The effort paid off. *Weird Tales* published four of his stories in 1928; one of them was the first *Solomon Kane* tale, "Red Shadows" (August 1928). With Solomon Kane, Howard started his first continued series, featuring the dour Puritan swordsman and his never-ending fight against evil, from the shores of Elizabethan England to the demon haunted jungles of Africa. The readers loved the sto-

RED SHADOWS
ROBERT E. HOWARD

Red Shadows. Donald M. Grant 1968. Jacket art by Jeff Jones. © 1968 Glenn Lord.

ries. Within a year Robert E. Howard had become a successful writer and he never again worked at anything else. From 1928 til his death, his stories or poetry appeared in nearly three out of every four issues of *Weird Tales*.

In 1929 Howard began to write for other pulp magazines. He had a number of boxing stories accepted by *Fight Stories* and made his first sale to *Argosy* after having submitted unsuccessfully to the magazine for years. That he wrote as well as he did about boxing was neither invention nor coincidence. Robert's interest in the sport probably began as early as his ninth or tenth year. According to one of his best friends at the time, Austin Newton, Howard read everything he could find about boxing and was well informed on the subject. Although they did not have any boxing gloves, the two boys spent much time sparring.

In his teenage years, Robert also began a vigorous, almost fanatical physical training regimen to build his strength and develop his muscles. Not surprisingly boxing was his favorite sport and Howard became a fair pugilist, who missed no opportunity for a good fight. He arranged and participated in numerous Saturday night fist fights at the local ice-house. By the time he was an adult, he stood nearly six feet tall and weighed 210 pounds.

HOWARD'S INSPIRATIONS

Howard wrote a variety of different stories and invented a host of memorable characters who appeared in magazine issue after issue. The inspiration for his many and various stories may be traced to a number of sources. Among the earliest and most influential were most likely the ghost stories told him as a child by his grandmother and by Aunt Mary Bohannon, an old part-African cook, while the family temporarily lived in Bagwell, Texas. Aunt Mary was light-skinned and had as a young slave been very beautiful. One time she told Robert about the mistreatment she had suffered at the hands of her evil and villainously jealous white mistress. These revelations stayed with Robert and probably influenced his later views on the misuse of power by those in authority over less fortunate people.

The stories told by his grandmother made a particularly powerful impression on the young boy. His grandmother, who was only one generation removed from south Ireland, had a dark and gloomy Gaelic disposition and there was no light side to her. Her stories was a fusion of the folklore of the Scottish-Irish settlements of the American Southwest and the Celtic myths, mixed with African slave legends and superstitions. One

0-425-03711-8 • $1.95 • A BERKLEY BOOK

ROBERT E. HOWARD

BLACK CANAAN

HORROR-FANTASY BY THE CREATOR OF

CONAN

ILLUSTRATED • FULL COLOR FOLD-OUT POSTER INSIDE

From the swamp it rose— and with it, a dark and bloodsome Age of Horror

Black Canaan. Berkley Books 1978. Cover art by Ken Kelly. © 1978 Glenn Lord.

of her tales that had an apparently lasting impact on her young grandson was about a ghostly wagon driving down the wasteland roads at night on its own power, not drawn by any horse, and loaded with severed heads and dismembered limbs. Another story related the legends of the yellow ghost horse, that ran up and down the stairs of an old plantation mansion where a evil woman lay dying. Many of her tales included an old, deserted and decaying plantation house, where the weeds grew high all around, and ghostly flights of pigeons lifted off from the decaying woodwork and porch rails in response to any intrusion. There were many other stories of the same kind and though they scared the wits out of Robert at the time, he could never hear enough of them. These anecdotes unquestionably provided the inspiration for some of Howard's southwest horror stories, including two of his most acclaimed tales, *Pigeons from Hell* and *Black Canaan*.

Robert E. Howard was also an avid reader of history and adventure fiction, and his library included titles by Edgar Rice Burroughs, Arthur Conan Doyle, Rudyard Kipling, Harold Lamb, T.E. Lawrence, Jack London, H.P. Lovecraft, Talbot Mundy, Edgar Allan Poe, Sax Rohmer, Sir Walter Scott, Mark Twain and others. With his interest for poetry, he also included the verse by G.K. Chesterton, Walter de la Mare, Omar Khayyam, Kipling, Lovecraft, Poe, Robert W. Service, Alfred, Lord Tennyson, and many more in his collection.

When Robert was 13, the family had temporarily moved to New Orleans where Dr. Howard attended a post-graduate medical course. In the city's public library, Robert discovered a book on early British history that mentioned the settling of the British Isles, before the coming of the Celts, by a small, dark-skinned Mediterranean race called the Picts. It has been suggested that the book may have been G.F. Scott Elliot's *The Romance of Early British Life* (Seeley & Co., London, 1909). Howard became fascinated with the history of the Picts and decided to someday invent and write a heroic past for them and their struggle under a great king against the Roman invasion. This inspiration became the basis for his later Bran Mak Morn stories.

As did H.P. Lovecraft, Howard also drew upon his dreams which were vivid and in many cases story-like. Continuous, narrative dreams were quite common to him and in most of the dreams his personality was entirely different from his actual character. He gave as examples of his dream characters a 16th century Englishman, a prehistoric man, a United States cavalryman, a Renaissance Italian, an 11th century Norman knight, a Goth, a 17th century Irish soldier, an Indian, a Serb fighting Turks, and a prizefighter. The settlement and development of the American West also played a greater part in his dream world, and he dreamed of himself being a fur-

Bran Mak Morn: The Last King. Wandering Star 2001. Jacket art by Gary Gianni. © 2001 Robert E. Howard Properties, LLC., and Gary Gianni.

trapper, a pioneer, a hunter, an Indian fighter, a trail-driver, a cowboy, and a gunfighter among other western characters.

Although Robert E. Howard had lived in the American Southwest all of his life, many of his dreams were laid in what to him were entirely alien environments. Places that Howard had never seen, but only imagined through his reading and research. He often dreamed of cold, northern lands of icy wildernesses under gray skies, and of bleak marshlands swept with the sea-winds from the nearby stormy sea. The Nordic dream lands were not civilized, but inhabited by light-eyed, skin clad barbarians. He claimed that in these dreams he was never a civilized man, but a barbarian, armed with sword and axe, fighting the elements, wild beasts or the armed legions of civilization.

The inspiration of Howard's dreams seems to be reflected in much of his work. As he had expressed on several occasions, he believed that barbarism was the natural state of mankind and that civilization was unnatural, a whim of circumstance. Therefore barbarism would always ultimately triumph. As an extension of this notion, it can be seen in many of Howard's stories that his sympathy is clearly on the side of barbarians arrayed against the powers, excesses and corruptions of established civilization.

In 1929 another of Howard's successful serial characters, King Kull of Valusia, appeared in the pages of the August issue of *Weird Tales* with the story "The Shadow Kingdom." Bran Mak Morn, the last king of the Picts, emerged for the first time in the November 1930 issue of *Weird Tales* with the publication of "Kings of the Night." That year the publishers of *Weird Tales* launched another magazine, *Oriental Tales,* and based on his knowledge and interest in history, Howard began to write and submit stories about the Crusades and the bloody conflict between Christians and Muslims to the magazine.

In August 1930, Howard wrote a letter to Farnsworth Wright, regarding H.P. Lovecraft's story "The Rats in the Wall" and the questionable use of a certain Gaelic phrase. Wright forwarded the letter to Lovecraft, who responded directly to Howard. Thereby began a voluminous correspondence between the two men, which would last to Howard's death and precipitate much intense debate on various subjects. In addition to Lovecraft, Howard also corresponded with other pulp magazine writers, including Clark Ashton Smith and August W. Derleth.

In 1939, three years after Howard's death and two years after Lovecraft passed away, August W. Derleth and Donald Wandrei founded Arkham House Publishers, Inc., in Sauk City, Wisconsin. The primary purpose of the enterprise was to reprint all of H.P. Lovecraft's stories in book form and perpetuate his work and literary legacy. Under August Derleth's editorship, Arkham House would later publish two volumes of Robert E. Howard's stories and one volume of his poetry.

Shadow Kingdoms. Wildside Press 2004. Jacket art by Stephen Fabian. © 2004 Paul Herman and Stephen Fabian.

The Great Depression

In 1932 the Depression struck and dealt the pulp magazine market a blow from which it never fully recovered. In the same year Howard created what was to be his most famous character, *Conan of Cimmeria.* To provide Conan with a suitable, yet flexible environment for his many adventures, Howard invented the Hyborian Age, a mythical age some 12,000 years ago, before Atlantis sank beneath the ocean and the beginning of recorded history. By telescoping history he could include different historical periods and cultures in this setting. Howard also had a propensity for using a mixture of historical, pseudo-historical and slightly altered names for peoples, nations and places in his Hyborian Age saga.

Of Conan's creation, Howard claimed that the character was not created by any deliberate or conscious process. While stopping in a small border town on the lower Rio Grande, the concept of the character suddenly materialized in his mind. Conan of Cimmeria, stepped out of nowhere, fully developed as a viable character and Howard began writing stories about the Cimmerian's adventures.

Robert E. Howard wrote fast and furious. He was a prolific writer and had to be. Writing for the pulp magazines required loads of material. If one wanted to make a living in the business, imagination and productivity were the road to success. It has been said that Howard had the habit of yelling out the storyline as he typed the adventures of his many characters on an old Underwood typewriter, a practice that could be unnerving for the neighbors and for anyone passing by the small frame house, especially at night.

As the Depression deepened during 1932, several magazines went out of business. Among them were the entire line of titles published by Fiction House, including *Fight Stories,* which had been Howard's main buyer of boxing-adventure stories. This left him with only *Weird Tales* and *Oriental Stories* and both were in financial troubles. Checks for published stories were often long overdue. Out of necessity, Howard hired an agent, Otis Adelbert Kline, and began to write detective and western stories for other markets. He did, however, continue to write for *Weird Tales.*

In spite of the efforts of his new agent, 1933 was not a good year for Robert E. Howard. Kline sold only one story as the Depression continued to take its toll on the publication industry. *Oriental Stories,* recently renamed *The Magic Carpet Magazine,* folded with the January 1934 issue, while still holding several of Howard's historical and sports adventure stories.

But all was not as bleak as it appeared. With the rebirth of Fiction House and some of its magazines, including *Action Stories* in 1934, Howard began to write a new series about a larger-than-life mountain man character, Breckinridge Elkins of Bear Creek. *Action Stories* purchased the stories and continue to publish one in every issue of the magazine until after Howard's death. One of Howard's very first characters, Francis X. Gordon, was revived, together with a new comparable Middle East adventurer, Kirby O'Donnell. A number of these stories sold to *Top-Notch*, *Complete Stories* and *Thrilling Adventures*.

NOVALYNE PRICE

In the fall of 1934, Novalyne Price, a young, attractive brunette, arrived in Cross Plains to be employed as a high school teacher. She was originally from the Brownwood area and had been introduced to Robert E. Howard the previous spring by Tevis Clyde Smith. Novalyne Price had aspirations of becoming a writer and soon after her arrival tried to contact Howard. Her first attempts by telephone were unsuccessful; Mrs. Howard would not let her talk to Robert. Not to be foiled that easily, Novalyne had a cousin drive her to the Howard home, where she was warmly welcomed by Robert, more so than by his parents.

This was the beginning of a turbulent relationship that would last to the late spring of 1936, when Novalyne left Cross Plains for Louisiana State University, where she had been accepted into a graduate program. Except for his mother, Novalyne Price was probably the only woman who ever came close to Howard and came to know him intimately. They enjoyed each other's company and spent hours talking about literature, poetry and a multitude of other subjects, but they were also two fiercely independent, opinionated and passionate young people, attributes which often resulted in arguments and temporary break-ups. That they cared deeply for each other is beyond questioning, but neither seemed to be willing to compromise in the relationship and make a more lasting commitment to each other.

Over the years, Mrs. Howard's health had been deteriorating and in early 1935, hospitalization and surgery at Temple, Texas, became necessary. She remained in the hospital for a month, but never recovered her health. The last year of her life was spent in various hospitals and sanatoriums, or at home under the care of her husband and son. The medical care of Mrs. Howard had saddled the family with excessive expenses and Howard felt that he needed to help with payment of the bills. For that reason, he made a decision to abandon his Conan tales and other stories for *Weird Tales* and seek a better-paying market. His last story for *Weird Tales* was "Red Nails"—one of his better Conan stories—which was published in the July 1936 issue.

With the shift of market, Howard enjoyed an all-time high for sales of stories in the spring of 1936. He was selling to *Spicy-Adventure Stories, Dime Sports Magazine* and *Star Western*. Another magazine, *Cowboy Stories,* had accepted the first in a series of tales about a Breckinridge Elkins-type hero named Buckner J. Grimes, and Howard also sold three other western stories featuring a new character, Pike Bearfield, to *Argosy*.

THE END OF THE TRAIL

Nevertheless the sun was setting on Robert E. Howard's career and life. In early June 1936, Mrs. Howard was seriously ill and slipped into a coma. At eight o'clock in the morning of June 11, Robert asked the nurse attending if his mother would ever recover and recognize him again. When the nurse expressed her opinion in the negative, Howard walked to his 1935 Chevrolet parked outside the house, got into the car, pulled a borrowed .380 Colt automatic pistol from the glove compartment and shot himself in the temple. He died eight hours later at four o'clock, June 11, 1936. His mother died the next day without regaining consciousness. It was suggested that she died of either cancer or tuberculosis. On the morning of June 14, 1936, mother and son were interred together in a family plot that Robert had purchased just a week before at Greenleaf Memorial Cemetery in Brownwood, Texas.

After Robert had shot himself, Dr. Howard found a strip of paper in the billfold in his son's hip pocket. On the paper was typed the following lines:

"All fled—all done, so lift me on the pyre,

The feast is over, and the lamp expire."

According to Howard scholar Rusty Burke, it appears to be a rewriting of two lines of Viola Garvin's little known poem "The House of Caesar."

Novalyne Price received a Western Union telegram at Louisiana State University a day later. It was from a friend, Pat Allen, dated June 11, 1936, and read: "Bob Howard killed himself this morning. His mother very low." The tragic news struck the young woman a stunning blow. It took her a long time to accept the reality of Robert's death and much longer to recover from the traumatic impact of the event.

The sudden and meaningless death of Robert E. Howard was an unimaginable and great loss, not only because of the unnecessary demise of a human life in its prime, but also because of the loss of an irreplaceable and extraordinary talent. At the age of 30, Howard had become one of the best modern American writers of heroic fantasy, adventure stories, sports action tales, western stories—both realistic and humorous—gothic horror stories and historical fiction.

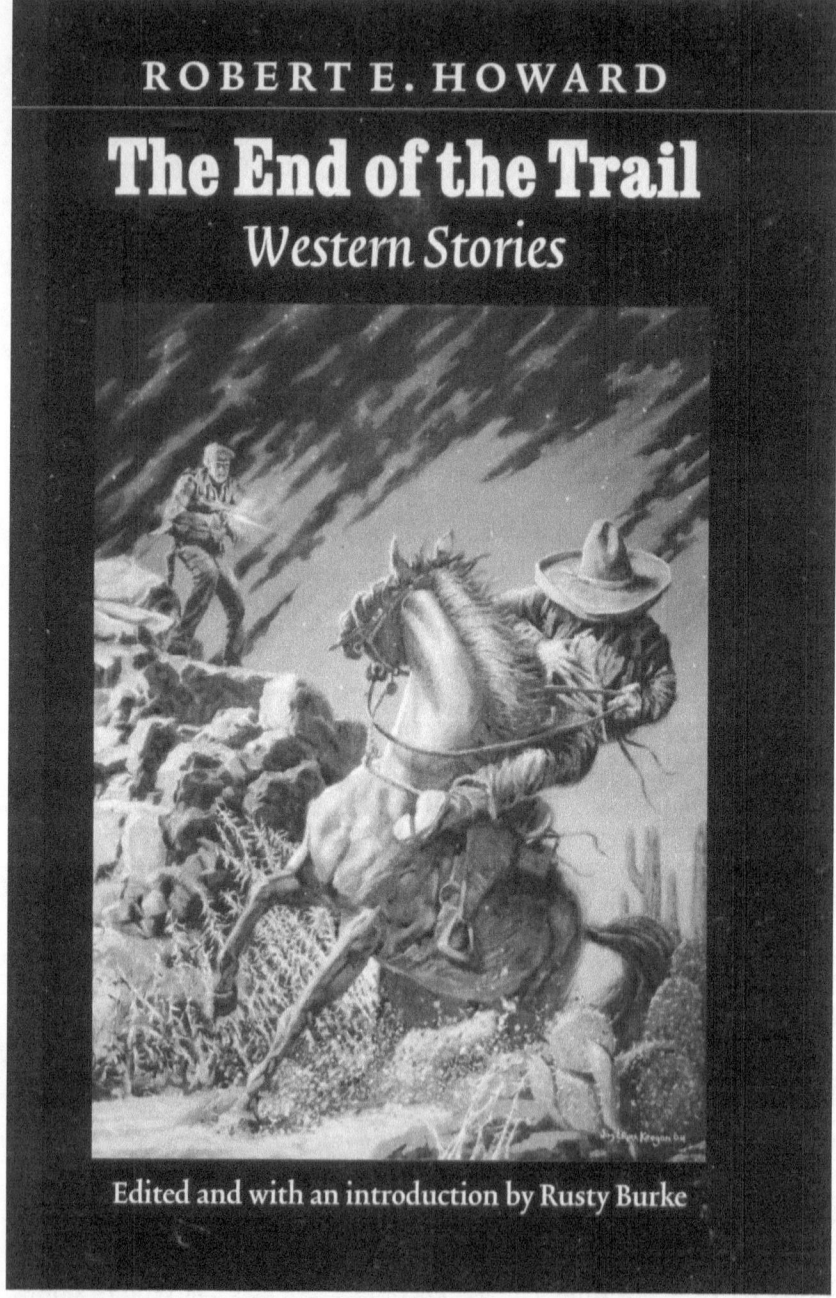

The End of the Trail. University of Nebraska Press 2005. Jacket art by Jim and Ruth Keegan. © 2005 REH Properties, Inc., and Jim and Ruth Keegan.

Nevertheless there is little doubt that he had not yet achieved his full potential. Few writers hit their stride at that young an age. Edgar Rice Burroughs was 36 years old when he sold his first story, *Under the Moons of Mars* to *All-Story;* Mark Twain was 41 when he wrote *The Adventures of Tom Sawyer;* Talbot Mundy (William Lancaster Gribbon) had reached the age of 55 when his masterpiece, *Tros of Samothrace*, was published, and Victor Hugo was 60 years old when he wrote *Les Misérables.* One can only speculate how far Robert E. Howard's unique gift and imagination would have taken him if he had chosen to live, develop his writing skills and continue to produce his stories, novels and poetry until the natural end of his life.

2

The Robert E. Howard Legacy

LETTERS

On June 29, 1936, Dr. Isaac M. Howard wrote the following letter to H.P. Lovecraft:

> Mr. H.P. Lovecraft
> 66 College Street
> Providence, Rhode Island
>
> My Dear Mr. Lovecraft:
>
> It is barely possible through some other source that you may have heard of the death of Robert E. Howard, my son. If not, I will say that after three weeks of vigilant watching at his mother's bedside, on the morning of June 11, 1936, at eight o'clock, he slipped out of the house, entered his car which was standing in front of the garage, raised the windows and fired a shot through his brain. The cook standing at the window at the back part of the house, saw him go get in his car. She thought he was fixing to drive to town as he usually did. When she heard the muffled sound of the gun, she saw him fall over the steering wheel. She ran in the house and called the physician who was in the house. The doctor was taking a cup of coffee in the dining room and I was talking with him. We rushed to the car and found him. We thought at first that it was a death shot but the bullet had passed through the brain. He shot himself just above the temple. It came out on the opposite side, just above and behind the left ear. He lived eight hours and never gained consciousness.
>
> I was watching Robert as this was premeditated, and I knew it, but I did not think that he would kill himself before his mother went. His mother was in coma and had been for many hours when this occurred. There were two trained nurses in the house and doctors there all the time. He did not ask a doctor, neither did he ask me, but he asked

a nurse if she thought his mother would ever regain consciousness enough to know him, and the nurse told him she feared not. This was unknown to me. Had I known, I might have prevented this, because I know now that he fully had made up his mind not to see his mother die.

Last March a year ago, again when his mother was very low in the King's Daughters Hospital in Temple, Texas, Dr. McCelvey expressed a fear that she would not recover; he began to talk to me about his business, and I at once understood what it meant. I began to talk to him, trying to dissuade him from such a course, but his mother began to improve. Immediately she began to improve, he became cheerful and no more was said. Again this year, in February, while his mother was very sick and not expected to live but a few days, at that time she was in the Shannon Hospital in San Angelo, Texas. San Angelo is something like one hundred miles from here. He was driving back and forth daily from San Angelo to home. One evening he told me I would find his business, what little there was to it, all carefully written up and in a large envelope in his desk. Again I begged him not to do it, but he positively did not intend to live after his mother was gone.

As the months grew on, his mother showed some improvement. He accepted her condition as one of permanent improvement and one that would continue. I knew well that it would not, but I kept it from him. Two weeks before she died, she began to decline rapidly. I saw the awful worry that came over him. I was following him and watching him closely, but did not think he would do anything until his mother was gone.

In that I was mistaken, because he never intended to see his mother die. The night before his death, he assumed an almost cheerful attitude, seemed very much interested about me, as if he intended to take the lead and take care of me. He came up to me in the night, put his arm around me and said: "Buck up, you are equal to it, you will go through it all right." He completely disarmed me of the intention of his death, but I knew well what to expect afterwards. He died without ever showing the least return of consciousness at four o'clock, June 11, 1936. His mother lingered thirty-one hours, never regaining consciousness.

I buried them both in the Greenleaf Cemetery at Brownwood, Texas. I selected caskets exactly alike. He had purchased a burial lot a week before this happened. It was in the restricted portion of the cemetery. The purchase carried with it a perpetual up-keep.

When he bought the lot, he went to the sexton and wanted to know if it was a bonafide contract and if it would be taken care of. He said to the sexton: "I want to know if the lot will be kept in order. My father and I will go away and never come again." Mr. Bass, the sexton, was under the impression that he was contemplating something in which we would all go, but he did not expect to kill me, but knew that the shock would kill me. He was careful to keep nurses and doctors around me, but no doubt thought I would die from shock, and which I think the last few lines he ever typed would indicate. These lines were found on a strip of paper in his bill fold in his hip pocket after he shot himself. The lines follow:

All fled—all done, so lift me on the pyre—
The Feast is over and the lamps expire.

I do not know whether these words were a quotation or original, but they were typed no doubt shortly before his death.

I do not know what was in his mind. I have tried to interpret this as being the last of all the family, The Feast the thirty years of love of the family life in our home. Robert loved me with a love that was beautiful. He loved my companionship above that of anyone else and every time opportunity afforded, he spent his time with me in preference to anyone else; but being a country doctor and practicing medicine in a country comparatively thinly settled, I was away from home most of the time, but when I was permitted to be home, our hours were spent pleasantly on discussion of men, women, animals, out-door life, adventure, history of long-lived frontiersmen, and such like. He was a great reader. It made me so happy to sit and listen. He acquired a knowledge, by reading, of history that I never knew. Lest I worry you with this I will close, but will say in conclusion, Mr. Lovecraft, that Robert was a great admirer of you. I have often heard him say that you were the best weird writer in the world, and he keenly enjoyed corresponding with you. Often expressed hope that you might visit in our home some day, so that he, his mother and I might see and know you personally. Robert greatly admired all weird writers, often heard him speak of each separately and express the highest admiration of all. He said they were a bunch of great men and he admired all of them very much.

The Howard Payne College of Brownwood has asked for letters from correspondents. If it is agreeable with you, I will furnish them with some of your correspondence to him as he has some in his files and they are interested in letters.

His books were given to the Howard Payne College and will be known as the Robert E. Howard Memorial Collection. It is so arranged that it is possible to add to it as friends see fit. If you have a book that you would like to add to it with an autograph, it will be greatly appreciated.

Yours very truly,

Dr I M Howard

I am mailing you a bundle of papers that contains the full of it all.

The following memoriam was published three months later, in the September 1936 issue of *Fantasy Magazine:*

Robert Ervin Howard: A Memoriam
By H.P. Lovecraft

The sudden and unexpected death on June 11 (1936) of Robert Ervin Howard, author of fantastic tales of incomparable vividness, forms weird fiction's worst loss since the passing of Henry S. Whitehead four years ago.

Mr. Howard was born at Peaster, Texas, January 22, 1906, and was old enough to have seen the last phase of southwestern pioneering—the settlement of the great plains and the lower Rio Grande valley, and the spectacular rise of the oil industry with its raucous boom towns. His father, who survives him, was one of the pioneer physicians of the region. The family has lived in South, East and West Texas, and western Oklahoma; for the past few years at Cross Plains, near Brownwood, Texas. Steeped in the frontier atmosphere, Mr. Howard early became a devotee of its virile Homeric traditions. His knowledge of its history and folkways was profound, and the descriptions and reminiscences contained in his private letters illustrate the eloquence and power with which he would have celebrated it in literature had he lived longer. Mr. Howard's family is of distinguished southern planter stock—of Scotch-Irish descent, with most ancestors settled in Georgia and North Carolina in the eighteenth century.

Beginning to write at fifteen, Mr. Howard placed his first story three years later while a student at Howard Payne College in Brownwood. This story, "Spear and Fang," was published in *Weird Tales* for July, 1925. Wider fame came with the appearance of the novelette, "Wolfshead," in the same magazine in April 1926. In August, 1928, began the tales dealing with Solomon Kane, an English Puritan of relentless dueling and wrong-redressing practices whose adventures took him to strange and primordial cities in the African jungle. With these tales Mr. Howard struck what proved to be one of his most effective accomplishments— the description of vast megalithic cities of the elder world, around whose dark towers and labyrinthine nether vaults linger an aura of pre-human fear and necromancy which no other writer could duplicate. These tales also marked Mr. Howard's development of that skill and zest in depicting sanguinary conflict which became so typical of his work. Solomon Kane, like several other heroes of the author was conceived in boyhood long before incorporation in any story.

Always a keen student of Celtic antiquities and other phases of remote history, Mr. Howard began in 1929—with "The Shadow Kingdom," in the August *Weird Tales*—that succession of tales of the prehistoric world for which he soon grew so famous. The early specimens described a very distant age in man's history—when Atlantis, Lemuria and Mu were above the waves, and when the shadows of pre-human reptile men rested upon the primal scene. Of these the central figure was King Kull of Valusia. In *Weird Tales* for December, 1932, appeared "The Phoenix on the Sword"—first of those tales of King Conan the Cimmerian, which introduced a later prehistoric world, a world of perhaps 15,000 years ago, just before the first glimmerings of recorded history. The elaborate extent and accurate self-consisting with which Mr. Howard developed the world of Conan in his later stories is well known to all fantasy readers. For his own guidance he prepared a detailed quasi-historical sketch of infinite cleverness and imaginative fertility.

Meanwhile, Mr. Howard had written many tales of the early Picts and Celts, including a notable series revolving around the chieftain Bran Mak Morn. Few readers will ever forget the hideous and compelling power of that macabre masterpiece "Worms of the Earth," in *Weird Tales* for November, 1932. Other powerful fantasies lay outside the connected series—these included the memorable serial, "Skull-Face," and a few distinctive tales with a modern setting such as "Black Canaan," with its genuine, regional background and its clutchingly compelling picture of the horror that stalks through the moss hung, shadow-cursed, serpent-ridden swamps of the American far south.

Outside the fantasy field, Mr. Howard was surprisingly prolific and versatile. His strong interest in sports—a thing perhaps connected with his love of primitive conflict and strength—led him to create the prize fighting hero, Sailor Steve Costigan, whose adventures in distant and curious parts delighted the readers of many magazines. His novelettes of oriental warfare displayed to the utmost his mastery of romantic swashbuckling, while his increasingly frequent tales of western life—such as the Breckinridge Elkins series—showed his growing ability and inclination to reflect the backgrounds with which he was directly familiar.

Mr. Howard's poetry—weird, warlike, and adventurous—was no less notable than his prose. It had the true spirit of the ballad and the epic, and was marked by a pulsing rhythm and potent imagery of the extreme distinctive cast. Much of it, in the form of supposed quotations from ancient writings, served to head the chapters of his novels. It is regrettable that no published collection of his has ever appeared, and one hopes that such a thing may be posthumously edited and issued.

The character and attainments of Mr. Howard were wholly unique. He was, above everything else, a lover of the simpler, older world of barbarian and pioneer days, when courage and strength took the place of subtlety and stratagem, and when a hardy, fearless race battled and bled, and asked no quarter from hostile nature. All his stories reflect this philosophy, and derive from it a vitality found in few of his contemporaries. No one could write more convincingly of violence and gore than he, and his battle passages reveal an instinctive aptitude for military tactics which would have brought him distinction in times of war.

Skull-Face and Others. Arkham House Publishers 1946. Jacket art by Hannes Bok.
© 1946 August Derleth.

His real gifts were even higher than the readers of his published works would suspect, and had he lived, would have helped him to make his mark in serious literature with some folk epic of his beloved southwest.

It is hard to describe precisely what made Mr. Howard's stories stand out so sharply; but the real secret is that he himself is in every one of them, whether they were ostensibly commercial or not. He was greater than any profit-making policy he could adopt—for even when he outwardly made concessions to Mammon-guided editors and commercial critics, he had an internal force and sincerity which broke through the surface and put the imprint of his personality on everything he wrote. Seldom, if ever, did he set down a lifeless stock character or situation and leave it as such. Before he concluded with it, it always took on some tinge of vitality and reality in spite of popular editorial policy—always drew something from his own experience of life instead of from the sterile herbarium of desiccated pulpish standbys. Not only did he excel in pictures of strife and slaughter, but he was almost alone in his ability to create real emotions of spectral fear and dread suspense. No author—even in the humblest fields—can truly excel unless he takes his work very seriously; and Mr. Howard did just that even in cases where he consciously thought he did not. That such a genuine artist should perish while hundreds of insincere hacks continue to concoct spurious ghost and vampires and space-ships and occult detectives is indeed a sorry piece of cosmic irony!

Mr. Howard, familiar with many phases of southwestern life, lived with his parents in a semi-rural setting in the village of Cross Plains, Texas. Writing was his sole profession. His tastes in reading were and included historical research of notable depth in fields as dissimilar as the American southwest, prehistoric Great Britain, and Ireland, and the prehistoric Oriental and African World. In literature he preferred the virile to the subtle, and repudiated modernism with sweeping completeness. The late Jack London was one of his idols. He was liberal in politics and a bitter foe of civic injustice in every form. His leading amusements were sports and travel—the latter giving rise to delightful descriptive letters replete with historical reflections. Humor was not a specialty, though he had on the one hand a keen sense of irony, and on the other hand an abundant fund of heartiness, cordiality, and conviviality. Though having numerous friends, Mr. Howard belonged to no literary clique and abhorred all cults of "arty" affection. His admiration ran toward strength of body and character than toward scholastic prowess. With his fellow authors in the fantasy field he corresponded interestingly and voluminously, but never met more than one of them—the gifted E. Hoffmann Price, whose varied attainments impressed him profoundly—in person.

Mr. Howard was nearly six feet in height, with the massive build of a born fighter. He was, save for his Celtic blue eyes, very dark; and in later years his weight averaged around 195. Always a disciple of hearty and strenuous living, he suggested more than casually his own famous character—the intrepid warrior, adventurer and seizer of thrones, Conan the Cimmerian. His loss at the age of thirty is a tragedy of the first magnitude, and a blow from which fantasy literature will not soon recover. Mr. Howard's library has been presented to Howard Payne College, where it will form the nucleus of the Robert E. Howard Memorial Collection of books, manuscripts and letters.

THE ROBERT E. HOWARD MEMORIAL COLLECTION

As mentioned in his letter to Lovecraft, shortly after his son's funeral Dr. Isaac M. Howard gathered all of Robert's books, papers and pulp magazines, and donated them to the library at Howard Payne College in Brownwood, Texas. According to the *Brownwood Bulletin*, June 29, 1936, the collection included about 300 titles of mostly history and biography, plus fifty volumes of current drama and poetry, and a complete file of magazines containing Robert's prose and verse. It was intended to be the foundation of the Robert E. Howard Memorial Collection.

The library did not seem particularly interested in the magazines and because of the risque *Weird Tales* covers, the librarian found some of the material indecent. While the more offensive magazines were consigned to obscurity in the basement of the library, where the paper quickly began to deteriorate due to mold and humidity, others were placed in general circulation and subject to damaging and rough handling. When Dr. Howard became aware of this state of affairs, he immediately went to Brownwood and reclaimed his son's magazines and other papers. The books, however, stayed at the library.

As the years passed, the concept of a Robert E. Howard Memorial Collection at the Howard Payne College Library was largely forgotten and the books ended up on the shelves for public circulation. After forty years in relative obscurity, and in response to a renewed public interest in his work, the Howard books were separated once again into a memorial collection. In the meantime many of the books had been lost, stolen, discarded or misplaced and it was only because of the dedicated and thorough effort by a librarian, Mrs. Corrine Shields, who pulled together 268 titles which she believed might have been in the original Howard collection, that this separation became possible. On the basis of Mrs. Shield's work, Dr. Charlotte Laughlin, a teacher at Howard Payne College, published the first of four articles, "Robert E. Howard's Library: An Annotated Checklist," in *Paperback Quarterly, A Journal for Paperback Collectors* (Pecan Valley Press, Brownwood, Texas), beginning in the spring of 1978.

Three more Howard library books were discovered during the run of Dr. Laughlin's articles and sometime later when L. Sprague de Camp and his wife, Catherine Cook de Camp, were doing their research at the library for the Robert E. Howard biography *Dark Valley Destiny*, a few more volumes were located. In 1978 Glenn Lord made another transcription of the Howard library list. It differed slightly from that of Dr. Laughlin and was published in the 12th mailing (July 1978) of *The Hyperborean League*, an amateur press association publication. A proposed listing of 247 titles was compiled by Stephen Eng from Glenn Lord's and Dr. Laughlin's lists, and on the basis of a considerable amount of independent research. The result was published as *Appendix A: Robert E. Howard's Library* in Don Herron's *The Dark Barbarian* (Greenwood Press, 1984). According to Rob Roehm, only 68 titles previously owned by Robert E. Howard are presently kept at the Howard Payne University's Library Treasure Room.

Dr. Howard outlived his wife and son by eight years. Deeply affected by the sudden loss of his family and suffering from cataracts and diabetes, he managed to continue his work as a physician. In November 1942, he made an arrangement with an associate, Dr. Pere M. Kuykendall, to help with the work in the physician's clinic, the West Texas Clinic and Hospital in Ranger, Texas. The war had made the lack of physicians critical.

Two years later on November 12, 1944, Dr. Howard died of a heart attack. All that he owned at the time he willed to Dr. P.M. Kuykendall. Among these possessions were a couple of thousand dollars in a bank account, a collection of Robert's magazines and other papers, and the copyrights to Howard's literary work. Dr. Howard had left instructions in his will that a trunk full of Robert's papers should be forwarded to E. Hoffmann Price in California. According to correspondence between Price and August Derleth at the time, the trunk was shipped soon after Dr. Howard's death and received by Price.

THE RIGHTS TO ROBERT E. HOWARD'S LITERARY'S WORK

The Robert E. Howard Estate was closed in November 1936 and the estate of Dr. Isaac M. Howard closed in 1945 and ceased to exist at that time as a legal entity. From Dr. Howard, Dr. Kuykendall inherited "the rights to Robert E. Howard's literary work." Robert E. Howard had engaged Otis Adelbert Kline as his literary agent in 1933 and Kline continued as the agent for the Howard heirs until his death in 1946. Shortly thereafter, the Kline Agency was sold to Oscar J. Friend, who remained agent for the heirs until his death in 1963.

In February 1954, Oscar J. Friend wrote to Dr. Kuykendall and proposed that the Conan of Cimmeria character was too valuable to let disappear with the end of the currently running Gnome Press series. Friend suggested that he would look for an author to continue the character. In a response, Dr. Kuykendall expressed his agreement with the continuation of Howard's works. He also stated that he would be willing to sell and release all rights to Robert E. Howard's literary work for the sum of $3,000.00. Friend replied with a counteroffer of $1,250.00. Dr. Kuykendall did not accept, but suggested that the Conan series should be continued as originally proposed by Friend. In December 1954, Friend increased his offer to $2,000.00 to be paid in quarterly installments. In a letter of February 1955, to Dr. Kuykendall's attorney, Beverly S. Dudley, Oscar J. Friend stated that it was his understanding that Dr. Kuykendall's proposition and his (Friend's) counter-proposition on the Howard properties were definitely off as of now. Dr. Kuykendall's decision to keep the Howard rights was a wise one. By mid-year of 1976, the earnings from Howard's literary works paid to Dr. Kuykendall's widow and daughter were close to $30,000, less the agent's fee.

When Dr. Pere M. Kuykendall died in 1958, the Howard rights went to his wife, Alla Ray Kuykendall, and their daughter, Alla Ray Kuykendall Morris. In late 1964, Oscar J. Friend's widow and daughter decided to close the agency, and the Kuykendalls asked them to recommend someone else to handle the Howard material. At the time, L. Sprague de Camp was asked, but declined on the grounds of conflict of interest. He recommended Glenn Lord, a staunch Howard devotee from Pasadena, Texas, who accepted and became agent for the heirs in March 1965.

Shortly after he was engaged as agent, Glenn Lord in an attempt to collect as much of Howard's material as possible, contacted E. Hoffmann Price with regards to the shipment of papers he had received from Dr. I.M. Howard. Price recalled having let someone borrow a number of tear sheets and other material. This person was contacted and claimed that he had passed the matters on to Francis T. Laney, the editor of the fanzine *The Acolyte*. Laney had died, but Lord pursued the contact with the original borrower, and indicated that he would be willing to pay for any recovered Howard material. The offer apparently did the trick and for a few hundred dollars Glenn Lord received a trunk full of manuscripts, letters, magazines, newspapers and other material, including many rare items. Glenn Lord remained the agent for the heirs, the gatekeeper and caretaker of the Howard material until September 1993.

With the successful marketing of the Lancer 11-volume, mass market paperback Conan series in the late 1960s, it became clear that Conan was a potentially profitable literary property that needed copyright protection. For that purpose the Kuykendalls, L. Sprague de Camp and others formed Conan Properties, Inc., in the 1970s, which thereby became "the owner of all rights in Conan, including trademarks, copyrights, registered copyrights, characters and stories."

Unfortunately CPI was not managed proficiently or objectively and Howard's original Conan stories were kept out of print, in favor of an array of poor products such as Conan pastiches, comic books, a disastrous TV show and an equally poor animated TV series. It appeared that CPI was not as interested in conserving and presenting Conan as created by Robert E. Howard as it was in using the copyright to prevent others from doing this, while marketing a number of inferior products under the Conan trademark.

After L. Sprague de Camp's death in November 2000, the shareholders of CPI sold Conan Properties, Inc., to Stan Lee Media. This did not improve either the objectivity or productivity of CPI. Less than a year after purchasing CPI, Stan Lee Media filed for bankruptcy and CPI went up for sale on the open market. It was eventually purchased by Paradox Entertainment in 2002. The legal copyright clause is written as, "Conan Properties International, LLC., a wholly owned subsidiary of Paradox Entertainment controls all rights to Conan, associated characters and the Hyborian Age as created by Robert E. Howard and expanded upon by acclaimed authors and artists for decades."

When Mrs. Morris died in 1995, she left the rights to Howard's literary work to Zora Mae Bryant, who was married to Mrs. Morris's cousin Elliott Bryant. Mr. Bryant passed away years before Mrs. Morris, but Mrs. Morris and Mrs. Bryant remained close. From Mrs. Bryant the literary rights went to her children, Jack Baum and Terry Baum Rogers, who formed Robert E. Howard Properties, LLC., in 1996. Before then, Kull Productions, LLC., Red Sonja Corporation and Solomon Kane Properties, LLC, had been established. Robert E. Howard Properties, LLC., retained the right to the remainder of Robert E. Howard's literary works. The Baums and the de Camp family had sold their interests in Conan Properties International, LLC., some years before. In early 2006, the Baums sold their rights in Robert E. Howard Properties, LLC., to Paradox Entertainment, which is now the owner of the majority of rights to Robert E. Howard's characters and stories.

THE HOWARD REVIVAL

At the time of his death, Robert E. Howard had written more than three hundred stories, about seven hundred poems, numerous unpublished fragments and synopses, several novel-length works and a plethora of letters, articles, essays and miscellaneous writings; all in the relatively short span of a dozen years. When he passed away, many of the stories and poems were still in the hands of the editors at various magazines, to which they had been submitted and accepted but not yet published. *Weird Tales*, a notoriously slow payer, owed Howard $1,350.00 when he died. The debt was eventually paid to his father.

A few weeks after Howard's death, his agent at the time Otis Adelbert Kline, sent a collection of early Breckinridge Elkins stories, which Howard had tied loosely together as a novel, by adding a love interest Glory McGraw, to an associate English agent who sold the manuscript to Herbert Jenkins in London. The first Howard hardcover book, *A Gent from Bear Creek*, was published the following year. The book is the undisputed key Howard title. Twelve copies are known to exist today, only one with its original dust jacket.

A Gent from Bear Creek. Herbert Jenkins 1937. Jacket artist unknown. Cover image © 1976 Glenn Lord.

During the rest of the 1930s and into the 1960s, magazines such as *Action Stories, Argosy, Cowboy Stories, Famous Fantastic Mysteries, Fantastic, Fantastic Universe, Fantasy Magazine, Fight Stories, Golden Fleece, Magazine of Horror, Spicy-Adventure Stories, Weird Tales* and other magazines continued to publish Howard's material. A small booklet produced by Bill Crawford in 1945 featured the story "The Garden of Fear" and although it was the only story by Howard out of five (one was by H.P. Lovecraft), it bore his name and the title of his story on the cover.

In 1946 Arkham House Publishers, Inc., released what the editor and co-founder of the small specialty publishing house, August Derleth, thought were the best of Howard's stories in an omnibus volume titled *Skull-Face and Others*.

Late in the 1940s, the publisher at Gnome Press, Martin Greenberg, recognized the commercial potential of a Conan series and published the novel *The Hour of the Dragon* under the title *Conan the Conqueror* in 1950. The book sold well enough that Gnome Press followed up by publishing five more Conan titles: *The Sword of Conan* (1952), *King Conan* (1953), *The Coming of Conan* (1953), *Conan the Barbarian* (1954), and *Tales of Conan* (1955). The first three books were edited by John D. Clark, the last three by L. Sprague de Camp, who also revised some of the stories. All the material in *Tales of Conan* was edited, revised or rewritten by de Camp. A seventh book, *The Return of Conan* written by Bjørn Nyberg and edited by L. Sprague de Camp was added to the series in 1956. It contains no Howard material. Noticing the public interest in the Gnome Conan books, Ace Books published *Conan the Conqueror* in 1953 in a mass market paperback, double edition, back-to-back with Leigh Brackett's *The Sword of Rhiannon*.

In 1957 Arkham House published the first hardcover volume of Howard's poetry under the title *Always Comes Evening*. The poems were selected by Glenn Lord and the printing of the book subsidized by Lord. Nineteen-sixty-one saw the appearance of "The Howard Collector," a high quality, periodic amateur press journal containing fiction, essays, poems and letters by and about Robert E. Howard. The journal was published by Glenn Lord and ran for 18 issues until 1973.

The third and last Robert E. Howard volume by Arkham House Publishers, a collection of weird, supernatural and fantasy stories, was selected by August Derleth and published in 1963 with the title *The Dark Man and Others*.

At this time, Ace Books was successfully, although unauthorized by the Burroughs estate, publishing a number of Edgar Rice Burroughs' science fiction novels that quietly had slipped into the public domain. Ace saw similar potential in *Almuric*, a Burroughs-inspired novel by Howard, narrating the adventures of a teleported human on a distant and perilous

Conan the Conqueror. Gnome Press, Inc., 1950. Jacket art by David Kyle and John Forte. © 1950 Gnome Press, Inc.

The Sword of Conan. Gnome Press, Inc., 1952. Jacket art by David Kyle. © 1952 Gnome Press, Inc.

2—The Robert E. Howard Legacy

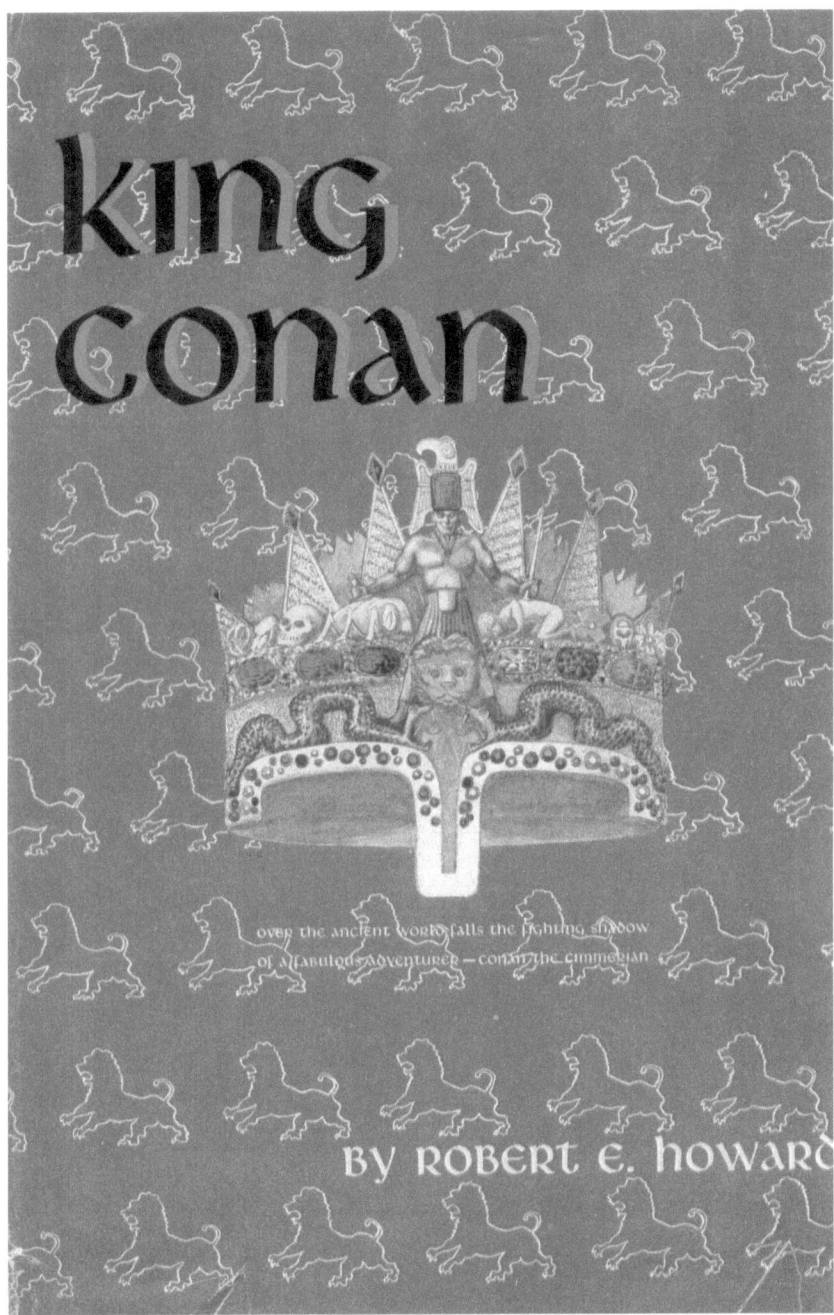

King Conan. Gnome Press, Inc., 1953. Jacket art by David Kyle. © 1953 Gnome Press, Inc.

Always Comes Evening. Arkham House Publishers 1957. Jacket art by Frank Utpatel. © 1957 Glenn Lord.

THE DARK MAN
THE JOURNAL OF ROBERT E. HOWARD STUDIES

The Dark Man—1990. © **Necronomicon Press.**

planet. A mass market paperback edition was released by Ace Books in 1964.

The following year, Donald M. Grant, West Kingston, Rhode Island, who would be prominent in the future publication of Howard hardcover books, released the first American edition of *A Gent From Bear Creek*. The book was photo offset from the Jenkins first edition. A second collection of Breckinridge Elkins stories with the title *The Pride of Bear Creek* was published by Grant in 1966.

The Dark Man and Others. Arkham House Publishers 1963. Jacket art by Frank Utpatel. © 1963 August Derleth.

LANCER, D.M. GRANT, FAX, ZEBRA AND BERKLEY

As it happened, 1966 turned out to be a banner year for Robert E. Howard. From his death and to that time, only a score of faithful fans remembered him and continued to buy and read what might appear on the market under his name. That was about to change. Persuaded by L. Sprague de Camp, Lancer Books, Inc., launched in 1966 an 11-volume mass market paperback series based on the Conan stories. With a stroke of genius, Lancer editor Larry Shaw hired the fantasy artist Frank Frazetta to paint eight of the covers for the paperbacks. The combination of Howard's stories and Frazetta's covers sold well and the series was reprinted several times. It brought the works of Howard to a much broader audience and the interest in his stories and poetry saw an unprecedented rise in the late 1960s and 1970s.

While the Lancer series was commercially successful and brought a universal revival and broader appreciation of Robert E. Howard's work, the downside was that many of the stories were textually compromised because of the editing, rewriting or expansions done by L. Sprague de Camp and his collaborator at the time, Lin Carter. Other Howard titles published by Lancer Books were *King Kull* in 1967, *Wolfshead* in 1968, and *The Dark Man and Others* in 1972.

The entire Lancer Conan series was reprinted by Ace Books in the mid–1970s, edited by L. Sprague de Camp. A 12th volume, *Conan of Aquilonia*, written by L. Sprague de Camp and Lin Carter was added to the series. The Conan series was reprinted in 20 printings into the mid–1980s. Dell Publishing Co. released *Bran Mak Morn* in a mass market paperback edition with a superb Frank Frazetta cover in 1969. The same year Centaur Press published *The Moon of Skulls*, followed by *The Hand of Kane* (1970) and *Solomon Kane* (1971) in paperback editions.

Donald M. Grant continued the publication of Howard hardcover volumes with *Singers in the Shadows* (1970), *Red Blades of Black Cathay* (1971), *Marchers of Valhalla* (1972), *The Sowers of the Thunder* (1973), and *Worms of the Earth* (1974). From 1974 through 1989, Grant published a series of 11 limited edition books of Conan stories. Each volume contained one or two Cimmerian tales and was illustrated by various more or less talented artists. The series began with *The People of the Black Circle* (1974) and ended with *The Hour of the Dragon* (1989). During this period, Grant also published several other hardcover Howard titles, most of them illustrated. In total Donald M. Grant published 37 Robert E. Howard titles, ending in 1990 with Howard's autobiographical novel, *Post Oaks and Sand Roughs*.

In addition to the commercial printings, the 1970s was also a time for the emergence of numerous private printings of Howard material. Some of the best known were Roy A. Squires' five handsome, limited printings of

Marchers of Valhalla. Donald M. Grant 1972. Jacket art by Robert B. Acheson. © 1972 Glenn Lord.

poetry published between 1972 and 1977. George T. Hamilton entered the Howard publication race in 1975 with *Verses in Ebony* and a matched set of seven booklets, beginning with "Blades for France" in 1975 and ending with "Spears of Clontarf" in 1978. Several other small publishing enterprises added to the number of special publications.

The Sowers of the Thunder. **Donald M. Grant 1973. Jacket art by Roy G. Krenkel. © 1973 Glenn Lord.**

The People of the Black Circle. Berkley/Putnam 1977. Jacket art by Ken Kelly. © 1977 Glenn Lord.

The Hour of the Dragon. Berkley/Putnam 1977. Jacket art by Ken Kelly. © 1977 Glenn Lord.

The Robert E. Howard zenith in the 1970s propagated a multitude of privately produced and published fanzines or amateur press publications of varying quality. Most of them did not last beyond a few issues, but some continued publication—although in most cases infrequently—for several years. One remarkable example of perseverance is the Robert E. Howard

Verses in Ebony. George T. Hamilton 1975. Cover art by Kirwan. © 1975 Glenn Lord and Kirwan.

United Press Association (REHupa) that began publishing special mailings to its members in 1972 and continues to this day.

Another hardcover book publisher, FAX Collector's Editions, Inc., began publication of Howard story collections with *The Incredible Adventures of Dennis Dorgan* in 1974 and published four more volumes, ending with a Richard Lupoff collaboration, *The Return of Skull-Face* in 1977.

Zebra Books entered the fray in 1975 with a mass market paperback edition of *The Sowers of the Thunder* and published 13 more titles till 1977. At the time Robert E. Howard's books were selling so well that Zebra capitalized on its success by adding the line, "Heroic fantasy in the tradition of ROBERT E. HOWARD" to the front cover of any book that might fit even loosely into the category of heroic fantasy. One of the more memorable uses of this marketing device was the Zebra 1977 four-volume issue of Talbot Mundy's *Tros of Samothrace/The Purple Pirate*—probably one of the finest pieces of historical fantasy written—with Robert E. Howard's name printed in larger letters on the cover than the author's. The irony was that it was Talbot Mundy who had influenced and inspired Howard, not vice versa, so properly speaking Robert E. Howard would be "In the tradition of Talbot Mundy."

The cover of Andrew J. Offutt's Cormac Mac Art pastiches *Sword of the Gael* and *The Undying Wizard*, also Zebra Books printings, carried, as other similar titles, the words, "In the tradition of CONAN based on the character created by ROBERT E. HOWARD" with Conan's and Howard's name in much larger types than Offutt's.

Ace Books, the publisher of the first book edition of *Almuric*, continued its run of Howard stories in 1979 with *The Gods of Bal-Sagoth* and published 15 more paperbacks ending in 1987 with *Swords of Shahrazar*. Most of the books were reprints of the same titles published earlier by Zebra or Berkley Books. When Ace Books began reprinting Howard pastiches, they followed Zebra's strategy by printing a cover banner, "Mightier than CONAN? ROBERT E. HOWARD's Other Hero CORMAC MAC ART" on Offutt's *The Sword of the Gael* and similar titles, with Conan's and Howard's name in larger type than the author's. In the 1970s and 1980s, the name Robert E. Howard sold mass market paperbacks by the thousands. The salient incongruity was that many of the books sold were not his work.

Berkley Medallion issued a three-volume Conan paperback collection in 1977, followed by another 14 Howard titles that ended with reprints of Glenn Lord's two Zebra Book anthologies, *The Book of Robert E. Howard* and *The Second Book of Robert E. Howard*, in 1980. In 1977 Berkley-Putnam released three hardcover volumes in both book club and trade editions, of the Conan collection: *The Hour of the Dragon*, *Red Nails* and *The People of the Black Circle*. The nine Conan tales contained in the three books were edited by Karl Edward Wagner and

The Sowers of the Thunder. Zebra Books 1975. Cover art by Jeff Jones. © 1973 Glenn Lord.

Almuric. Ace Books 1964. Cover art by Jack Gaughan. © 1964 Ace Books.

Swords of Shahrazar. FAX Collector's Edition 1976. Jacket art by Michael W. Kaluta. © 1976 Glenn Lord and Michael W. Kaluta.

Red Nails. Berkley Books 1977. Cover art by Ken Kelly. © 1977 Glenn Lord.

based on the original text from *Weird Tales*. This makes these books remarkable since they contain the first unaltered Conan stories in publication since their original appearance in *Weird Tales*. It was the intention of Wagner to publish all of the Conan stories as originally published in *Weird Tales*, but a copyright dispute with Conan Properties, Inc., unfortunately prevented the continuation of this worthwhile project.

The Movies

Even Hollywood was now paying attention to the Howard boom and in 1982 released its first movie based on Robert E. Howard's best known character, Conan of Cimmeria. The title of the movie was *Conan the Barbarian*; it was directed by John Milius and starred Arnold Schwarzenegger, James Earl Jones and Sandahl Bergman. While the movie did little for Robert E. Howard's reputation—the script bore only a sketchy resemblance to any Conan story—it was reasonably successful at the box office and made an instant star of Schwarzenegger. A sequel titled *Conan the Destroyer* followed in 1984, directed by Richard Fleischer and again starring Arnold Schwarzenegger with Grace Jones. The movie script was even further from the original Conan material than its predecessor. Nevertheless the two Conan movies carried Arnold Schwarzenegger to stardom and started him on a successful career in the action movie genre, a factor which undoubtedly was of no small significance in his successful campaign for the governorship of California in 2004.

Another Howard inspired movie, titled *Red Sonja*, was released in 1985. The movie was also directed by Richard Fleischer and once again starred Arnold Schwarzenegger, in the Conan-type role as Kalidor and Brigitte Nielsen as Red Sonja. There is nothing in the script recognizable from Howard's tale about Red Sonya of Rogatino, who appeared in "The Shadow of the Vulture" published in *The Magic Carpet Magazine* in 1934. Even the spelling of the character's name is different.

In 1996 Sony Pictures released a movie, *The Whole Wide World,* based on Novalyne Price Ellis' biographical book, *One Who Walked Alone* (Donald M. Grant,1986), about Robert E. Howard's final years. The movie was directed by Dan Ireland and starred Vincent D'Onofrio and Renée Zellweger. In spite of a stellar performance by the two stars, a script true to the original text and a fine atmospheric setting, the movie did not receive the acclaim or public attention it deserved.

The most recent movie based on Howard's writings was *Kull the*

Conqueror directed by John Nicolella and released in 1996, starring Kevin Sorbo—of TV *Hercules* fame—and Tia Carrere. The script was mediocre at best and had only a few names and scenes in common with Howard's outstanding yarns about the Atlantean fugitive who becomes the enigmatic king of Valusia.

In 2000 Warners Brothers paid $2.5 million for the movie rights to the Conan character for a third movie, which was to be titled, *King Conan: Crown of Iron*. The director of the original Conan movie, John Milius, was hired as writer and director, as were Larry and Andy Wachowski (of *Matrix* fame) as creative partners and producers. After some time Conan Properties International, LLC., became disenchanted with the slow progress of the movie in the hands of Warner Brothers and decided not to allow Warner, Milius or the Wachowski brothers to renew the option on the material when it expired. One reason for the production hold up was that the Wachowskis had to finish their work on the *Matrix* sequels before they could start on the Conan movie.

Conan Properties International, LLC., had decided to produce the new Conan movie and began looking for a studio which could produce a lower budget film. CPI wanted to make a less violent and more audience-friendly movie on a smaller scale, using the format of *Spider-Man* and *The Scorpion King*, and with a younger actor in the title role. The project was undertaken by the Swedish-based Paradox Entertainment, that had purchased 20 percent of the Conan Sales Company, which according to a company press release, held all intellectual property rights in and associated with the character Conan.

For various reasons, the production of the CPI movie version did not happened and eventually CPI sold the Conan movie rights back to Warner Brothers. Warner Brothers has suggested that they want to produce the movie within the next year, but it appears that the project is still in limbo. One of the most problematic aspects is to find the right writer, director and actor for the title role. Arnold Schwarzenegger has been mentioned on numerous occasions as the frontrunner for the role of an aging King Conan, but it is doubtful that he would be interested or have the time to do the work along with his official duties as governor of California.

A Solomon Kane movie has tentatively been in the works for some time under the banner of Solomon Kane Properties, LLC. Wandering Star's deluxe edition *The Savage Tales of Solomon Kane* (1998) was originally published as a promotional lead-in or forerunner to the movie. How far the production may be at this time is not publicly known. It has been announced that a Bran Mak Morn movie might also be in the making, but no further details are available at the time of writing.

The Textually Pure Howard

Coincidentally with the rise of the personal computer in the mid-1980s, the Howard boom began to lose momentum as public interest waned. The computer soon became a primary source of entertainment for the younger generation and computer gaming quickly took preference over leisure reading. Nevertheless the Howard boom had produced a new generation of Robert E. Howard devotees, more sophisticated, perhaps better educated and certainly more discriminating.

Another phenomenon created by the upsurge in Howard's popularity was the proliferation of revisions, expansions and pastiches, particularly of the Conan character by other fantasy writers. Most of these imitations were tolerable at best and all were sorely lacking when compared to the original; but they resulted in one positive turn of event. They produced a demand by the more knowledgeable Howard followers for the pure Howardian text and rejection of all else, including editorial corrections, revision and deviation from the original material. The new Howard readers wanted the true, unexpurgated and unaltered text.

Their voices were heard and in 1995–1996, Baen Publishing Enterprise released a mass market paperback, seven volume collection of Howard's non–Conan stories, in which an attempt had been made to restore the original text. Two years after the successful Baen series, the Science Fiction Book Club released a hardcover volume collecting the three Conan book club editions originally published by Berkeley-Putnam in 1977 and edited by Karl Edward Wagner under the title *The Essential Conan*. It included the same nine stories as the three-volume series, but the text had been cleaned up and previous typographical errors were corrected.

The British publisher Wandering Star published a limited, luxury edition of *The Savage Tales of Solomon Kane* in 1998. The book was aptly illustrated by Gary Gianni and produced as a promotional forerunner for a forthcoming Solomon Kane movie. The text was taken in part from the original typescripts and scans from the Baen 1995 paperback edition. During the proofreading process, some deviations from the original typescripts found their way into the text, however, all such departures are documented in the book.

The book sold well and Wandering Star followed up with *The Ultimate Triumph* in 1999. It was also a limited, luxury edition of Howard stories and letters focused on the subject of barbarism vs. civilization, with the original, unexpurgated text. The book was illustrated with a wealth of art by the master fantasy artist Frank Frazetta.

In 2000 the British publisher Victor Gollancz issued a two-volume set of oversized paperback books titled *The Conan Chronicles*. The books were

The Essential Conan. The Science Fiction Book Club 1998. Jacket art by Ken Kelly. © 1977 Glenn Lord.

The Savage Tales of Solomon Kane. Wandering Star 1998. Jacket art by Gary Gianni. © 1998 Solomon Kane Corporation and Gary Gianni.

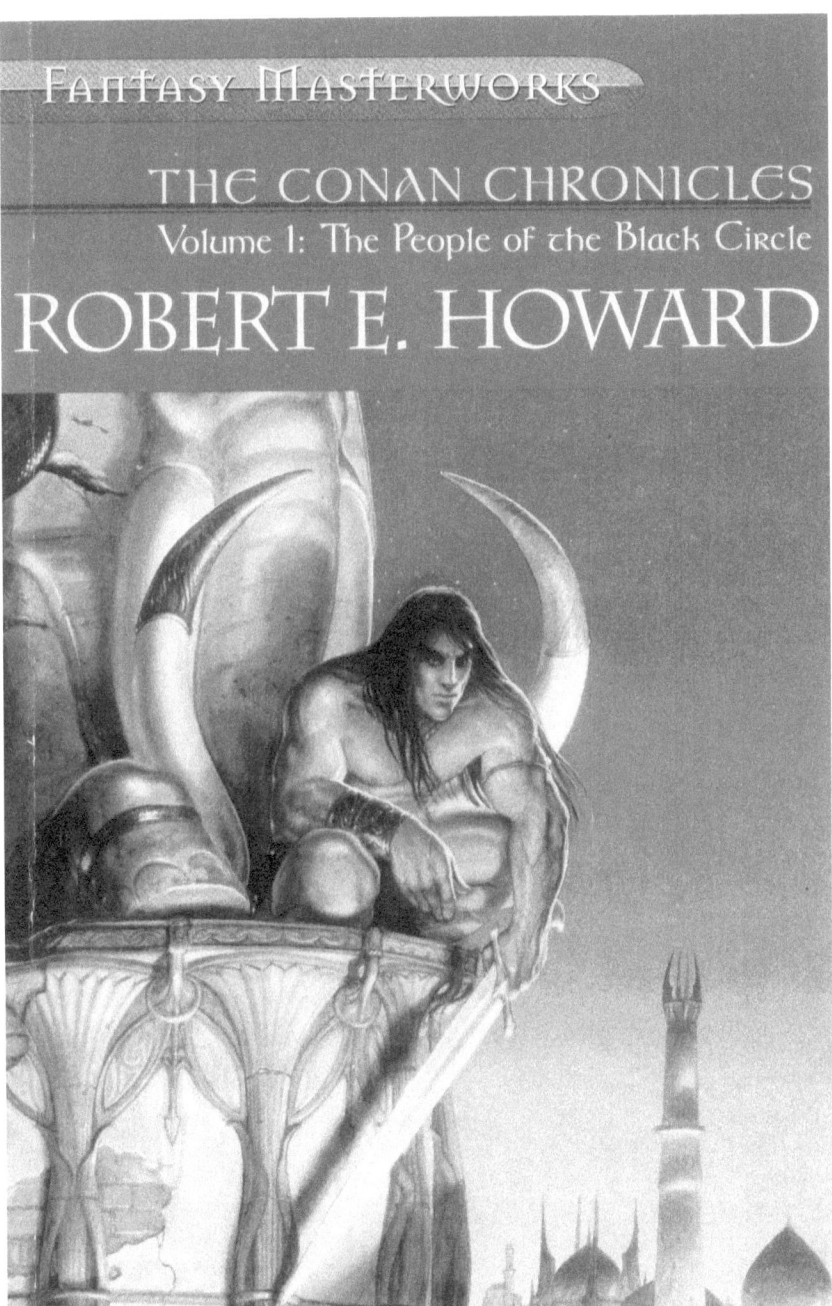

The Conan Chronicles. Vol. 1. Gollanz Fantasy Masterworks 2000. Cover design by Richard Carr, art by John Howe. © Robert E. Howard.

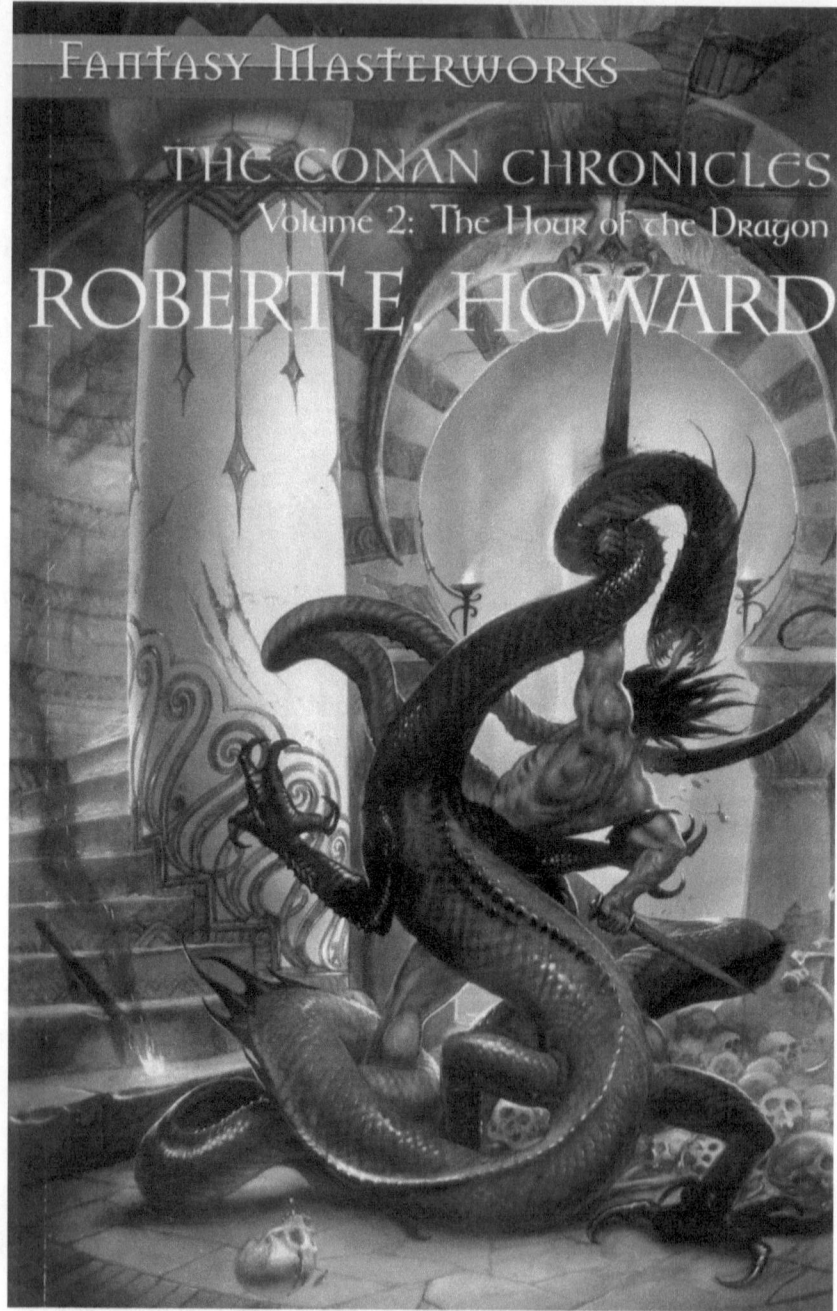

The Conan Chronicles. Vol. 2. Gollanz Fantasy Masterworks 2001. Cover design by Richard Carr, art by John Howe. © Robert E. Howard.

edited by Stephen Jones and contained the known Conan series of 28 tales. An effort was made to publish the stories as they originally appeared in *Weird Tales*, however, the majority were reprinted from various less textually true sources. The stories are arranged in the chronological order of Conan's biography as suggested by P. Schuyler Miller and John D. Clark, and not in the order that Howard wrote them. *The Conan Chronicles* was a welcome addition to the extant, unaltered Howard texts, but suffers unfortunately from an excessive amount of typographical and grammatical errors, which made reading some stories less enjoyable.

The next year Wandering Star published a limited, luxury edition of *Bran Mak Morn: The Last King,* illustrated by Gary Gianni. This was followed in 2002 by a limited, facsimile edition of Howard's original typescripts for *The Black Stranger,* presented in a folder illustrated by Gianni. Years earlier the story had been revised and published by L. Sprague de Camp under the title *The Treasure of Tranicos.*

The first volume in a limited, luxury edition, three-volume set of Conan stories, *Conan of Cimmeria. Vol. I (1932–1933)*, illustrated by Mark Schultz and as true to Howard's original typescript as possible was released by Wandering Star in 2002 (available in 2003). The second volume in the series, *Conan of Cimmeria. Vol, II (1934)*, illustrated by Gary Gianni, was published in 2003 (available in 2004). When completed the three-volume set will contain all the known Conan tales and may be considered the definitive Conan series.

Del Rey-Ballantine reprinted Wandering Star's 2002 *Conan of Cimmeria. Vol. I* under the title *The Coming of Conan the Cimmerian* in 2003, in an affordable, softcover trade edition with all the text and illustrations of its expensive predecessor. *Conan of Cimmeria. Vol. II* was reprinted in the same format, under the title *The Bloody Crown of Conan* in 2004. Both of the Del Rey Conan books were reprinted as hardcover book club editions the same year. Also in 2004, Del Rey reprinted Wandering Star's 1998 *The Savage Tales of Solomon Kane* in the same format as the two previously published Conan books. The text had been corrected for any errors or deviations from the original typescripts. The book was reprinted as a hardcover book club edition in 2005. The same year Wandering Star's 2001 *Bran Mak Morn: The Last King* was reprinted by Del Rey in a fully illustrated softcover trade edition and a hardcover book club edition. A Del Rey trade cloth edition of *The Coming of Conan the Cimmerian* has been announced for release late December 2005 at a cover price of $29.95.

In 2003 Wildside Press began publishing a collection of hardcover books of the lesser known Howard stories, starting with *The Complete Action Stories* and followed by six more volumes. In late 2004 the same publisher launched a 10-volume limited hardcover series of Robert E. Howard's fantasy writings. The series is edited by Paul Herman and sub-titled *The Weird Works of R.E. Howard*. It will reprint all the *Weird Tales* stories in chronological order. The first volume, *Shadow Kingdoms*, was published in December 2004, followed by *The Moon of Skulls* in April, *People of the Dark* in August, and *Wings in the Night* in December 2005.

Along the same lines, Girasol Collectables, Inc., in Mississauga, Ontario, Canada, announced in October 2005 the facsimile publication of all of Robert E. Howard's writings from the original run of *Weird Tales* Magazine. *The Weird Writings of Robert E. Howard* includes all the stories, illustrations, poems and relevant letters to the editor, scanned from the original magazine pages and collected in two hardcover volumes. The first volume was published in February 2006, and volume 2 became available later in the spring. Under Canadian copyright law, all of Howard's work published in this edition is considered to be in the public domain north of the border.

For reasons unknown, but probably of a financial nature, Wandering Star did not publish the third and final volume of the limited edition trilogy, *Conan of Cimmeria Vol. III (1934–1936)*, as planned in 2005. Del Rey/Ballantine, however, published a reprint of this work with the title *The Conquering Sword of Conan* in both a hardcover book club edition and a trade softcover edition in November 2005. The book is illustrated by Gregory Manchess. The Del Rey trade edition became the true first edition of this title.

The latest revival of the interest in Robert E. Howard's work also started a rebirth of the small press printings and amateur press publications, but in a more professional and discriminating manner than in the free-for-all Howard melee of the 1970s. Necronomicon, among others, has released several excellent Howard items, including a new scholarly publication, *The Dark Man: The Journal of Robert E. Howard Studies* (now published by Seele Brent Publications). Other noteworthy scholarly journals are Leo Grin's handsome *The Cimmerian* and *The Cimmerian Library*; Damon C. Sasser's *REH: Two Gun Raconteur*, and Jim Van Hise's *Sword & Fantasy*. A collection of Howard's poetry in hardcover format is in the works spearheaded by graphic designer Jim Keegan. Since Howard wrote approximately 700 poems, this is a major undertaking. The book is scheduled for release in 2006, the one hundredth anniversary of Howard's birth, but may be postponed or shelved on account of a copyright dispute.

In April 2005 the University of Nebraska Press published a new Bison series of five Robert E. Howard books, consisting of *The Black Stranger and Other American Tales, Boxing Stories, The End of the Trail, Lord of Samarcand and Other Adventures of the Old Orient* and *The Riot at Bucksnort and Other Western Tales*. All five titles are published in both hardcover and soft cover editions.

Moon of Skulls. Wildside Press 2004. Jacket art by Stephen Fabian. © 2004. Paul Herman and Stephen Fabian.

Sword & Fantasy—2005. © James Van Hise.

The Black Stranger and Other American Tales. University of Nebraska Press 2005. Jacket art by Mike Mignola. © 2005 Robert E. Howard Properties, LLC and Mike Mignola.

Boxing Stories. University of Nebraska Press 2005. Jacket art by Gary Gianni.
© 2005 REH Properties, Inc., and Gary Gianni.

CROSS PLAINS AND PROJECT PRIDE

In 1989 a community organization known as Project Pride purchased the old Howard house in Cross Plains. This was made possible by contributions from local citizens, from Howard fans across the country and from Alla Ray Kuykendall Morris, the heir to Howard's literary properties at the time. Following the necessary repairs and restoration, the house was listed in 1994 on the National Register of Historical Places.

The Howard house is maintained by Project Pride as a museum and provides the frame for the Robert E. Howard Days, held in June each year. Hosted by Project Pride and arranged by the members of the Robert E. Howard United Press Association, this event, which includes speakers, tours, banquet, auction and other activities, has been growing in popularity and attendance from year to year. In 2000, a pavilion was built on an adjoining lot to accommodate both the Robert E. Howard Day visitors and other Cross Plains community events.

At the time of writing, the legacy of Robert E. Howard seems relatively secure and Conan of Cimmeria, Solomon Kane, Bran Mak Morn, King Kull, Steve Costigan, Breckenridge Elkins and all the other memorable characters who sprang from the fertile mind of the young Texas writer will continue to captivate and entertain us for a long time to come. For those of us who are getting on in years and remember when the pulps and books gave us a world of bold adventures and derring-do, before the advents of television and the computer, that is a comforting thought.

Thank you, Bob Howard!

3

A Robert E. Howard Cast of Characters

The following gallery of characters created by Robert E. Howard is not all-inclusive. During his short but prolific career, Howard created a multitude of characters from prehistoric swordsmen, sorcerers, pirates and medieval knights to modern day adventurers, fist fighters and detectives. It would require much more space than is available to give equal recognition to every character. A choice has been made on the basis of popular appeal and how well Howard developed the character primarily reflected in the number of related stories written.

Howard's writing was to a large extent directed by what the pulp magazine editors wanted at the time. As a consequence some of the more interesting characters, whom we may have liked to hear more about, barely made it into print, while others probably were overdone to satisfy public demand. Several of Howard's characters, who appeared in only one or a few stories, had great appeal and development potential if they had been given more favorable consideration by editors and readers.

The stories listed at the end for each character under "Other Stories" are arranged in alphabetical, not in chronological or publication, order.

AGNES DE CHASTILLON

Agnes de Chastillon, or Black Agnes de La Fere, is with Sonya of Rogatino (*The Shadow of the Vulture*), Helen Tavrel (*The Isle of Pirate's Doom*), Valeria of the Red Brotherhood (*Red Nails*), and Bêlit (*Queen of the Black Coast*), one of the more prominent warrior women created by Howard. On the day of her arranged wedding, the strong-willed and free-spirited Agnes stabs to death her betrothed, whom she loathes. She escapes from her small 15th century French village, joins a mercenary rogue and

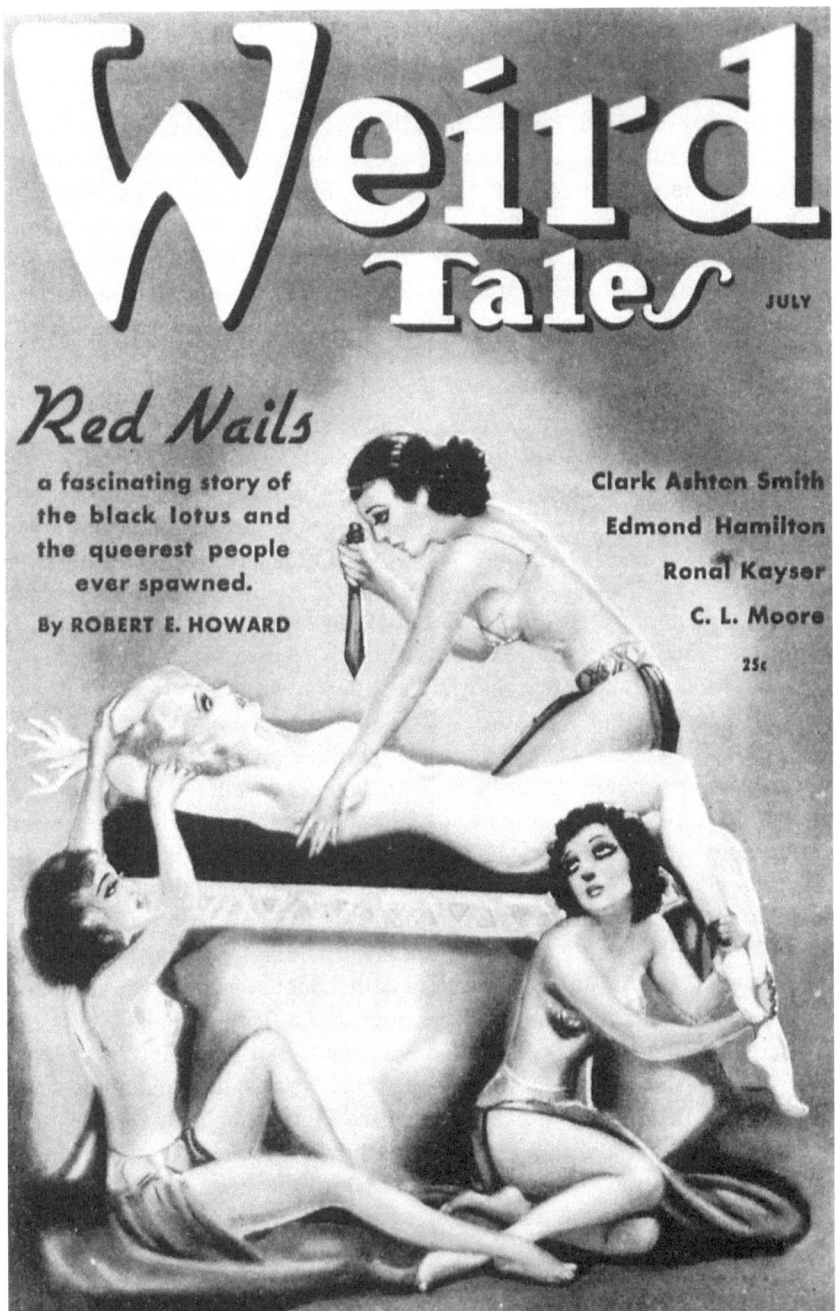

Red Nails. Cover art by Margaret Brundage. *Weird Tales,* July 1936. © 1976 Glenn Lord.

with an apparent innate flair for the blade, uncannily quickly becomes an accomplished sword fighter.

Agnes de La Fere is a beautiful, strong and pragmatic woman, who handles herself well in the violent milieu of her times. In writing *Sword Woman,* the first Dark Agnes tale, it seems likely that Robert E. Howard might have been inspired by C.L. Moore's *Jirel of Joiry* stories, which he had read and enjoyed. Jirel also appeared in *Weird Tales* before *Sword Woman* was written. Since the Dark Agnes tales did not sell and were not published before after Howard's death, one must assume that in spite of the unique appeal and charisma of the character, a sword woman was not what the pulp magazine editors wanted at the time.

First appearance: "Sword Woman," *The Nemedian Chronicles for REH: Lone Star Fictioneer*, No. 2, 1975.

Other stories: "Blades for France"; "Mistress of Death."

BRAN MAK MORN

As a young boy, Howard read a book on early English history, which mentioned the initial settling of the British Isles by a race of small, dark-skinned, Mediterranean people who became known as the Picts. The mystery of these ancient tribesmen fascinated Howard and he resolved to someday write about them and their struggle against other tribes, the Roman invasion and eventually against their own decline, degeneration and demise. Forever the advocate of whom he considered to be the underdog, even when contradictory to historical facts, Howard wrote several stories and poems about the doomed race and thereby created a valorous final chapter for the Picts under one last, great warrior king, Bran Mak Morn.

Historically, the Picts were a seafaring and agricultural people who first appeared c. AD 300. They were equally adept at farming, pirating and warfare, and fought numerous battles against the Britons, Celts, Scots and Norsemen. Later they became allied with the Ulster Scots and other local tribes and participated vigorously in the revolt against the Roman presence in Northern Britain. By the 4th century the Picts had become the leading Caledonian nation and the military superpower of a greater part of Scotland, which became known as Pictland or Pictavia.

Nevertheless, invoking the literary license granted all writers of historical fiction, Robert E. Howard chose to present the Picts as a race in decline, a people past its glory days, a genetically corrupt and physically degenerating nation, slowly vanishing into the darkness of extinction. Since the bloodline of the Pictish kings has been kept pure, Bran Mak Morn himself does not share his people's genealogy and its consequences, but he

WORMS OF THE EARTH

Worms of the Earth. Orbit Books 1976. Cover art by Chris Achilleos. © 1969 Glenn Lord.

shares its fate. He knows that regardless of any effort to prevent the inevitable, his is a dying nation and yet he fights not only against his human enemies, but also to preserve what is left of the once proud Pictish heritage.

In Bran Mak Morn, Howard has created one of his most enigmatic and tragic characters. A great leader who, unlike most of Howard's other heroes, is not focused primarily on his own fate and fortune, but is fully devoted to the impossible task of averting the cruel destiny of his people.

First appearance: "Kings of the Night," *Weird Tales,* November 1930. (Howard's first Pict story, "The Lost Race," appeared in *Weird Tales,* January 1927, but it does not include Bran Mak Morn.)

Other stories: "Bran Mak Morn," "Bran Mak Morn—a Play," "Children of the Night," "The Dark Man," "The Drums of Pictdom" (poem), "The Little People," "Men of the Shadows," "A Song of the Race" (poem), "Worms of the Earth."

BRECKINRIDGE ELKINS

When Fiction House suspended publication of *Fight Stories* and *Action Stories* in 1932 under the impact of the Great Depression, Howard lost two important markets for his Sailor Steve Costigan stories and other boxing-adventure tales. From July 1929 through March 1932, 18 of his stories were published in the two magazines. The loss of this important market was a blow to Howard's financial status and it was probably with some relief that he learned *Action Stories* would resume publication in the fall of 1933. In a letter to August Derleth in December that year, Howard wrote that while he had been only minimally successful in selling to this market before, he was currently working on a series of stories featuring a new character aimed at *Action Stories*. The character was a Pecos Bill type western hero, a giant mountain man named Breckinridge Elkins, who roamed the Humboldt Mountains.

Howard carried through on the idea and thus Breckinridge Elkins of Bear Creek, Nevada, the larger than life, toughest, and strongest mountain man ever to ride the trails of the west, with his old cap-and-ball .44 strapped around his waist, appeared on the pages of *Action Story* in the March 1934 issue with the tale "Mountain Man."

The Breckinridge Elkins stories became so popular that from his debut with "Mountain Man" and until Howard's death in June 1936, every issue of *Action Stories* contained a Breckinridge Elkins story. Several other stories in the hands of the editors at the time were published thereafter.

In creating and developing the Breckinridge Elkins character and his environment, Howard showed a mastery of what may be called the humorous western tale. Told in dialect, the stories, the characters and the wild happenings in these yarns are outrageously funny, yet underneath the swift action, satire and humor, one can feel the undercurrent of Howard's great love for the west and his admiration for the various human types who populated it before it became tamed.

While composing these tales appears to have been well within Howard's range and ability, they are far from easy to write in a convincing and interesting way. No one has ever succeeded in writing this type of western as well as Howard, which might be why pastiche writers have not attempted to capitalize on the Breckinridge Elkins stories as they have done with Conan, Bran Mak Morn and Cormac Mac Art.

First appearance: "Mountain Man," *Action Stories,* March 1934.

Other Stories: "The Apache Mountain War," "The Conquerin' Hero of the Humbolts," "Cupid from Bear Creek," "The Curly Wolf of Sawtooth," "Educate or Bust," "Evil Deeds at Red Cougar," "The Feud Buster," "A Gent From Bear Creek"; "Guns of the Mountain," "The Haunted Mountain," "High Horse Rampage," "Mayhem and Taxes," "Meet Cap'n Kidd," "No Cowherders Wanted," "The Peaceful Pilgrim," "Pilgrims to the Pecos," "Pistol Politics," "The Riot at Cougar Paw," "The Road to Bear Creek," "The Scalp Hunter," "Sharp's Gun Serenade," "Striped Shirts and Busted Hearts," "War on Bear Creek," "When Bear Creek Came to Chawed Ear," "While Smoke Rolled."

BUCKNER JEOPARDY GRIMES

Towards the end of his career, Howard abandoned many of his earlier characters and series and focused primarily on tales and characters of the west. He was fortunate to find a ready market for his western stories, first in the revived *Action Stories* and later in *Argosy* and *Cowboy Tales.*

Buckner J. Grimes of Knife River, Texas, is pretty much cut from the same cloth as Breckinridge Elkins and Pike Bearfield. It seems obvious that Howard, for financial reasons, created the three characters in order to sell the popular western stories to three different magazines. All the series were cut short by Howard's untimely death and several of the tales purchased previously to this event were published later in 1936 and 1937. Howard's humorous westerns were among his last work and in many respects his most finished and accomplished work.

First appearance: "A Man-Eating Jeopard," *Cowboy Stories,* June 1936.
Other stories: "Knife River Prodigal," "Texas John Alden."

Conan the Cimmerian

Of all Robert E. Howard's *Weird Tales* stories and serial characters, no one has captured the public imagination as the Cimmerian swordsman and his adventures in the ancient world of the Hyborian Age. Taken as a whole, the Conan series is the story of a young Nordic, barbarian tribesman who becomes a thief, a mercenary, a pirate, a warrior, a chieftain and eventually king of Aquilonia, the most illustrious kingdom of the time.

In order to give Conan a sufficiently colorful environment, with unlimited possibilities for various plot backgrounds, Howard invented the Hyborian Age. This was a time set approximately 12,000 years ago, on the threshold of recorded history. The Hyborian Age in effect combined and telescoped several different historical periods and various human cultures, and provided a unique and multifaceted stage for the Cimmerian's many adventures. In total, Howard wrote 26 Conan stories, including unfinished items and fragments, one novel and a poem. The majority of the stories were published in *Weird Tales* between December 1932 and October 1936.

Many of the Conan stories were later revised and rewritten by other writers, and published in books, mass market paperbacks and other publications. In later years, other writers have added to the series and produced their own versions of Conan adventure stories and novels.

Lancer Books' publication of an 11-volume Conan mass market paperback series from 1966–1969 launched a revival of public interest in the Cimmerian and the series was reprinted repeatedly. The interest in Conan spread to the comic book industry and in 1970 *Marvel Comics* began the "Conan the Barbarian" comic book series which ran to 1993. The success of the series created the spin-off of other Conan comic books and magazine series such as "King Conan," "Conan the King," "The Savage Sword of Conan" and "The Conan Saga."

The celebrity of the character also spawned two movies: *Conan the Barbarian* (1982) and *Conan the Destroyer* (1984), both starring Arnold Schwarzenegger as the Cimmerian. Neither of them were particularly noteworthy or true to any of the original Conan stories by Howard. A third Conan movie, *King Conan: The Crown of Iron*, has been in the making, on again and off again, since 2000.

On the origin of Conan, Robert E. Howard wrote to Clark Ashton Smith in December 1933, that he felt the creation of Conan had come about through the influence of some unexplainable, outside force. According to Howard he had been barren of ideas for months and unable to work on anything sellable, when Conan suddenly appeared in his mind. From there on the adventures of the Cimmerian swordsman in the Hyborian Age flowed from the typewriter without much effort on his part. The stories kept

THE CIMMERIAN

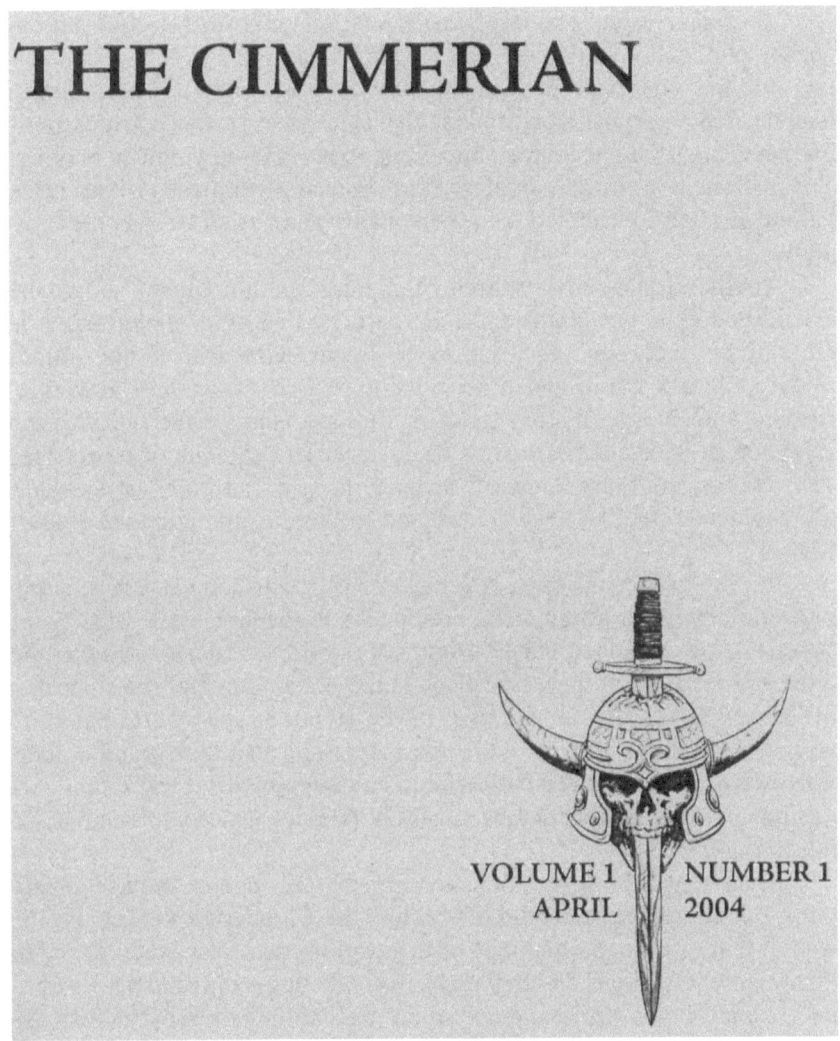

The Cimmerian—2004. © **Leo Grin.**

coming, one piling upon the next in rapid succession and gave him little time for writing anything else for several weeks. He felt as if Conan had taken control of his mind and left no room for anything else than recording the Cimmerian's tales.

Howard may have engaged in some small measure of imaginative contemplation here, for as we know, the first Conan story written and subsequently accepted for publication by *Weird Tales* was "The Phoenix on the Sword," a rewrite of the rejected King Kull tale "By This Axe I Rule." The second Conan story, "The Frost-Giant's Daughter," was rejected and did not see publication until well after Howard's death.

On the character of Conan, Howard told Clark Ashton Smith that he had subconsciously taken the characteristics of various real-life personages he had known, including prize-fighters, gunmen, bootleggers, oil field bullies, gamblers, and honest workmen. All of these individuals had contributed to the personality and traits of Conan the Cimmerian.

Another prospective source of inspiration for Conan should be considered of equal importance. Howard was an avid reader and it is more than likely that the fiction of Edgar Rice Burroughs, Talbot Mundy, Harold Lamb and other adventure writers, as well as Celtic, British and Norse history and mythology, may have led to the invention of several of Howard's characters. The exploits of personages such as Tarzan, Tros, Beowulf, Roland, El Cid and other larger-than-life characters may all have contributed to the creation and evolution of Conan.

In 1936 two Conan fans, P. Schuyler Miller and John D. Clark, wrote a chronology of the Cimmerian, entitled "A Probable Outline of Conan's Career." They arranged the 17 originally published Conan stories in the order the authors felt they took place in the life and time of the character. Miller and Clark also drew a map of the Hyborian Age world based on Howard's notations. A draft of the chronology and map were sent to Robert E. Howard, who reviewed the material and suggested several minor corrections, but his responses was generally positive and complimentary to the chronology.

In his reply Howard commented broadly on Conan's life and adventures, but stated that he could not predict the Cimmerian's eventual fate. He felt that he was chronicling Conan's exploits as if they were related to him mentally by the character, rather than creating them, and gave this as the reason why the stories did not follow any chronological order. As a living adventurer, he suggested, so did Conan tell the tales of his life randomly and as they came into his mind.

After having made the corrections suggested by Howard and adding one more story, Miller and Clark published the chronology in *The Hyborian Age* (LANY Corporative Publishers, 1938).

In the 1950s, L. Sprague de Camp updated Miller and Clark's chronology by adding the posthumously published Conan stories, pastiches, revisions and finished story fragments. The chronology was eventually adopted by the Conan copyright holder at the time, Conan Properties, Inc., as the official Conan biography. It was required thereafter that all new Conan tales should fit into the chronology, without conflicting

3—*A Robert E. Howard Cast of Characters* 89

The People of the Black Circle. Cover art by Margaret Brundage. *Weird Tales*, September 1934. © 1976 Glenn Lord.

with any previous story or event. It is unclear if this requirement is still in effect.

The issue of the Conan chronology has been the cause of a great deal of deliberation, controversy and dispute since 1973 when Kevin Miller was the first to question the validity of the Miller-Clark Conan chronology (*Amra*, Vol. 2, No. 59, February 1973). Placing all the Conan stories correctly in their proper chronological order, when not even Howard seemed to be sure or particularly concerned about their sequencing, seems a daunting task, which in the end would be more a result of guesswork than constructive research.

The questions is: Do we really need a Conan chronology to enjoy the stories? And particularly one that is based primarily on speculation rather than the writer's personal design and perspective. Every Conan story can stand alone and in my opinion it is more rewarding to disregard the chronology—and the chronology argument—and read the stories in the order that Howard wrote them. This will keep the reader's attention on the quality of the story itself, rather than the aging of the character, and provide a better insight into the making of Howard the writer, as he matured and developed his craft. That would appear to be more important than which tale should come before or after another story.

First appearance: "The Phoenix on the Sword," *Weird Tales,* December 1932.

Other stories: "Beyond the Black River," "Black Colossus," "The Black Stranger," "The Devil in Iron," "Drums of Tombalku," "The Frost-Giant's Daughter," "The God in the Bowl," "The Hall of the Dead," "The Hand of Nergal," "The Hour of the Dragon," "The Hyborian Age," "Jewels of Gwahlur," "The People of the Black Circle," "The Pool of the Black One," "Queen of the Black Coast," "Red Nails," "Rogues in the House," "The Scarlet Citadel," "Shadows in the Moonlight," "Shadows in Zamboula," "The Slithering Shadow," "The Snout in the Dark," "The Tower of the Elephant," "The Vale of Lost Women," "A Witch Shall Be Born," "Wolves Beyond the Border," "Cimmeria" (poem).

CORMAC FITZGEOFFREY (HISTORICAL FICTION)

In June of 1930, the editor of *Weird Tales,* Farnsworth Wright, told Howard that his publishing house was launching a new magazine which was to be named *Oriental Stories.* On the same occasion Wright asked Howard if he would be interested in submitting stories to the new magazine, within the theme of its title. Howard, who had always been interested in history and historical fiction, agreed. For years he had read *Adventure*

Magazine, one of the most prestigious magazines on the market featuring writers such as Harold Lamb and Talbot Mundy, who would become a major influence on Howard's historical fiction, but in spite of numerous submissions he had not been able to sell any of his work to *Adventure Magazine.*

With his profound interest in ancient and medieval history, there is little doubt that Howard was keenly enthusiastic about writing historical fiction. He expressed this passion in a letter to H.P. Lovecraft in September 1933. He wrote that he wished he could devote the rest of his life to rewriting history in the form of fiction and that he found the sources of history to be infinite. However, he also expressed some doubt that he could make a living writing historical fiction, since the market for such work was limited and the requirements narrow. He commented also that it took him a long time to write these tales.

Howard's first successful attempt to write for *Oriental Tales* was a story named "The Voice of El-Lil." It was published in the October 1930 issue. Next followed a joint venture with his friend Tevis Clyde Smith, who did the research for the story. The title was "Red Blades of Black Cathay" and it appeared in *Oriental Tales* in February 1931.

In the April 1931 issue a Howard story titled "Hawks of Outremer" featured a crusader knight with the name Cormac FitzGeoffrey of Norman-Gaelic descent. The place of the story is Palestine (Outremer) and the time approximately AD 1220 or 70 years before the Christian kingdom in the Middle East fell to the Muslim armies. Howard describes FitzGeoffrey as a very large man, dark complexioned, black-haired, scarred, blue-eyed and grim-faced to the point of being sinister looking. An unmatched master with the sword and possessing a savage disposition, FitzGeoffrey was the personification of the crusading European knights who ravaged the lands and cities of the Middle East.

Howard's historical fiction, which takes place in Palestine, the Middle East and the near orient, all featured Gaelic, Celtic or Nordic knights with the appearance, demeanor, skills with weapons and dark disposition as FitzGeoffrey. In "Red Blades of Black Cathay" the Norman knight Godric de Villehard faces down the Mongol hordes of Genghis Khan. The lead character in "The Sowers of the Thunder" is the Frank Red Cahal, a knight of Irish descent. In "Lord of Samarkand" we meet the Scotsman Donald MacDeesa and in "The Lion of Tiberias," the lead character is the Danish knight John Norwald.

In 1933 and once more influenced by the financial iron grip of the Great Depression, an attempt was made to boost sales by changing the name of *Oriental Tales* to *The Magic Carpet Magazine.* Howard's story "The Lion of Tiberias" appeared in the July 1933 issue and he had two more stories, "Alleys of Darkness" and "The Shadow of the Vulture," published before the magazine folded in January 1934.

It was unfortunate that the pulp magazine market, as unstable as it was because of the financial difficulties of the time, could not support the publication of more of Robert E. Howard's historical fiction. To a large degree these stories have been overshadowed by the much more aggressively promoted Conan series and other popular tales. This is regrettable. Howard put a great deal more effort, time and research into his historical fiction than he did in the Conan tales and the majority of his other stories. The stories that comprises Howard's historical fiction work are bloody, dark and somber tales, but they have a certain grim realism that many of his other stories are lacking. They are among the very best of his work.

First appearance: "Hawks of Outremer," *Oriental Stories*, April 1931. Other stories: "The Blood of Belshazzar," "The Slave Princess."

Cormac Mac Art

The Gaelic pirate and renegade Cormac Mac Art of Erin, also known as *an Cliuin*, the wolf, is representative of the characters that Howard created in the late 1920s, when he tried to sell to the adventure magazines. It was an attempt to break into a different market which was more prestigious and paid better at the time than *Weird Tales*.

Before joining the Danish Viking raider Wulfhere, the Skull-splitter, Cormac Mac Art had first led his own band of Irish pirates and plundered the coastal cities of Britain, Spain and Gaul. The stories are set in Britain's post-Roman period and the dawning of the Arthurian age. The departure of the Romans had left Britain divided in largely three Celtic kingdoms, which were constantly under attack by Saxons, Angels and Danes.

As realized by other writers before and after, there is a gold mine of material here for the historical fiction writer and Howard tried his hand at the tales of the age, with his two characters Cormac Mac Art and Turlogh Dubh O'Brien.

Howard completed two Cormac Mac Art stories, *The Night of the Wolf* and *Swords of the Northern Sea*, but did not sell either. Two other stories were left unfinished. They were found in Howard's papers after his death and completed by other writers.

First appearance: "The Night of the Wolf," *Bran Mak Morn*, Dell Publishing Company, 1969.

Other stories: "Swords of the Northern Sea," "The Temple of Abomination," "Tigers of the Sea."

FRANCIS XAVIER GORDON (EL BORAK)

One of the first characters Howard created was Frank Gordon, an American adventurer traveling in the orient. At the time Howard was probably not more than 10 years old, but as with other of his characters, he did not commit Gordon to paper before sometime later. It seems likely that the Frank Gordon stories were inspired by the works of Talbot Mundy, Harold Lamb, Richard Francis Burton, Rider Haggard and Thomas E. Lawrence. After Howard began to write professionally at about 15 years of age, he targeted his Frank Gordon stories at magazines such as *Adventure Magazine* and *Argosy All-Story Weekly*, but none of them sold.

In 1933 Howard revived Frank Gordon under the name Francis Xavier Gordon, together with a new, similar oriental adventurer, Kirby O'Donnell. Several of the Gordon and O'Donnell stories sold to *Top-Notch, Complete Stories* and *Thrilling Adventures.*

Francis X. Gordon is a former Texas gunfighter from El Paso, who has found a home in the Middle East, adventuring and treasure hunting in the mountains, deserts and mysterious cities of one of the most forbidden regions of the world. After years in Afghanistan and other remote places in the Middle East, Gordon has adapted so completely to the dress, demeanor, life style and languages that he passes easily for a native anywhere. His skills with weapons, and particularly the curved tulwar, have made him a formidable fighter and won him recognition by all, friends and enemies alike, as El Borak—The Swift. The stories take place during the First World War when the British officer Lawrence of Arabia, whom Gordon knows, was prominent in leading the Arabian revolt against the Turks.

First appearance: "The Daughter of Erlik Khan," *Top-Notch*, December 1934.

Other stories: "Blood of the Gods," "The Coming of El Borak," "Country of the Knife," "El Borak *(1)*," "El Borak *(2)*," "Hawk of the Hills," "Intrigue in Kurdistan," "The Iron Terror," "Khoda Khan's Tale," "The Land of Mystery," "The Lost Valley of Iskander," "North of Khyber," "A Power Among the Islands," "The Shunned Castle," "Son of the White Wolf," "Three-Bladed Doom (long version)," "Three-Bladed Doom (short version)."

The Lost Valley of Iskander. Orbit Books 1976. Cover art by Chris Achilleos. © 1974 Glen Lord.

JAMES ALLISON

In the early 1930s, Howard wrote a series of stories featuring a character named James Allison, using the device of ancestral memory or incarnation. Allison, who lives in the present time, is a disabled and depressed individual who has the ability to remember his other lives. In "The Valley of the Worm," Allison is Niord a member of the Aesir tribe. In "The Garden of Fear" he is Hunwulf of the Aesirs and in "The Marchers of Valhalla" he is Hialmar, also an Aesir. In all the stories, James Allison, the cripple, appears as the powerful barbarian warrior, strong, cunning and skilled in the use of arms.

During his lifetime, Howard sold only two of his James Allison tales. *Weird Tales* accepted "The Valley of the Worm" and "The Garden of Fear" was bought by *Marvel Tales,* a short-lived semi-professional magazine. The latter story was reprinted by the same publisher, William Crawford, in a small anthology chapbook in 1945. After Howard's death, the manuscript of another major James Allison tale, "The Marchers of Valhalla," was found among his papers. It had been submitted to *The Magic Carpet Magazine* in 1933 but rejected. The story was published in a hardcover edition by Donald M. Grant in 1972.

First appearance: "The Valley of the Worm," *Weird Tales,* February 1934.

Other stories: "Black Eons," "Brachan the Kelt," "The Garden of Fear," "Genseric's Fifth-Born Son," "The Guardian of the Idol," "The Marchers of Valhalla," "The Tower of Time."

KIRBY O'DONNELL

The Irish-American adventurer and treasure hunter Kirby O'Donnell is close to Francis X. Gordon in both character and personality. Fascinated by the Middle East and Afghanistan in particular, O'Donnell has adopted the way of the Kurds. He dresses like them, speaks their language and darkened by the sun, he passes for one of them as Ali el Ghazi.

Howard describes O'Donnell as being above medium height, with broad shoulders and wiry muscles that gave him strength out of proportion to his weight. A natural fighter with a temper easily set ablaze, he is also known as "El Shirkuh"—the mountain lion. The time frame of the stories appears to be the late nineteenth to early twentieth century. Like Francis X. Gordon, who was revived about the same time as O'Donnell was created in the early 1930s, the latter was probably inspired by the adventure

Swords of Shahrazar. Berkley Books 1978. Cover art by Ken Kelly. © 1978 Glenn Lord.

stories of Talbot Mundy, Harold Lamb, Rider Haggard and the exploits of T. E. Lawrence in Arabia.

Kirby O'Donnell is another character who was interesting enough and with sufficient adventurous potential in the grim landscape of Afghanistan, at a time that was seething with political unrest, to further develop through other stories. The Kirby O'Donnell stories were written towards the end of Howard's career, and it's possible that if he had lived we would have heard more from Ali el Ghazi, the false Kurd.

First appearance: "Swords of Shahrazar," *Top-Notch,* October 1934.

Other stories: "The Curse of the Crimson God," "The Treasures of Tartary."

KULL OF ATLANTIS

The enigmatic Atlantean fugitive, Kull, who conquers the throne of the ancient and troubled kingdom of Valusia, was one of the only characters that Howard committed to paper immediately upon conception. He was 19 years old when he wrote the first Kull story, "Exile of Atlantis," in 1925, but it was not before August 1929, that the first published King Kull tale, "The Shadow Kingdom," appeared in the pages of *Weird Tales.* The only other King Kull story to see publication while Howard was still alive was "The Mirrors of Tuzun Thune" in September 1929, also in *Weird Tales.*

Howard finished several other King Kull tales, all of which eventually saw publication in one form or another. In time, these stories made Kull, along with his brother-in-arms, the Pict Brule the Spear-slayer, one of Howard's more popular and charismatic characters. The tales of King Kull are set in the Howardian Pre-Cataclysmic age, the distant past before Atlantis, Lemuria and Mu sank beneath the ocean waves and great geological upheavals changed the world map and impacted human cultures. The Age of King Kull was the remote time ancestry to the Hyborian age, which became the era of one of Howard's best known characters, Conan the Cimmerian.

In addition to the tales written by Robert E. Howard, King Kull gained sufficient popularity to generate his own Marvel comics magazine, "Kull the Conqueror" (1971–1985), followed by a limited magazine series, "Kull and the Barbarians" (1975). In 1996 a movie, *Kull the Conqueror* based on Howard's character, and starring Kevin Sorbo, was released. One of the only episodes in the movie that was true to Howard's writing was the scene where Kull shatters the old stone tablet of Valusian law with his axe and declares: "By this axe I rule."

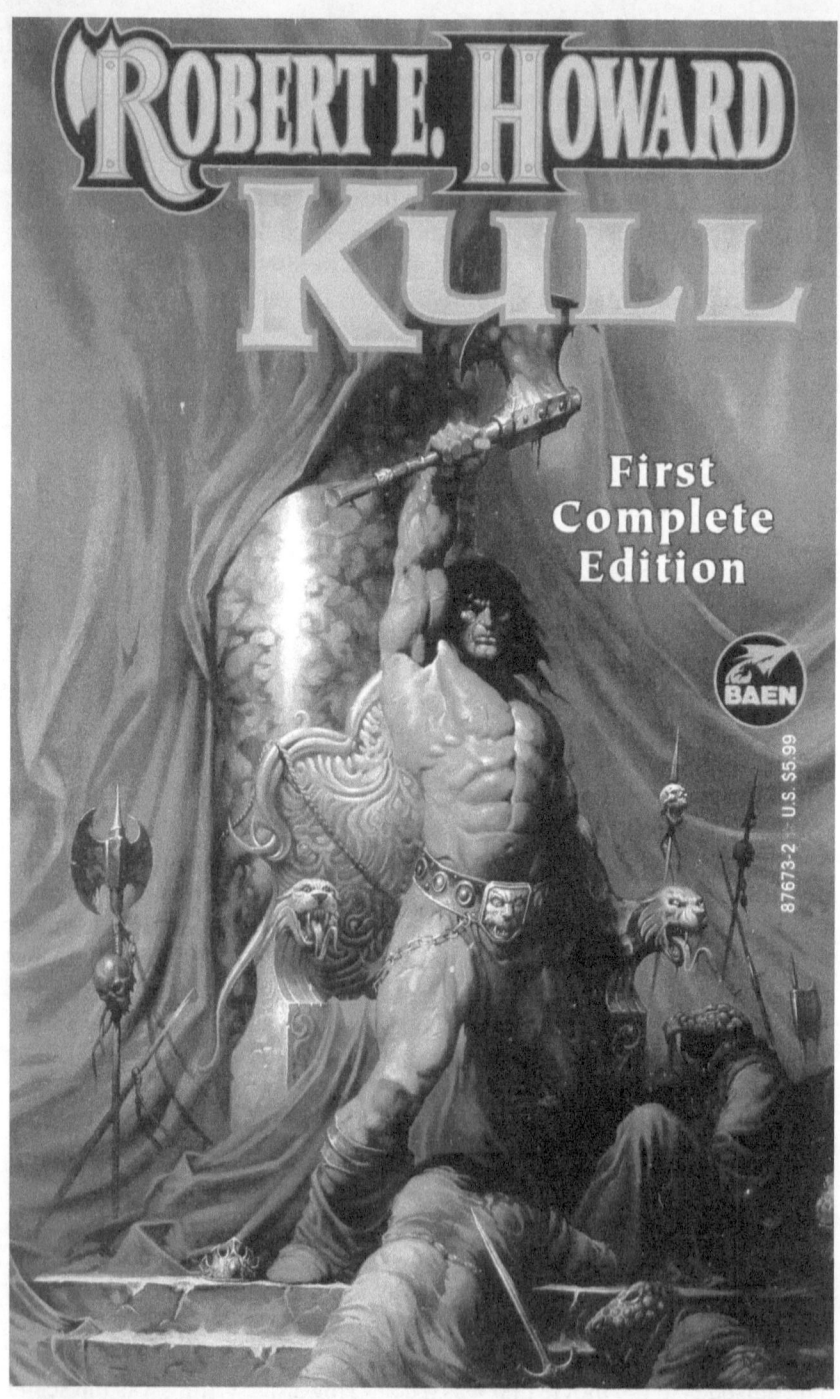

Kull. Baen Publishing Enterprises 1995. Cover art by Ken Kelly. © 1995 Baen Books and Glenn Lord.

This forceful declaration was originally the title of a King Kull story that Howard wrote but was unable to sell. He later rewrote it as a Conan story and sold it to *Weird Tales* under the title "The Phoenix on the Sword." It was the first Conan story to be published in the December 1932 issue.

Perhaps more than any other of his characters, King Kull of Valusia is the personage most identifiable with Robert E. Howard himself, his sentiments, melancholies and not infrequent dark and nebulous moods.

First appearance: "The Shadow Kingdom," *Weird Tales,* August 1929.

Other stories: "The Altar and the Scorpion," "The Black City" (fragment), "By This Axe I Rule!" "The Curse of the Golden Skull," "Delcardes Cat," "Exile of Atlantis," "The King and the Oak" (poem), "Kings of the Night," "The Mirrors of Tuzun Thune," "The Skull of Silence," "The Striking of the Gong," "Swords of the Purple Kingdom."

PIKE BEARFIELD

With the Breckinridge Elkins stories selling successfully to *Action Stories* on a regular basis from 1934, Howard decided to switch the main focus of his writing to similar western stories, but with different lead characters. When John F. Byrne, the editor of *Fight Stories* and *Action Stories,* moved from Fiction House to *Argosy* in early 1936, he asked Howard to create a series for that magazine like the Breckinridge Elkins stories.

The result was a series of stories about Pike Bearfield of Wolf Mountain, Texas. The Bearfield stories are very much like the Elkins tales, although the lead character in the former is not as well developed. Yet the stories are great reading and very funny, almost burlesque in some ways. Howard sold three Pike Bearfield tales to *Argosy,* but he also sold two more traditional western stories ("The Dead Remember" and "Vulture's Sanctuary") to the magazine. Unfortunately none of the five *Argosy* stories were published before Howard's death.

First appearance: "A Gent from the Pecos," *Argosy,* October 1936.

Other stories: "The Diablos Trail," "Gents on the Lynch," "The Riot at Bucksnort," "While Smoke Rolled."

RED SONYA

Red Sonya of Rogatino, the red-haired Russian warrior woman, is a minor Howard character who appears only in one story, "The Shadow of the Vulture." The story takes place in 1529, and centers on Süileyman the

Magnificent's siege of the city of Vienna. In spite of her limited appearance, Red Sonya caught the public's and publishers' imagination as few other Howard characters have done. With a change in the spelling of her name to Red Sonja, the red-haired sword woman had her own comic book series, published by Marvel Comics, that ran from 1977 through 1986.

From Howard's description of Red Sonya, it is unlikely that he would have been particularly pleased with the juvenile exploits of the voluptuous, sword wielding, chain-mail bikini clad, comic book heroine. In 1985 the movie *Red Sonja,* starring Brigitte Nielsen and Arnold Schwarzenegger, premiered to mixed reviews. A series of Red Sonja paperbacks by David C. Smith and Richard Tierney were published in the early 1980s. None of these character exploitations have anything to do with Robert E. Howard's original work.

First (and only) appearance: "The Shadow of the Vulture," *The Magic Carpet Magazine,* January 1934.

SOLOMON KANE

The 16th century Puritan duelist Solomon Kane was the first of Howard's characters to become serialized in the pulp magazines and one of his most celebrated. Kane lived at the time of Elizabeth I of England, Sir Francis Drake and Sir Richard Grenville. In *Fantasy Magazine,* July 1935, Howard is quoted as having said that he conceived Solomon Kane at the age of sixteen, while still in high school, but did not commit the character to paper until several years later. According to Howard, Solomon Kane was most likely inspired by his own admiration for the cold, steel-nerved duelists of the sixteenth century.

Kane, a native of Devon, England, is a tall, wiry man of strong faith, and considerable physical strength, endurance and tenacity. Somberly dressed in black and armed with a brace of pistols, a dirk, a rapier which he masters and an ancient magic staff given to him by an African sorcerer, Kane restlessly travels the world, righting wrongs and fighting evil wherever and in whichever form he might find it.

The Solomon Kane character became sufficiently popular to generate its own limited issue comic book series published by Marvel Comics, from September 1985 to July 1986. A movie featuring Solomon Kane has been in the negotiation and planning stage for the last several years.

First appearance: "Red Shadows," *Weird Tales,* August 1928.

Other stories: "Blades of the Brotherhood," "The Castle of the Devil," "The Children of Asshur," "Death's Black Riders," "The Footfalls Within,"

"Hawk of Basti," "The Hills of the Dead," "The Moon of Skulls," "The One Black Stain" (poem), "Rattle of Bones," "The Return of Sir Richard Grenville" (poem), "The Right Hand of Doom," "Skulls in the Stars," "Solomon Kane's Homecoming" (poem), "Wings in the Night."

STEVE ALLISON—THE SONORA KID

Robert E. Howard had a great compassion for the old west—the west that his ancestors had pioneered, and the west he had glimpsed the very end of as a young child. As part of that fondness came an enchantment with the colorful human characters who were part and parcel of the old western landscape: the cowboy, the miner, the gambler, the mountain man, the Indian fighter, the lawman, the gunfighter and the outlaw—especially the outlaw. Howard was fascinated by characters such as Billy the Kid, John Wesley Hardin and Jesse James. The admiration for the true gunfighters of the old west came to Howard at an early age and in his early teens, he began to write a series of stories about a Texas gunfighter named Steve Allison or the Sonora Kid. This character was contemporary with his original creation of Frank Gordon, the Middle East adventurer, who later became Francis X. Gordon (El Borak).

In the early 1930s, when Howard was seeking to break into other and more lucrative markets for his stories, he revived Steve Allison as he had revived Francis Gordon. He wrote a number of conventional western stories featuring a Steve Allison, who made the borderland between Texas and Mexico his home territory. The Sonora Kid was a young man—most gunfighters were—of medium height, slim, suntanned, with steel-gray eyes and a cold, steady gaze. He was uncannily fast with his two ivory-handled Colt .45s and having grown up in a land of Mexican knife-fighters, he was also well versed in the use of the blade.

In the late spring of 1933, Howard delivered the first two Steve Allison stories, "The Devil's Joker" and "Knife, Bullet and Noose," to his newly hired agent, Otis Adelbert Kline, in the hope of finding a buyer for his new western series. Unfortunately none of the Steve Allison stories sold during Howard's lifetime. Most of the stories would eventually be published in limited edition, small press printings.

First appearance: "Knife, Bullet and Noose," *The Book of Robert E. Howard,* Zebra Books, New York 1976.

Other stories: "Brotherly Advice," "Desert Rendezvous," "The Devil's Joker," "Red Curls and Bobbed Hair," "The Sonora Kid—Cowhand," "The Sonora Kid's Winning Hand," "The West Tower."

STEVE COSTIGAN—DENNIS DORGAN

One of Howard's most popular characters, the quick-fisted and hard-hitting sailor Steve Costigan, was introduced in the July 1929 issue of *Fight Stories.* At the time Howard was selling stories to a number of magazines and a series of Steve Costigan adventure tales appeared in *Action Stories* and *Fight Stories* in 1930 and 1931. The Costigan stories were popular and Howard wrote them at a quick pace. When the finished stories began to pile up faster than they could be submitted, Howard decided to clone the Costigan character and rewrite some of the stories with another protagonist.

This was the start of the adventures of Sailor Dennis Dorgan. Minor changes included the name of Costigan's ship and loyal companion dog, but otherwise the stories remained true to the original character. The locale is the Far East with its many exotic ports and mystical cities, among them Singapore, Hong Kong and Shanghai. In most of these well-told tall tales, there is usually a tremendous fist fight, a dramatic rescue, a kidnapping, a treasure hunt, or some arcane oriental affair, after which Sailor Costigan or Sailor Dorgan, as the case may be, barely manages to extricate himself in time for the next exotic port-o-call and new adventures.

The Costigan-Dorgan stories are light, humorous and extremely enjoyable adventure tales, which as much of his other works, show Howard's ability to move from one dramatic setting to another and from the extremely bleak, brutal and dark narrative to the humorous and lighter story-telling. It is interesting to notice that Steve Costigan was also the name that Howard chose for his own character in his semi-autobiographical novel, *Post Oaks & Sand Roughs,* written in 1928 and published by Donald M. Grant in 1990.

First appearance of Steve Costigan: "The Pit of the Serpent," *Fight Stories,* July 1929.

Other stories: "Alleys of Peril," "The Battling Sailor," "Blue River Blues," "The Bull Dog Breed," "By the Law of the Shark," "The Champion of the Forecastle," "Circus Fists," "The Fightin'est Pair," "Fist and Fang," "Flying Knuckles," "General Ironfist," "Hard-Fisted Sentiment," "The Honor of the Ship," "The House of Peril" (as "Blow the Chinks Down"), "Night of Battle," "One Shanghai Night" (as "Dark Shanghai"), "Sailor Costigan and the Swami," "Sailor's Grudge," "The Sign of the Snake," "The Slugger's Game," "Sluggers of the Beach," "Texas Fists," "Vikings of the Gloves," "Waterfront Fists," "Waterfront Law" (or "The TNT Punch"), "Winner Take All."

First appearance of Dennis Dorgan: "Alleys of Darkness," *The Magic Carpet Magazine,* January 1934.

Other stories: "Alleys of Treachery" (as "The Mandarin Ruby"), "Cultured Cauliflowers" (as "In High Society"), "Iron-Clad Fists" (as "A Knight of the Round Table"), "A New Game for Dorgan" (as "Playing Journalist"), "Sailor Dorgan and the Destiny Gorilla" (as "The Destiny Gorilla"), "Sailor Dorgan and the Jade Monkey" (as "The Jade Monkey"), "Sailor Dorgan and the Turkish Menace" (as "The Turkish Menace"), "Sailor Dorgan and the Yellow Cobra" (as "The Yellow Cobra"), "A Two-Fisted Santa Claus" (as "Playing Santa Claus").

STEVE HARRISON

With the appearance of the hard-boiled detective stories in the pulp magazines of the early 1920s, spear-headed by writers such as Dashiell Hammett and later by Raymond Chandler, these tales quickly became popular reading and numerous detective magazines were launched. When Robert E. Howard was looking to expand his sales of stories into other markets in the early 1930s, he wrote and sold several detective stories to *Strange Detective Stories, Super-Detective Stories* and *Thrilling Mystery.*

His reason for diversifying and breaking into a totally new market was primarily financial. His mother's illness had placed a considerable financial burden on the family and Howard felt an obligation to help with the bills. *Weird Tales,* which was his primary source of income, was slow to pay and Howard needed to move in any direction that might be more financially productive. The detective story, however, was not Howard's forte and it is questionable if he could work up much enthusiasm for the genre while writing the stories. Only weeks before his death, Howard stated that he currently found it difficult to write anything but western stories. He had at that time abandoned the crime story genre, which he felt he had not been successful in. He did not personally care for detective stories and could barely endure reading one, much less writing one.

Nevertheless Howard must have put his dislike for the genre aside and gone to work. He created several lead characters for his detective stories, but Steve Harrison was the one that he most often featured. Waterfront detective Steve Harrison is a broad-shouldered, deep-chested man of medium height. Black-haired and blue-eyed, he is a man of action, tough, competent and very good at his job, which constantly puts him in harm's way.

Several of Howard's Steve Harrison stories have a weird or oriental element, among others the schemes of the diabolical mongol Erlik Khan. It would appear that the tales featuring Erlik Khan may have been inspired by Sax Rohmer's Fu Manchu stories, which at the time were enormously popular. It is no secret that Howard's negative feelings about detective stories may have influenced his writing and while they cannot be counted among his better work, they are still enjoyable, action-packed and well-worth reading.

First appearance: "Fangs of Gold," *Strange Detective Stories,* February 1934.

Other stories: "The Black Moon," "Graveyard Rats," "The House of Suspicion," "Lord of the Dead," "The Mystery of Tannernoe Lodge," "Names in the Black Book," "The Silver Heel," "The Tomb's Secret," "The Voice of Death."

Turlogh Dubh O'Brien

This is another of Howard's Gaelic warrior characters, cast from the same mold as Cormac Mac Art, and, as Cormac was created for potential sales to the adventure magazine market. Turlogh Dubh O'Brien is an outcast from his own Irish clan, who ranges far and wide and battles Saxons, Norsemen and other contemporary people.

The Turlogh adventures are set in the politically tumultuous times, about half a century preceding the Battle of Hastings in 1066 and the subsequent Norman conquest of Britain. It is a period of British history that is seething with unrest as many diversified peoples and tribes were struggling for the power to rule the lands the Romans had left behind when the empire fell.

Howard completed two Turlogh stories which he sold to *Weird Tales.* After his death three more fragments or unfinished, related Turlogh stories were found. They were completed by other writers and published privately.

First appearance: "The Gods of Bal-Sagoth," *Weird Tales,* October 1931.

Other stories: "The Dark Man," "The Grey God Passes," "The Shadow of the Hun," "Spears of Clontarf."

4

COLLECTING ROBERT E. HOWARD

A. Identification, Condition, Grading

Collecting the works of Robert E. Howard is a challenge, and probably more so than collecting many other 20th Century American authors. Howard wrote primarily for the pulp magazines and while he did prepare, submit and had some manuscripts rejected by book publishers, his major market remained the pulps, especially *Weird Tales, Action Stories* and *Fight Stories*. He was an exceptionally productive writer and generated a considerable volume of short stories, poems and miscellaneous writings in the twelve years prior to his untimely death.

Three major factors seem to have motivated Robert E. Howard to write. First and probably most importantly, writing provided the freedom he cherished so highly; freedom to work when he wanted to, and not be accountable to anyone but himself. Secondly, his writings gave him a reasonable income at a time when the Great Depression cut deepest, made employment hard to come by, and ravaged the paychecks of those who did find work. Thirdly, Howard liked to write. It gave him an outlet for his intensity and passion. As he created his characters and stories, he lived the action in his mind as it unfolded on the paper in the typewriter. In every character he created could be found something of himself, his passion, sentiments, yearnings, melancholies or his rage against realities that he found unacceptable, but had no control over. In his relatively short career as a writer, Howard produced a gigantic amount of material, and the potential collector will soon discover that gathering samples of all that he wrote is a difficult or nearly impossible task.

Other By-Lines

During his writing career Robert E. Howard wrote primarily under his own by-line and material published after his death is nearly always identified with his proper name. As authors who write for various media simultaneously often do, however, Robert E. Howard wrote and was published under a number of different by-lines. These include Mark Adam, William Decatur, Patrick Ervin (most often used), Patrick Howard, Patrick Mac Conaire, R.T. Maynard, Max Neilson, John Taverel, and Sam Walser.

Pastiches, Revisions and Posthumous Collaborations

Since the late 1970s and especially in the past 10 to 15 years frequent criticism has been expressed about the numerous pastiches, revisions, and posthumous collaborations of Howard's work by other writers. Few other, if any, 20th century American authors have been so imitated and plagiarized as Robert E. Howard and particularly his best known character, Conan of Cimmeria.

While Howard was still alive, Jack Byrne did some rewriting of the boxing stories he published at *Fiction House*, cutting 10,000 words from *Iron Men*, while the editors at *Argosy All-Story* made cuts to *Crowd Horror*. After Howard's death in 1936, Otis Adelbert Kline rewrote some of his western stories to get them published. Following Howard's original synopsis, someone (probably Otto Binder) wrote the conclusion to *Almuric* and another writer (perhaps Oscar Friend) rewrote *The House of Arabu* for *The Avon Fantasy Reader*.

In the 1950s L. Sprague de Camp edited, revised and rewrote many of the Conan stories for the Gnome series and this continued with de Camp's, Carter's and Nyberg's revisions and pastiches for the Lancer series. In more recent times, the Robert E. Howard pastiche writing has been taken up in a big way by fantasy writers such as Poul Anderson, Leonard P. Carpenter, Lin Carter, L. Sprague de Camp, David Drake, Roland Green, John C. Hocking, Robert Jordan, Sean A. Moore, Björn Nyberg, Andrew J. Offutt, Steve Perry, John Maddox Roberts, Harry Turtledove, Karl Edward Wagner and James M. Ward. Conan and other Howard characters sell books and it would appear that anyone with some measure of writing skills has jumped on the bandwagon for a profitable ride.

The obvious issue is that none of these pastiche writers are Robert E. Howard, hence, what they write and whatever story they may concoct, it is not Howard's. Some indiscriminate readers may not know the difference and believe that any book with the name "Conan" in its title is the work of Robert E. Howard. Other less informed readers probably think that Conan is the original creation of Carpenter, Green, Jordan, Offutt or whoever else might be the author of a particular Conan pastiche.

I don't believe that pastiches have a place in a collection of Robert E. Howard's work. They are primarily commercially driven plagiarism of characters, concepts or scenarios created by another writer. I would also exclude revisions, expansions and rewriting by other authors, unless there is at least a recognizable element of original Howard material included.

Another category of faux Howard is the posthumous collaboration. The term is an oxymoron. How can someone no longer alive be a collaborator? Perhaps I am being contentious, but that expression has always grated on my nerve endings. Unless there is a considerable amount of genuine Howard material in such "collaborations," they do not belong in the collection.

Identification

The foremost objects of desire for serious book collectors are the first editions, the first printings of their chosen author. In the case of Robert E. Howard's works, published in book form after his death, the term "First Edition" has been used loosely and in some cases incorrectly. Qualifying statements such as "first edition, thus," or "first book edition" would have been more appropriate. There are a number of first editions of Howard's works, both prose and poetry, which have been published in various formats after his death, but the majority of true first printings remain the stories and poems published in the pulp magazines in the 1920s and 1930s. This is where the collector who wishes to acquire the bulk of the first printings of Howard's work must go.

The pulp magazines were cheaply produced from newspaper print which contained a degree of acidity that made them susceptible to browning, flaking and rapid deterioration. They were disposable and meant to be read only once or twice before being discarded. Because of the poor quality, what we today would consider "fine" or "very good" copies are scarce and demand top prices. To assemble a complete set of the pulp magazines in which Howard's works first appeared, in collectable condition, would be a formidable undertaking and financially out of reach for most collectors living on an average income.

No hardcover book by Howard was published while he was alive; another circumstance which sets him apart from most other collected authors. The first hardcover title, *A Gent from Bear Creek,* was published in England in 1937, and is known to exist in just twelve copies with only one in the original dust jacket. This leaves the hardcover book collector with the 1950 to 1955 Gnome Press, six-volume Conan series as a starting point. These books are not scarce, but copies in "fine/fine" condition are difficult to come by. The Gnome Press series was inexpensively produced and printed on paper with a high acid contents, which make the inside pages inclined to browning and flaking. The bulk of Howard's stories

A Gent from Bear Creek. Zebra Books 1975. Cover art by Jeff Jones. © 1975 Glenn Lord.

included in the books are reprinted from pulp magazines and have been edited, rewritten or expanded by other writers. There is a seventh Gnome Press Conan book, *The Return of Conan*, but it contains none of Howard's original material and is not a genuine Howard collectible.

From Gnome Press, the collector may move on to the hardcover editions by Arkham House, Donald M. Grant, Fax Collector's Edition, Berkley-Putnam, Wandering Star, Wildside Press, Girasol Collectables and the University of Nebraska Press, some of which are designated as "first edition," "first American edition" or "first illustrated edition." Much of the material found in these books are edited reprints from earlier books or pulp magazines, but some may contain new or textually corrected material. This is particularly true of the books published in the last 10 years, when a greater effort has been made to present the unaltered, Howard text, reprinted from the pulp magazines or the original typescripts when available.

Advance reading copies (ARC) or uncorrected proof copies (UPC) are limited pre-publication, plainly formatted releases of trade edition books. Uncorrected proof copies may be considered true firsts, since they are released months before the trade edition. They are usually distributed free to newspapers and magazines that feature book reviews, to book sellers and to individual book reviewers as a marketing device. In the case of Robert E. Howard titles, uncorrected proof copies are fairly recent. Examples are the newly issued ARC titles by Del Rey Books as pre-publication promotion for their trade edition reprints of Wandering Star's "Robert E. Howard Library of Classics."

For the mass market paperback collector, there is a wealth of much repeated and reprinted Howard material. This is also the most affordable collecting category of Howard's published works. The major paperback publishers are Ace Books, Lancer Books, Dell Publishing Co., Centaur Press, Prestige (Lancer), Zebra Books (Kensington Publishing), Berkley Medallion Books, Bantam-Ballantine Books and Baen Publishing Enterprise. Orbit, Sphere and Panther Books are published in the United Kingdom. Each of these companies has released several titles, many of them reprinted from earlier hardcover or paperback editions. There is a prodigious amount of repetition in the mass market paperback books by Howard and textual deficiencies, editions, revisions, or additions by other writers, along with typographical errors are not uncommonly repeated in reprints.

The paperback market is strongly commercially driven and titles that appear to sell well have been reprinted again and again. Together Lancer Books, Inc., and Ace Books, for example, have reprinted the 1966 to 1969 Lancer Conan series in more than 25 printings over 20 years. Other publishers have followed suit and kept reprinting as long as the books were selling.

A particularly intriguing aspect of Howard collecting can be found in the field of small press or private publications. These printings are usually issued in very limited editions, containing only one or a few stories or poems and are often printed on high quality paper, utilizing the best material and craftsmanship. The finest and most collectible are Roy A. Squires's and George T. Hamilton's limited printings, followed by items published by Jonathan Bacon, Gibbelin's Gazette, Cryptic Publications and Necronomicon Press.

Because of their limited numbers and in most cases, but not always, high quality printing and material, all of these publications have seen substantial increases in value since they were first published. They are usually issued in the form of saddle-stapled pamphlets or chapbooks and bound in wraps, with one thing in common. They are not easy to find and demand premium prices in any condition at or above "very good."

Amateur press journals or privately published magazines relating to Robert E. Howard and his writings constitute another element of collecting worth considering. These small magazines, mailings or fanzines were particularly numerous from the late 1960s through the 1970s. Some contained good, interesting information, new Howardian items and were skillfully edited and designed. Others were hopelessly amateurish, ineptly illustrated and published more for egocentric reasons than for contributing to the knowledge of Robert E. Howard.

Some disappeared after a single or a few issues, others lasted for several years and a few are still in business. The last decade has seen a revival of the amateur press publication and new journals of a higher standard in both contents and printing are available today. The most prominent amateur press publications of yesteryear were "The Howard Collector," "AMRA," "REH: Lone Star Fictioneer," "Fantasy Crossroads," and "The Robert E. Howard United Press Association (REHupa)," of which the latter is still going strong. The current amateur press publications include "The Dark Man," "The Cimmerian," "Sword & Fantasy" and the recently revived "REH: Two Gun Raconteur" and "The Howard Review."

Collecting the works of Robert E. Howard can be a formidable undertaking and it is almost inevitable that a collector imposes some limitations on what type of material should or should not be collected. For those who could use some guidance on which items are considered collectible, I can recommend Don Herron's article "A Robert E. Howard Checklist," published in the July-August 2000 issue of *Firsts—The Book Collectors's Magazine,* pages 36–37. This issue is dedicated to collecting Robert E. Howard and contains three well-illustrated articles by Don Herron. At the time of writing, it was still listed by the publisher as an available back issue at

$6.00, and well worth the money. The address is: *Firsts Magazine,* P.O. Box 65166, Tucson, AZ 85728–5166 or call (520) 529–1355.

Book Sizes

The standard system of designating book sizes is based on the size of the sheet used and the size into which it is folded to make each signature. The five most common sizes are: folio (fo): greater than 12" in height; quarto (4to): 10" to 12" in height; octavo (8vo): 8" to 10" in height; duodecimo (12mo): 7" to 8" in height; and sextodecimo (16mo): 6" to 7" in height.

Acidic paper

The paper used in the production of books, newspapers and magazines contains varying degrees of acid, which accelerates the aging and associated deterioration process. This is evident in the gradual browning (tanning) and brittleness of pages in many older books. Newspaper print, mass market paperback books, older comic books and pulp magazines are particularly susceptible to this process because of the paper's high acid content. During the war years, 1941 through 1945, special government restrictions were imposed on the publishing industry to save resources, and many publications from this period were printed on cheaper, thinner and more acidic paper. Today more acid-free paper is being manufactured and used in publishing, yet not all modern books are printed on acid-free paper. The paper in mass market paperback books still has a moderate acid content.

Dust jackets

Dust jackets or wrappers are paper covers used to protect the binding of hardcover books. The earliest can be traced back to the early to mid–19th century. The dust jacket is an important part of a book. Without the original dust jacket, the book is incomplete and has considerably less value. On the average the dust jacket may constitute as much as 80 percent or more of a book's value. An example is the first edition of Robert E. Howard's book *Skull Face* (Sauk City: Arkham House Publishers, Inc., 1946), that sells for about $150 to $250 without its dust jacket, while a copy with the original jacket demands a price of $600 to $800 depending on the book's condition.

Take care of the dust jackets. It is well worth the cost to preserve the original jacket of any collectible book with a clear Mylar(r) cover. This will protect the book from shelf wear, handling and spills, and make the book look more attractive. A prominent source for dust jacket covers and other book preservation products is the Brodart Co., 100 North Road, P.O. Box 300, McElhattan, PA 17748 (www.brodart.com).

Condition

As location is the premier consideration in real estate sales, condition is the foremost consideration in the collectible book trade. Along with scarcity and demand, the physical condition of a book is the all-important factor that determines collector desirability and subsequently value. Regardless of the scarcity of a book or magazine, if it is in poor condition it is not considered collectible and consequently is of little value.

Because of inconsistencies in the way the condition of books has been described in the past, the antiquarian book trade has adopted a scale that assigns a specific grade to a book in accordance with its physical condition. The purpose of the universal grading scale is to achieve standardization of how the condition of a book is described in print, as it may be listed in catalogs, advertisements, inventories or on Internet sites, and facilitate fair and equitable commerce in books.

Grading

The proper grading of collectible hardcover books, paperback books and pulp magazines is a skill which can be learned only through experience and must be executed with a high degree of objectivity. This is particularly important to keep in mind when commercial interest is involved and a step up or down in grade can mean a difference of income earned or lost. Without entering into a philosophical discourse on the improbability of human objectivity, it is my personal experience that book grading is not uncommonly done with bias and subjectivity.

Grading is a preliminary step for selling or buying a book or to establish the book's value for insurance or inventory purposes. Whenever possible it is preferable to have an experienced, impartial appraiser grade the books. Where this is not workable, the grading must be done with objective detachment and honesty. Follow the grading scale as closely as possible and list all flaws and defects. The standard book grading scale may be applied universally, but it is better to use a format-specific scale. When possible do not use a comic book scale for grading hardcover books or dust jackets, and do not use a standard book scale for grading mass market paperback books or pulp magazines. Each format has its own characteristics, flaws and defects, which will influence the grading and its accuracy.

The dust jacket is graded separately from the book. Unless protected with a Mylar(r) cover from the time of printing, the dust jacket will usually show more wear than the book itself. This is a natural result of handling, reading and shelving. It is therefore not uncommon that the dust jacket grades lower than the book, a condition reflected in a description such as (FN/VG) which indicates a "fine" book in a slightly worn, but still "very good" dust jacket.

Hardcover Books and Dust Jackets

Very Fine (VF) is the highest grade given. It describes a book that is pristine, flawless, complete in every aspect and appears as if it just came off the press. There are no visible signs of wear and no defects, imperfections or blemishes. The dust jacket is original, pristine, flawless and as new, showing no wear or defects, fingerprints, nail marks or white along the edges. The jacket shows high reflectivity and strong color. Books in this condition are scarce.

Fine (FN) is the highest grade that many booksellers will use. It describes a book that is close to very fine and complete, but lacking the crispness of a very fine book. It has no visible flaws or defects, but may show very slight signs of aging or wear. It has been well taken care of. The dust jacket is original, not price-clipped and without tears or chips. There may be light signs of aging and wear along edges and folds, but with only a minimum of white seen. The jacket shows good reflectivity and color. Any flaws and blemishes must be noted. A fine book is a very collectible item.

Very Good (VG) is the most common grade given to collectible books. It describes a book that is visibly used, with signs of wear, but complete. It is without major defects and the binding is still tight and sound, with only the slightest spine-lean. There may be an owner signature, inscription, bookplate, remainder mark or other minor blemishes in the book. The dust jacket is original and complete, but may be price-clipped and shows moderate aging and wear. White may be seen along edges and on corners, and there may be minor chipping and short closed tears on the edge of the jacket. The jacket shows some reflectivity and good color. All flaws, defects and blemishes must be noted.

Good (GD) is the lowest grade given to a collectible book. It describes the average used book that is noticeably worn, but is still complete. Moderate to pronounced spine-roll, moisture stains, creased pages and fading or discoloration of boards. Inside pages may be browning and beginning to show brittleness. The dust jacket is original, but with signs of fading and loss of color. Chips, tears and wear of edges, corners and folds are common flaws. Small pieces may be missing from the jacket, but it is not fragmented. The jacket shows loss of reflectivity and of color. All flaws, defects and blemishes must be noted.

Fair (FR) is an uncollectible grade. It describes a book that is heavily worn and incomplete, but with text pages and inside plates intact, although some may be loose. It is a reading copy only and should be listed as such. It may have several major defects such as cracked hinges, missing end papers, water damage, fading, discoloration of boards or heavy browning and flaking of pages. The dust jacket is original, but with larger pieces missing, fragmented and with visible signs of wear, fading and aging. The jacket shows no reflectivity and poor color. All flaws, defects and blemishes must be noted.

Poor (PR) is the lowest uncollectible grade. It describes a book that is heavily worn and defective. Major defects such as severely damaged binding, torn, loose or missing pages, cracked hinges, water damage, discoloration and flaking are common and must be noted. The dust jacket is original, but badly damaged, discolored and fragmented. What is left of it shows no reflectivity and little color. All flaws, defects and blemishes must be noted.

Ex-library copies (Ex-Lib), regardless of their condition and grade, must always be described as such with all their flaws, such as ex-library labels, lending card pockets, location and date stamps. Except for very rare books, ex-library copies are not considered collectible.

Book Club Editions (BCE), regardless of their condition and grade, must always be listed as such.

The condition of books that fall between the above listed categories may be further defined by adding plus (+) or minus(-) to a grade to indicate a better or lesser copy. For example VG+ and FN-. Some sellers and collectors may also use terms such as "near very good" or "near fine" in describing a book's condition. Others may use the terms "mint," "as new" or "near mint" instead of "very fine." This is acceptable, but creates more categories, more confusion and a wider range of interpretations. There are no such grades or definitions as "otherwise very fine," "fine for its age," "very good except for..." or any other conditional qualifications of the standard grades

Grading Dust Jackets

Dust jackets are paper wraps whose main purpose is to protect the binding of a book. For that reason, the average dust jacket is subjected to a certain amount of handling and wear. While some overall wear of an older dust jacket should be expected, tears, flaking or chipping of edges and corners will downgrade a jacket. Missing pieces will further downgrade the jacket in accordance with how large a piece of the jacket is gone and how this may affect the jacket's illustration or text. Fragmentation will drop the grade of a dust jacket to "fair" and therefore an uncollectible.

Price clipping (the removal of the piece of the jacket's front or rear flap on which the price was printed) is another defect that may or may not downgrade a jacket. On a common dust jacket the drop in value would be slight, but if the price is the only indicator of a first state jacket, the value of a price-clipped dust jacket will drop and the jacket should be listed as possibly a later issue. Dust jackets cut in pieces and pasted into the book will decrease the value of the book by as much as one or two full grades.

Facsimile Dust Jackets

With today's computer and color reproduction technology, facsimile dust jackets have proliferated at an amazing rate in the last ten years. Early color copies and photographic reproductions have been replaced by laser printed facsimiles, dye-ink replications and reconstruction jackets. Most are copies of the original first edition jacket and the better ones are so close to the original that it can be difficult to tell the difference. Some show the word "facsimile" or other indicators that the jacket is a copy or reproduction, but others do not. As a book ages, so does its dust jacket with the inevitable signs of wear, rubbing, fading, chipping, small tears, etc. If the dust jacket on an older book is new and fresh with a "very fine" look and feel, it is most likely an overrun or facsimile jacket. The Robert E. Howard hardcover books most frequently found without the original dust jacket are the Arkham House and Gnome Press editions. Excellent facsimile dust jackets are available for all these titles for approximately $20.00 each. A quality facsimile or reproduction dust jacket protects and enhances the appearance of a book and may furnish information printed on the original dust jacket, such as contents, author profile, reviews, other titles, etc., but it does not affect the value of the book as a collectible. The value of a book in a facsimile jacket is the same as the value of the book without a dust jacket.

Mass Market Paperback Books

Very Fine (VF) is the highest grade given. It describes a paperback book that is immaculate, unread, flawless, complete in every aspect, and appears as if it just came off the press. There are no visible signs of wear and no defects, imperfections or blemishes. The binding is tight and square with sharp corners. No spine creases. Covers show high reflectivity and strong colors. There are no fingerprints, creases or nail marks on the cover. No white is showing at top or bottom of the spine or along the edges of the cover. Paperback books in this condition are scarce.

Fine (FN) is the highest grade that many booksellers will use. It describes a paperback book that is close to very fine and complete, but lacking the crispness of a very fine book. It is unread and has no visible flaws or defects, but may show light signs of aging or shelf-wear. The binding is tight and square. Corners are sharp. The cover shows good reflectivity and strong colors. There are no nail marks, spine reading creases or any other creases on the front and back cover. A thin sliver of white may show at top or bottom of the spine, or along the edges of the cover. All flaws, defects and blemishes must be noted. A fine paperback book is a very collectible item.

Very Good (VG) is the most common grade given to collectible paperback books. It describes a book that is visibly used, with signs of wear but complete. It is without major defects and the binding is still fairly tight and square, with only light spine-lean. There may be an owner signature, inscription, seller's stamp, date stamp or other minor blemishes in the book. Inside pages may begin to discolor. The cover shows some reflectivity and good colors. There may be a few nail marks, a single spine reading crease or maybe one other crease on the front or back cover. More white may show at top or bottom of the spine, or along the edges and corners of the cover. Corners may be blunted. All flaws, defects and blemishes must be noted.

Good (GD) is the lowest grade given to a collectible book. It describes the average used paperback book. It is noticeably worn, but still complete. The binding is no longer tight or square and have moderate to severe spine-roll. There may be moisture stains or wrinkles, creasing, discoloration or browning of pages which may begin to show brittleness. The cover shows little reflectivity and dull colors. There are several spine reading creases which may obscure the title and other creases on the front and back cover. Flaking or chipping at the top or bottom of the spine, or along the edges and corners of the cover is common. Corners are blunted with bent tips. All flaws, defects and blemishes must be noted.

Fair (FR) is an uncollectible grade. It describes a paperback book that is heavily worn and incomplete, but with the text block intact although some pages may be loose. It is a reading copy only and should be listed as such. It may have several major defects such as severe spine-roll, loose cover, missing front matters, water damage, fading, discoloration or heavy browning and flaking of pages. The cover shows loss of reflectivity and dull colors. The cover is creased, soiled, torn or missing. Heavy flaking or chipping at the top or bottom of the spine, or along the edges and corners of the cover is common. Corners are blunted with bent corner tips. All flaws, defects and blemishes must be noted.

Poor (PR) is the lowest uncollectible grade. It describes a paperback book that is heavily worn and defective. Major defects such as severely damaged binding, torn, loose or missing pages, loose binding, water damage, discoloration and flaking are common and must be noted. The cover is badly damaged, discolored, creased, torn and with pieces missing. All flaws, defects and blemishes must be noted.

The condition of paperback books that fall between the above listed categories may be further defined by adding plus (+) or minus(-) to a grade to indicate a better or lesser copy. For example VG+ and FN-. Some sellers and collectors may use terms such as "near very good" or "near fine" in describing a paperback's condition. Others may use the terms "mint," "as new" or "near mint" instead of "very fine." One paperback price guide, for example, lists seven collectible grades ranging from "fine" through "good minus." This is acceptable, but creates more categories, more confusion and a wider range of interpretations of the grades. The majority of collectible paperback books are found in the grades "very good" or "good."

Pulp Magazines

Very Fine (VF) is the highest grade given. It describes a magazine that is immaculate, unread, flawless and complete in every aspect, and appears as if it just came off the press. There are no visible signs of wear and no defects, imperfections or blemishes. The spine is flat with no flaws. Corners are sharp and the staples are not rusty. The cover overhang has no tears or chips. The pages are off-white and supple. The cover shows high reflectivity and strong colors. Pulp magazines in this condition are very rare.

Fine (FN) is the highest grade in which pulp magazines are likely to be found. It describes a magazine that is close to very fine and complete, but lacking in crispness. It has no visible major flaws or defects, but may show light signs of reading, aging or shelf-wear. The spine is flat and complete. Corners are sharp and the staples are not rusty. The cover shows good reflectivity and colors. A small date stamp or initials on the cover are acceptable. The cover overhang may have very minor tears and there may be light stress marks along the spine. The pages are beginning to yellow, but are still supple with no flaking. All flaws, defects and blemishes must be noted. A fine pulp magazine is not common and very collectible.

Very Good (VG) is the most common grade given to collectible pulp magazines. It describes a magazine that is visibly used, with signs of wear, but complete and still above average. It is without major defects and the spine is still fairly flat with only slight spine-roll. Staples may be rusting or rusty with some minor spots of discoloration of the cover or pages. There may be a seller's stamp, date stamp, signature or other minor blemishes on the cover or inside the magazine. Inside pages are beginning to change color toward a brown tint, but are not flaking. The cover shows little reflectivity and less bright colors. There may be minor tears, chipping or creases of the spine and cover overhang. Corners are no longer sharp but blunted. All flaws, defects and blemishes must be noted.

Good (GD) is the lowest grade given to a collectible magazine. It describes the average used and well-read magazine. It is noticeably worn, but still complete. The spine is no longer flat and has moderate to severe spine-roll. There may be rusty staples, moisture stains or wrinkles, creasing, discoloration or browning of pages to the point of brittleness and light flaking. The cover shows no reflectivity and dull colors. There is also spine flaking and missing pieces, which may obscure the title, and other creases on the front and back cover. More severe flaking or chipping along the edges and corners of the cover overhang. Corners are blunted with bent corner tips. All flaws, defects and blemishes must be noted.

Fair (FR) is an uncollectible grade. It describes a magazine that is heavily worn and incomplete, but with the text intact. It is a reading copy only and should be listed as such. May have several major defects such as severe spine-roll, loose or missing pages, water damage, browning and heavy flaking of pages. There are rusty staples and corresponding discoloration. The cover shows loss of reflectivity and dull colors; it is marred, creased, soiled, torn or missing. There is heavy flaking or chipping of the spine, and along the edges and corners of the cover overhang. Corners are blunted with bent or missing corner tips. All flaws, defects and blemishes must be noted.

Poor (PR) is the lowest uncollectible grade. It describes a magazine that is heavily worn and defective. Major defects include severely damaged, torn, loose or missing pages, water damage, severe browning of pages and flaking, rusty staples and associated staining. The cover and spine are badly damaged, discolored, creased, torn, missing or with pieces missing. All flaws, defects and blemishes must be noted.

The condition of pulp magazines that fall between the above listed categories may be further defined by adding plus (+) or minus(-) to a grade to indicate a better or lesser copy. For example VG+ and FN-. Some sellers and collectors may also use terms such as "near very good" or "near fine" in describing a magazine's condition. This is acceptable, but creates more categories, more confusion and a wider range of interpretations of the grades. The majority of collectible pulp magazines are found in the grades "very good" or "good."

Major Flaws and Defects

In addition to the conditions listed in the grading scales, there are specific major flaws and defects that may influence the value of a book, paperback or magazine. High acid content in the paper, flaking, mildew, insect damage, water damage, smoke, rough handling and incorrect storage are some of the agents that result in the deterioration or destruction of thousands of valuable paper collectibles every year.

The term major defects as used here does not refer to normal wear, but are specific, identifiable things to look for which will lower the value, sometimes several grades depending on the severity of the defect. The list is a personal ranking of the most common major flaws and defects.

Missing cover or pages. Any cover, page or plate missing from a book or magazine, including end papers (which may have been removed to obliterate an inscription, name, notes or library markings) will instantly drop it to a "fair" copy and it is not considered a collectible.

Missing dust jacket. Without its original dust jacket, a book is incomplete. The lack of a dust jacket may drop a book's value by 75 to 80 percent or more, even when the book itself is graded fine. This is not likely, though, for without its dust jacket the book is unprotected and a grade of "good" or at best "very good" is more likely for a book without a jacket.

Water damage. This is a matter of degree, but any water damage such as stains, warping, wrinkling or color change (bleed) will drop the book or magazine to "good" or below. A barely perceptible ring from a water glass on the rear panel of a dust jacket or magazine, for example, will not detract as much as more serious damage. Collectors should avoid books that show signs of water damage, since there may be associated hidden problems such as decay in the spine, mildew, rotting stitching or disintegration of glue.

Cracked hinges. If the hinges of a book, also known as inner joints, are broken or nearly broken, which will show as a splitting or separation of the front or rear end paper, the book is nearly worthless. This is a major defect that cannot be remedied without extensive restoration. Books with broken hinges are graded no higher than "good." Collectors should avoid books with cracked or cracking hinges. Minor splits may be repaired, but this should be noted.

Spine roll. This is also known as leaning, slanting or sloping of the spine. When viewed from the head or tail of the book, the spine is not at

Tigers of the Sea. Donald M. Grant 1974. Jacket art by Tim Kirk. © 1974 Glenn Lord.

a right angle to the front and back boards, but leans more or less usually towards the front. Spine roll is caused by wrongly "breaking in" a new book, by repeated reading or storing the book at a slant on a bookshelf. It is a common defect and undesirable, although it can be corrected. Even moderate spine roll will drop a book one full grade.

Foxing. This defect is seen as spotting of pages and page edges by light, reddish-brown spots, predominantly caused by mildew. If the condition is arrested, a few spots may not lower the grade of the book much, but a more severe affliction can drop an otherwise decent book as low as "fair" or "poor," effectively removing it from the realm of collectible books.

Damage to the binding. Defects in the case or binding of a book include damaged or creased boards, bumped corners due to the book having been dropped, bumped and frayed head and tail of the spine, cracked spine, spine wrinkles and creases, rubbing, edge wear and torn cloth. Depending on the damages, the book may drop several grades to "good" or "fair."

Damage to the text block. Damage to the text block includes separation of pages at the gutter, tearing of pages, missing corners or parts of pages, creases and stains, browning or discoloration and flaking. Because of the acid content of the paper used in some books and magazines, natural aging may cause browning of pages or page edges. Unless excessive or accompanied with brittleness, which can make the page edges flake off when touched, a moderate, naturally occurring browning (or tanning) due to age does not downgrade a book. Separations, tears, creases, stains, water damage and other page defects, however, will downgrade a book in accordance with the extent of the damage.

Loose binding. As a book ages and is read and handled more often, the binding may become loose through normal wear. For books graded "good" or lower a certain amount of looseness may be expected. If the binding is excessively loose, which usually means that the hinges and spine are weakened and may be about to crack or break, the book is downgraded accordingly.

Inscriptions and bookplates. A previous owner of a book may write an inscription, a name or a date on the front end papers or half title. The writing may be small and neat, in which case it does not detract much from the book. In other cases, the writing may be large and sprawling or consists of extensive notations. In that case, the book should be downgraded accordingly. Bookplates are also used to show ownership of a book and while some are small, neat and tasteful, others are garish or offensive. The placement of the bookplate is also an issue. If covered by the dust jacket front flap, it is less obtrusive than if it is centered on the free front end paper. Except for inscriptions associated with the author or publisher(in which case the value of the book may increase), bookplates and writing will downgrade a book in accordance to the degree that it affects its appearance. Unless a bookplate is old and the glue dried up so that it can be loosened and removed with minimum effort and residue, it is better to leave it where it is and grade accordingly.

Remainder marks. These are stamps, dots, slashes or colored sprays on the head or tail of the text block, indicating that the publisher has relinquished a number of copies for resale at a reduced price. In most cases, the books are publisher's overstock sold directly to retail outlets. The presence of a remainder mark is undesirable from a collector's point of view and will drop the book one grade.

Unpleasant smells. A musty, moldy, mildewy odor or a strong smell of tobacco smoke emanating from the pages of a book or magazine when opened, will detract from its value. The smell may be caused by storage of the book in a high humidity location or because of smoking while reading. Books with this flaw should not be graded above "very good" regardless of condition.

Repairs and Restorations

Repairs of books and magazines can consist of many things and may range from the finest professional work to the most crude amateurish efforts. Minor professional repairs, such as closed tears, will usually not have any effect on the grade, but tape or glue residue will lower the grade. When tape is used to hold a dust jacket to the binding of a book, fasten loose pages or covers, and repair major page tears, cracked hinges, etc., it will downgrade the item one or more grades. The extent of repairs and the quality of the work will determine the effect it may have on its grading. Professionally executed repair may enhance the value of a book, while amateurish or poor quality attempts to fix a problem can plummet an otherwise acceptable copy to the bottom of the grading scale. Leave any necessary repair to a professional paper restorer.

To what extent a worn or damaged book or magazine should be restored depends largely on the scarcity and value of the item. If it is a less scarce, favorite novel or pulp magazine, professional restoration can bring new life and longevity for many more years of enjoyment. If is a scarce, valuable or collectible item, the merits of restoration become debatable. While some collectible books, dust jackets and magazines might benefit from professional restoration, the more extensively an item is restored, the

The Lost Valley of Iskander. FAX Collector's Edition 1974. Jacket art by Michael W. Kaluta. © 1974 Glenn Lord and Michael W. Kaluta.

less of the original work remains which in turn makes it less valuable and desirable. When deemed appropriate or necessary, restoration should be done sparingly and professionally.

As much as possible of the original material should be preserved. When done right restoration can fix minor problems, which may have little effect on value and in the best of cases enhance the item's worth. Dust jackets, boards and pages can be cleaned. Slight tears can be closed nearly invisibly and weak hinges can be reinforced. Loose pages and plates can be tipped in and small rips and splits in bindings can be glued in place. Such restorations do not replace any original part and are in most cases unobtrusive. Therefore they do not have any great impact on value. More extensive restoration, which may require replacement of original material, will drop the value, proportional to the amount of restoration done. Restoration should not be done to push an inferior copy up to a higher grade for commercial gains. The purpose of restoration is preservation of that which might otherwise be lost. As an alternative to restoration and for storage of valuable books and magazines, custom-made clam-shell book boxes or slip cases are recommended. All repairs and restorations must be listed when an item is offered for sale.

B. Values, Buying and Selling

Values

The values listed in the following bibliography are based on the conditions described previously. They are not definitive, but provide a guide for pricing a particular book or magazine based on current information. The prices suggested are retail prices that a collector can expect to pay; they are not the prices that a bookseller may pay for a book or magazine. Demand, scarcity and condition constitute the foundation of pricing; the greater the demand for a book, the scarcer it is and the better its condition, the higher the price. As with any other collectible, a book or magazine is worth only what someone is willing to pay for it. Use the information herein as a guide, but remember that the final word on pricing is the compromise between what a seller is asking and what a buyer is prepared to pay.

For the purpose of using this guide, the values listed for all books, mass market paperbacks and special publications are for titles in "fine" condition, and, for hardcover books, in an original issue "fine" dust jacket. The values listed for pulp magazines are for copies in "very good" condition.

Items in better condition will demand higher prices than those listed and items in lesser condition will cost less. The values of reprints have been listed where appropriate for completeness, but the listing is primarily for first edition and first printing copies.

The following table may be used to determine the value of lower or higher grade copies, using the grade "fine" as the baseline. The percentages listed indicate the increase or decrease in value for lower or higher grade copies.

Poor	*Fair*	*Good*	*Very Good*	*Fine*	*Very Fine*
10%	20%	50%	75%	100%	125%

BUYING BOOKS AND PULP MAGAZINES

Collectors have the options of purchasing books from booksellers (at shops, by mail or at conventions), from other collectors, or from sellers on the Internet. Prices are usually firm and based on the condition and current catalog value of a book. When buying from a bookseller, be prepared to pay the asking price. Rummage sales, estate and moving sales, auctions, and used book stores are other sources for books and magazines, but for acquiring high grade copies, find and develop a good relationship with several reputable booksellers. Let them know what your wants are and what you are prepared to pay. Some of the ways of finding booksellers who are selling Robert E. Howard books are through references from other collectors, Internet Web sites and visits to rare book stores.

Buying Books on the Internet. In the short time since the personal computer became a reality, the Internet has revolutionized the book trade and provided collectors with instant access to the world's rare book market. Book searches that would have required days, weeks or months to carry out by traditional means a few years ago can now be done within minutes. A book that has eluded a collector for years may now be found in less than ten minutes; not only one copy, but several of varying conditions and prices.

For the book seller, the Internet has also opened a whole new world of marketing possibilities and for a small fee, books that have lingered on the shelf waiting for a walk-in customer can now be spotlighted to millions of potential buyers.

Currently the largest book search service on the Internet is *www.abebooks.com*, the Advanced Book Exchange. At the time of writing it lists 5,779 Robert E. Howard titles, with new items being added or sold daily.

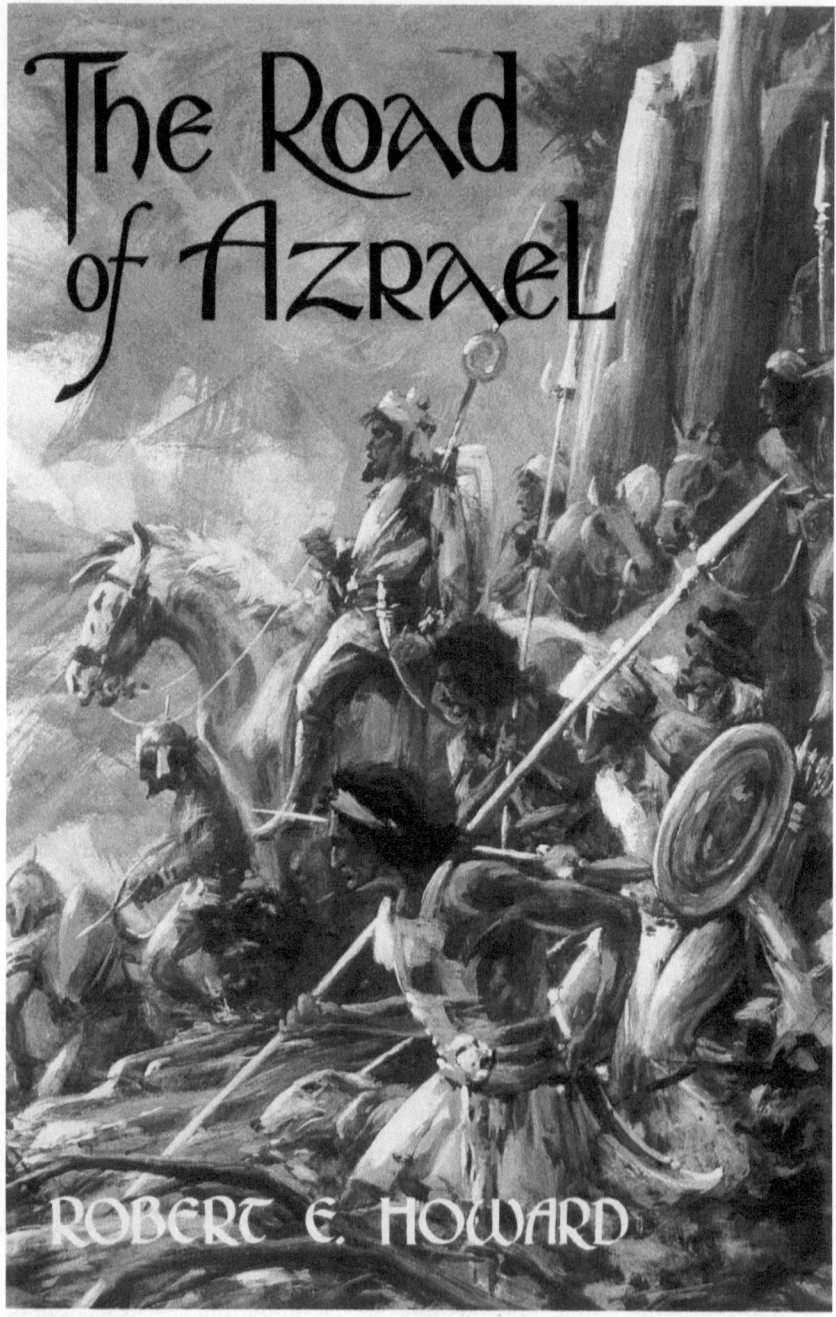

The Road of Azrael. Donald M. Grant 1979. Jacket art by Roy G. Krenkel. © 1979 P.M. Kuykendall.

Limited to hardcover books in dust jackets, the count is 908 titles, and for available *Weird Tales* pulp magazines only 15 issues. Another Web site well worth looking at is *www.abaa.com*, the Antiquarian Bookseller's Association of America (ABAA), which lists 142 Robert E. Howard titles, at the time of writing, with 49 being hardcover books in dust jackets. There are other commercial sites which may offer the occasional Howard title, but mostly the newer reprints. Many booksellers maintain their own Web site, but they can be difficult to locate unless one knows the name of the business or the address of the Web site.

This leaves the Howard collector with *www.abebooks.com* and *www.abaa.com* as the two largest book search services for buying collectible books. The titles offered on these two sites may be repeats since many booksellers list their books on both sites. The books offered by the ABAA are usually a better grade and more accurately described. Higher prices reflects the greater level of quality. The sellers know their books and their values. The books offered by abebooks.com are usually well described and fairly correctly represented, but there are occasional inaccuracies and inconsistencies in edition identification and description. I have personally had a few disappointing transactions with sellers on this site. Regardless of site reputation, description and price, buying books unseen on the Internet can be a gamble. Here are a few suggestions which can make the experience less risky.

Compare Price and Condition. Recently I found 14 copies of a key Howard title, *Skull-Face and Others* (Sauk City, Arkham House, 1946), on abebooks.com, all first editions in the original dust jackets. The books, though all listed in "very good" grade, were priced inconsistently. One copy described as "very good/very good" listed at $365.00 while another book also described as "very good/very good" was priced at $600.00. Other books in the same grade listed anywhere in between the two extremes. Such differences in grading and pricing are not uncommon. It is possible to pick up good copies for a reasonable price, if one is patient and takes the time to look and not jump on the first book that is available.

Contact the Seller. Most Web sites have a service that facilitates direct communication between a potential buyer and the seller through e-mail. Do not buy a high-priced book or pulp magazine unseen without contacting the seller and asking specific questions such as: a) Is this a true first edition or first printing? b) Is the binding tight and square, with no spine roll and good hinges? c) To what degree are the boards, spine and covers faded or discolored and is the text on the spine still readable? d) Are there any pages missing, or writing, bookplates, stamps, tears, tape repairs, stains or remainder marks? e) Is the dust jacket the original, issued

Waterfront Fists and Others. Wildside Press 2003. Jacket artist unknown. © 2003 Paul Herman.

with the book, or is it a later state dust jacket? f) Is the jacket price clipped, faded, chipped, repaired or are pieces missing? g) May I return the book or magazine for a refund if I am not satisfied?

This may seems like a lot of work, but it only takes a few minutes to e-mail the questions and when several hundred dollars is at stake, it is well worth the effort. If some of the answers are provided in the description of the book there is no need to ask. If the seller does not answer positively within a reasonable time (usually one to three business days), do not buy the book. If the seller answers your questions honestly and courteously, you are less likely to end up with a book or magazine that you would not have bought if seen beforehand. Some sellers will e-mail electronic scans or photographs of high-priced items.

Buying on Internet Auctions. Buying books through online auctions such as *www.ebay.com* or other sites is entirely different than buying from a bookseller and can be a chancy proposition. While the sellers on the aforementioned sites know their books and price accordingly, this is not always the case on auction sites. Sometimes the seller does not know the difference between a first edition and a reprint or how to grade a book or magazine. Or the condition and consequent value of a book may be misrepresented or inadequately described, giving the bidder little information to make a decision to buy or not. It is, however, possible to make some good deals on Internet auctions if one knows what to look for and how to develop a winning bidding strategy. As a rule of thumb, but depending on scarcity, the winning bid paid for most Robert E. Howard items on *www.ebay.com* is about 60 percent of the price charged by booksellers for the same item in comparable condition. Before bidding on a book or magazine, know its current catalog value and determine the top price that you are prepared to pay. The most important thing when buying at an Internet auction is to make sure that the seller has a return guarantee so a book or magazine purchased may be returned for a refund if it is not as described or is unsatisfactory.

When buying or selling on the Internet, it is inevitable that so-called "spoof" or "phished" messages with requests for information will be received unsolicited. These are messages which appear authentic, down to the graphics and logo of a legitimate Web site, but are unlawful attempts to obtain personal and financial information for fraudulent use. It is usually claimed that an audit or unauthorized use of the customer's account has necessitated a confirmation of all relevant information, including name, address, date of birth, Social Security number, credit card numbers, bank account numbers, passwords and other ID verification. The hook is that unless this information is provided within a few days, the customer's account will be closed and further access to the site denied. Do not respond in any way to such messages. Forward them at once to the legitimate Web site which they pretend to represent before deleting them. Do not open these messages!

Selling Books and Magazines

For the book collector who wants to dispose of duplicate copies, single titles or an entire collection of Robert E. Howard books and pulp magazines, there are five basic options available.

Sale to Collectors. This is the option that brings the best price. The greatest challenge is to find collectors who are interested in buying the book(s) or magazine(s) and can pay the asking price. Acquiring mailing lists from collectors' groups, advertisements in speciality publications and listings on the Internet are common promotional approaches.

Sale by Auction. Larger collections may be offered for sale through auction houses. Auctions attract booksellers and collectors and will often bring the best price for the least amount of work. The seller can set a minimum (reserve) price or leave the conditions of sale to the auctioneer. The percentage commission charged by the auction house per book is usually paid by the buyer.

Sale at Book Fairs and Conventions. Most larger cities have one or more book fairs, conventions or exhibitions per year. Some of these events are reserved for professional booksellers, but in many cases it is possible for anyone to rent space for a table with chairs and offer books for sale. The seller should be prepared to negotiate. Potential buyers expect to find bargains, but may also be nitpicking at insignificant flaws and unfairly criticize a book or its condition to bring the price down. This tactic cheapens the buyer and demeans the seller. Don't fall for it. Determine a fair price and stick to it.

Sale to Booksellers. When selling to booksellers, remember that this is how they make a living. They cannot buy at catalog prices if they want to stay in business. If a seller has a ready buyer or knows that there is a high demand for the item, he may be prepared to pay up to 70 percent of guide value. If a seller believes that the item is scarce enough to sell within a reasonable time, he may offer 30 to 40 percent of guide value, but if it is common and most likely will linger on the shelf (or Web site) for more than a year, don't expect more than 10 to 20 percent of guide value, if the seller wants the book at all. Instead of selling a book or a collection outright to a bookseller, one might consider trading for credit towards the purchase of other books. This may give more buying power than a cash deal, since most sellers would be willing to give more store credit than cash.

Internet Sales. There are presently three ways of selling books and magazines on the Internet:

Personal Web site. Many sellers post their own Web site with customer access to their inventory through a user-friendly, search engine, together with listings of services, news items, links and other matters of interest. Individual titles can be better represented and are easier to find on a personal Web site than getting lost in the thousands of titles listed by the book search services. The seller determines the price for the books offered for sale. A personal Web site might be listed in various Internet directories or a potential buyer will need to know the name of the seller or the Web site address to access it.

Book Search Services. Like *www.abebooks.com*, *www.abaa.com* and others, these services are massive databases containing millions of books and representing thousands of booksellers world-wide. For a nominal fee, abebooks.com, for example, will list books for sale, collect credit card payments, provide a small personalized Web site and a free download book database program to keep track of inventory, sales, invoices, etc. The seller sets the price. The downside is, that with more than 5,000 Howard titles online, the few items listed by a private seller may easily disappear into the enormity of such inventory unless they are exceptionally desirable or scarce. It may be a long time before the average book or magazine is sold through this market. While abebooks.com will list for anyone who registers successfully, abaa.com will accept listings only from members of the Antiquarian Bookseller's Association of America.

Online Auctions. If one is more interested in a quick sale than a higher profit, the online auction is the way to go. There are several possibilities, but *www.ebay.com* is probably the best known and has a large following world-wide. Auctions usually run for 7 days, but can be more or less if required. There is a listing fee and a percentage is deducted from the winning bid price. Ebay.com also provides online payment services and has a feedback system for buyers and sellers. The seller determines the auction starting price, and can set a reserve line which is the price below which the item cannot be sold. As mentioned before, one can expect about half the price for a book or magazine sold on an ebay.com auction than it would sell for on a book search service.

Regardless of which of these options the seller may choose, know the books offered for sale. Consider titles and editions and keep in mind that condition, supply and demand will influence values. Grade the books accurately and conservatively. A "very good" book should be graded as such, not as a "fine" copy. An informed buyer will know the difference. Study catalogs and price guides to get a realistic fix on the asking price.

Echoes from an Iron Harp. Donald M. Grant 1972. Jacket art by Alicia Austin. © 1972 Glenn Lord.

When selling on the Internet, insist that insurance or at least a delivery confirmation be paid before shipping. It is not uncommon that an item sold and shipped without either is claimed not to be received. This is accompanied by a fraudulent demand for a refund from an unscrupulous buyer who did receive the item but insists not to have. Also be careful when sending any personal or financial information into cyberspace.

5
A ROBERT E. HOWARD BIBLIOGRAPHY

Few bibliographies are complete. The present is no exception. The prolific Robert E. Howard wrote more than 300 stories, approximately 700 poems, several novel-length works, and countless letters, articles and essays. Many stories and poems remained unfinished or were abandoned as fragments, because he lost interest in them or they did not work for him. Some of his writings have been published only in limited editions, amateur press publications or other less accessible media, and many original typescripts are lost. This has left a volume of stories, fragments, poems and miscellaneous material which is difficult to locate and catalog.

Consequently a work such as this must be incomplete, missing some of the lesser known or more indefinite items. At the time of writing, Glenn Lord's book *The Last Celt* (Donald M. Grant, 1976) is still the definitive and most exhaustive published Robert E. Howard bibliography prior to December 1973. The present work is not intended to replace or supersede Glenn Lord's book, but rather to supplement it by inclusion of the main body of Robert E. Howard's works published after 1973.

Since the appearance of Howard's first story, "Spear and Fang," in *Weird Tales* in July 1925, his stories, letters, poetry and other writings have been published in a variety of formats, including pulp and fantasy magazines, hardcover books, limited edition books, mass market paperback books, anthologies, special printings and amateur press publications.

To organize such varied material, the bibliography has been arranged in five categories: 1) books, including material published in hardcover (casebound) and softcover editions; 2) mass market paperback books, including material published in paperback editions; 3) magazines, including material published in the pulps and other magazines; 4) special publications, including material published in privately printed, limited editions; and 5) amateur press journals.

In all instances I have used the titles under which the items were published, which may not be Howard's original title or the title under which the story or poem was first submitted for publication. Some titles were changed in the course of writing or submission by Howard himself; others were changed at the time of publication by editors or publishers. Other titles were changed when some of Howard's original work became subject to rewriting, revision, expansion and publication by other writers.

In addition to the American editions, Robert E. Howard's work has also been released extensively in the United Kingdom, Canada, Australia, New Zealand and other English-speaking countries by various publishing houses. Many of these editions have attractive cover art and are well worth collecting. The British publisher Victor Gollancz compiled and published the first textually unaltered collection of Conan stories, several reprinted from *Weird Tales* as Howard wrote them. Wandering Star, another British publisher, is in the process of publishing the "Robert E. Howard Library of Classics" in lavishly illustrated, luxury editions, textually corrected and collected in subject or character volumes.

Robert E. Howard's work has been translated and published in many foreign languages, including Bulgarian, Croatian, Czech, Dutch, Estonian, French, German, Italian, Japanese, Lithuanian, Polish, Russian, Spanish, and Turkish. The list of translated reprints and the proliferation of reprints by foreign publishers is nearly endless. Translations and foreign editions have been omitted except for United Kingdom titles.

For the collector who wants foreign editions of Howard's work, the possibilities are limitless; but a lifetime of collecting and a warehouse-sized library would probably not offer enough time or space for such an undertaking.

In all five of the following categories, individual titles are listed in the chronological order of publication. While this arrangement may seem more difficult to navigate than an alphabetically ordered system, the description of each item is preceded by a unique letter-number-letter code that is easily tracked through the appropriate index. Reprints of a title or variant editions are listed under the first edition in the chronological order of publication and indicated as a, b, c, and so forth, as may be appropriate.

A. BOOKS

The publication of Robert E. Howard's work in book format was a slow process. The first book appeared in London, England, in 1937 the year after his death. It would be another nine years before the next hardcover edition would be published in the United States. From then on the number of Howard titles in book form has increased slowly, gained momentum with the mass market paperback boom in the late 1960s, culminated in the 1970s and 1980s, and slowed to a more steady pace at the present time.

Since there were no books by Howard published during his lifetime, there are no author-signed copies. It may be possible to find books which have Howard's signature from a letter, receipt or signature sheet cut out and pasted in. Unless there is some other association, the complete instrument from which the signature was cut, would probably be of greater value by itself than affixed at random to a contemporary Howard title.

Except for reprints, the books are listed chronologically, in order of publication. The suggested values indicated are for titles in "fine/fine" condition. Books in better condition will demand higher prices, and books in lower grades may be purchased for less. The first noted value is for books in the original dust jacket; the second is for books without dust jackets or in facsimile jackets.

B1a A Gent from Bear Creek. Herbert Jenkins, London, England, 1937. Orange-golden binding with black lettering. 8vo. 312 pp. Copies printed not stated. Cover price 7s 6d. Jacket artist not identified. A very rare book. Only twelve copies are known to exist and only one of these have the original dust jacket.

Contents: *Striped Shirts and Busted Hearts; Mountain Man; Meet Cap'n Kidd; Guns of the Mountains; A Gent from Bear Creek; The Feud Buster; The Road to Bear Creek; The Scalp Hunter; Cupid from Bear Creek; The Haunted Mountain; Educate or Bust; War on Bear Creek; When Bear Creek came to Chawed Ear.* $30,000/3,500

B1b A Gent from Bear Creek. Herbert Jenkins, London, England, 1938. Inexpensive reprint of the first edition. 8vo. 312 pp. Copies printed not known. Cover price 2s 6d. Little is known about this printing and its binding. No copies are known to exist. It is possible that most were destroyed in the Second World War paper drive.

Contents: Presumed identical to the first edition.

B1c A Gent from Bear Creek. Donald M. Grant, West Kingston, Rhode Island, 1965. First American edition. Orange-Brown cloth binding with gilt lettering. 12mo. 312 pp. 732 copies printed. Cover price $4.00. Jacket art by Henry Eichner.

Contents: Photo offset from the Jenkins first edition. $125/30.

B1d A Gent from Bear Creek. Donald M. Grant, West Kingston, Rhode Island,1975. Dark Brown cloth binding with gilt lettering. 12mo. 312 pp. 1,500 copies printed. Cover price $7.00. Illustrated edition. Jacket art and three interior illustrations by Tim Kirk.

Contents: Photo offset from the Jenkins first edition. $50/15.

B1e   A Gent from Bear Creek and Other Tales. Wildside Press, Holicong, Pennsylvania, 2004. Edited by Paul Herman. Blue cloth binding with gilt lettering. 8vo. 222 pp. Copies printed not stated. Cover price $39.95. Jacket art by David Burton.
   Contents: As B1a, with an introduction by Paul Herman and two additional stories: *While Smoke Rolled* and *Texas John Alden*. $40/10.

B2a   Skull-Face and Others. Arkham House, Sauk City, Wisconsin, 1946. Black cloth binding with gilt lettering. 8vo. 475 pp. 3,004 copies printed. Cover price $5.00. Jacket art by Hannes Bok.
   Contents: *Foreword,* by August Derleth; *Which Will Scarcely Be Understood* (poem); *Robert Ervin Howard: A Memoriam,* by H.P. Lovecraft; *A Memory of R.E. Howard,* by E. Hoffmann Price; *Wolfshead; The Black Stone; The Horror from the Mound; The Cairn on the Headland; Black Canaan; The Fire of Asshurbanipal; A Man-Eating Jeopard; Skull-Face; The Hyborian Age; Worms of the Earth; The Valley of the Worm; Skulls in the Stars; Rattle of Bones; The Hills of the Dead; Wings in the Night; The Shadow Kingdom; The Mirrors of Tuzun Thune; Kings of the Night; The Phoenix on the Sword; The Scarlet Citadel; The Tower of the Elephant; Rogues in the House; Shadows in Zamboula; Lines Written in the Realization That I Must Die* (poem). $800/125.

B3a   Conan the Conqueror. The Gnome Press, Inc., New York, 1950. Edited by John D. Clark. Dark red cloth binding with dark blue lettering. 8vo. 255 pp. 5,000 copies printed. Cover price $2.75. Jacket design and art by David Kyle and John Forte. Endpaper map by David Kyle. Inexpensively produced and less durable; inside pages have a high acid contents and a tendency to browning and brittleness. This is one of the only full-length novels written by Robert E. Howard. It was first submitted and accepted under its original title "*The Hour of the Dragon"* by Pawling & Ness, Ltd., London, in 1934, but was not published when the company went into bankruptcy. The change of title was done primarily to capitalize on the name Conan.
   Contents: *Introduction,* by John D. Clark; *Conan the Conqueror.* $250/50.

B3b   Conan the Conqueror. T.V. Boardman & Co, Limited, London, England, 1954. Edited by John D. Clark. Black binding with silver lettering. 8vo. 255 pp. Copies printed not stated. Cover price 9s 6d. Jacket artist not identified. Frontispiece map of the Hyborian Age by David Kyle.
   Contents: *Introduction,* by John D. Clark; *Conan the Conqueror.* $100/30.

B4a   The Sword of Conan. The Gnome Press, Inc., New York, 1952. Edited by John D. Clark. Dark red cloth binding with black lettering. 8vo. 251 pp. 4,000 copies printed. Cover price $2.75. Jacket art and endpaper map by David Kyle. Inexpensively produced and less durable; inside pages have a high acid contents and a tendency to browning and brittleness.
   Contents: *The People of the Black Circle; The Slithering Shadow; The Pool of the Black One; Red Nails.* $250/50.

B5a   King Conan. The Gnome Press, Inc., New York, 1953. Edited by John

Skull-Face. Berkley Books 1978. Cover art by Ken Kelly. © 1978 Glenn Lord.

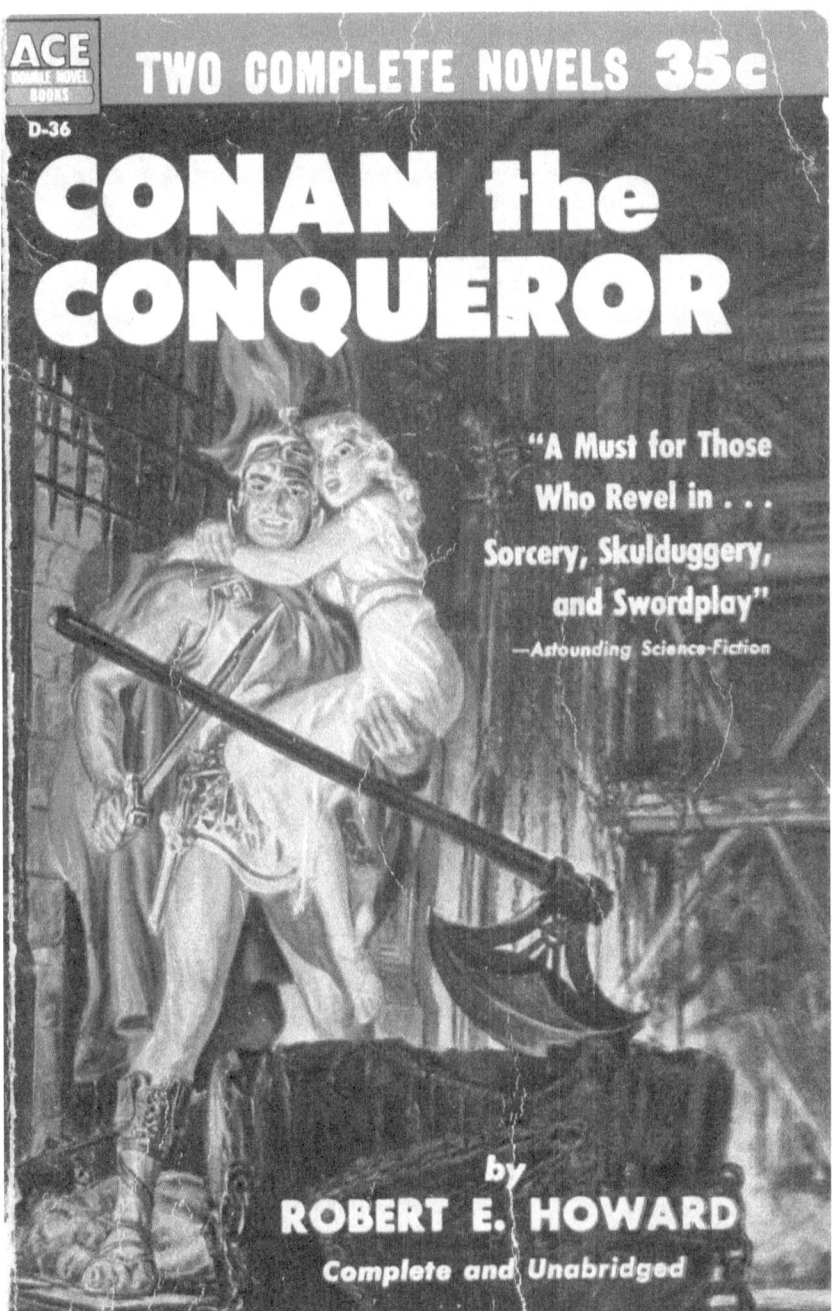

Conan the Conqueror. Ace Books 1953. Cover art by Norman Saunders. © 1953 The Gnome Press, Inc.

D. Clark. Red cloth binding with black lettering. 8vo. 255 pp. 4,000 copies printed. Cover price $3.00. Jacket art and endpaper map by David Kyle. Inexpensively produced and less durable; inside pages have a high acid contents and a tendency to browning and brittleness.

Contents: *Introduction,* by L. Sprague de Camp; *Jewels of Gwahlur; Beyond the Black River; The Treasure of Tranicos* (edited by L. Sprague de Camp); *The Phoenix on the Sword; The Scarlet Citadel.* $250/50.

B6a   The Coming of Conan. The Gnome Press, Inc., New York, 1953. Edited by L. Sprague de Camp. Red cloth binding with black lettering. 8vo. 224 pp. 4,000 copies printed. Cover price $3.00. Jacket art by Frank Kelly Freas. Inexpensively produced and less durable; inside pages have a high acid contents and a tendency to browning and brittleness.

Contents: Howard's Letter to P. Schuyler Miller; H.P. Lovecraft's Letter to Donald Wollheim; *The Hyborian Age* (with John D. Clark); *The Shadow Kingdom; The Mirrors of Tuzun Thune; The King and the Oak* (poem); *An Informal Biography of Conan the Cimmerian,* by John D. Clark and P. Schuyler Miller; *The Tower of the Elephant; The God in the Bowl* (edited by L. Sprague de Camp); *Rogues in the House; The Frost-Giant's Daughter* (edited by L. Sprague de Camp); *Queen of the Black Coast.* $200/40

B7a   Conan the Barbarian. The Gnome Press, Inc., New York, 1954. Edited by L. Sprague de Camp. Red cloth binding with black lettering. 8vo. 224 pp. 3,000 copies printed. Cover price $3.00. Jacket art by Ed Emshwiller. Inexpensively produced and less durable; inside pages have a high acid contents and a tendency to browning and brittleness.

Contents: *Black Colossus; A Witch Shall Be Born; Shadows in Zamboula; The Devil in Iron.* $250/50.

B8a   Tales of Conan. with L. Sprague de Camp. The Gnome Press, Inc., New York, 1955. All the stories in this volume have been edited, rewritten or expanded by L. Sprague de Camp. Red cloth binding with black lettering. 8vo. 219 pp. 4,000 copies printed. Jacket art by Ed Emshwiller. Inexpensively produced and less durable; inside pages have a high acid contents and a tendency to browning and brittleness. Some years after publication, unbound sheets were bound in several different color bindings, including green, black and gray.

Contents: *Introduction,* by P. Schuyler Miller; *Note,* by L. Sprague de Camp; *The Blood-Stained God; Hawks Over Shem; The Road of the Eagles; The Flame-Knife.* $120/15.

B9a   Always Comes Evening. Arkham House, Sauk City, Wisconsin, 1957. Compiled by Glenn Lord and printed for him by Arkham House. Black cloth binding with gilt lettering. 12mo. 86 pp. 636 copies printed. Cover price $3.00. Jacket art by Frank Utpatel. By a printing error, the spine lettering is backwards on all but the final 100 copies. This makes the 100 copies, with the corrected spine lettering, a second state printing.

Contents: *Foreword,* by Glenn Lord; *Introduction,* by Dale Hart; *Always Comes Evening; The Poets; The Singer in the Mist; Solomon Kane's Homecoming;*

Futility; The Song of the Bats; The Moor Ghost; Recompense; The Hills of Kandahar; Which Will Scarcely Be Understood; Haunting Columns; The Last Hour; Ships; The King and the Oak; The Riders of Babylon; Easter Island; Moon Mockery; Shadows on the Road; The Soul-Eater; The Dream and the Shadow; The Ghost Kings; Desert Dawn; An Open Window; The Song of a Mad Minstrel; The Gates of Nineveh; Fragment; The Harp of Alfred; Remembrance; Crete; Forbidden Magic; Black Chant Imperial; A Song Out of Midian; Arkham; The Voices Waken Memory; Babel; Song at Midnight; The Ride of Falume; Autumn; Dead Man's Hate; One Who Comes at Eventide; To a Woman; Emancipation; Retribution; Chant of the White Beard; Rune; The Road of Azrael; Song of the Pict; Prince and Beggar; Hymn of Hatred; Invective; Men of the Shadows; Babylon; Niflheim; The Heart of the Sea's Desire; Laughter in the Gulfs; A Song of the Don Cossacks; The Gods of Easter Island; Nisapur; Moon Shame; The Tempter; Lines Written in the Realization That I Must Die; Chapter Headings: *The Pool of the Black One; Kings of the Night; Red Blades of Black Cathay; The Phoenix on the Sword; The Scarlet Citadel; Queen of the Black Coast.* $750/150.

B9b   Always Comes Evening. Underwood-Miller, San Francisco, California, 1977. Maroon cloth binding with gilt lettering. 8vo. 110 pp. 2,500 copies printed. Cover price $10.00, not listed. Jacket art and interior illustrations by Keiko Nelson. Includes a laid-in facsimile print of the poem "The Song of Yar Ali Khan" written by Robert E. Howard while a student. A second edition dust jacket, designed by Mara Murray, was published in 1980 and added to remaining 1977 copies. It features a wrap-around, National Archive photograph of ritually preserved skulls of an ancient sect of monks, from the remains of a monastery near Mt. Sinai. The jacket has differently printed flaps from the 1977 edition and lists a cover price of $10.00. In spite of the title it is not an exact reprint of the first edition. The poems have been rearranged into categories, and a new poem "A Crown for a King" has been added.

Contents: *Introduction,* by Glenn Lord; I. Poems from Weird Tales: *Fragment; Song of a Mad Minstrel; Remembrance; The Moor Ghost; Dead Man's Hate; The Ride of Falume; Arkham; Crete; Desert Dawn; The Riders of Babylon; Shadows on the Road; The Harp of Alfred; Moon Mockery; A Song Out of Midian; The Ghost Kings; Forbidden Magic; Recompense; The Song of the Bats; Ships; The King and the Oak; Futility; Autumn; The Poets; Easter Island; Black Chant Imperial; An Open Window; Lines Written in the Realization That I Must Die; The Gates of Nineveh; The Hills of Kandahar; Which Will Scarcely Be Understood.* Sonnets out of Bedlam: *The Soul-Eater; The Dream and the Shadow; The Last Hour; Haunting Columns; The Singer in the Mist.* Verse from the Stories: *The Scarlet Citadel; The Pool of the Black One; Kings of the Night; Red Blades of Black Cathay; The Phoenix on the Sword; Queen of the Black Coast.* II. Other Poems: *Always Comes Evening; Emancipation; Invective; Hymn of Hatred; Prince and Beggar; The Tempter; The Road of Azrael; A Song of the Don Cossacks; To a Woman; Retribution; Solomon Kane's Homecoming; Song at Midnight; One Who Comes at Eventide; Rune; Men of the Shadows; Song of the Pict; Chant of the White Beard; Nisapur; Babylon; Niflheim; The Gods of Easter Island; The Heart of the Sea's Desire.* Voices of the Night: *Voices Waken memory; Moon Shame; Babel; Laughter in the Gulfs; A Crown for a King.* $50/15

B9c **Always Comes Evening.** Underwood-Miller, San Francisco, California, 1977. Black leather binding with gilt lettering. 8vo. 110 pp. 206 numbered copies printed. Cover price not listed. Jacket art and interior illustrations by Keiko Nelson. Signed by the artist. In slipcase. Includes a laid-in facsimile print of the poem "The Song of Yar Ali Khan" written by Robert E. Howard while a student.

Contents: As B9b. $150/50.

B10a **The Dark Man and Others.** Arkham House, Sauk City, Wisconsin, 1963. Black cloth binding with gilt lettering. 12mo. 284 pp. 2,029 copies printed. Cover price $5.00. Jacket art by Frank Utpatel.

Contents: *Introduction*, by August Derleth; *The Voice of El-Lil; Pigeons from Hell; The Dark Man; The Gods of Bal-Sagoth; People of the Dark; The Children of the Night; The Dead Remember; The Man on the Ground; The Garden of Fear; The Thing on the Roof; The Hyena; Dig Me No Grave; The Dream Snake; In the Forest of Villefére; Old Garfield's Heart.* $250/70.

B11a **The Pride of Bear Creek.** Donald M. Grant, West Kingston, Rhode Island, 1966. Orange-Brown cloth binding with gilt lettering. 12mo. 221 pp. 812 copies printed. Cover price $4.00. Jacket art by Henry Eichner. This is the same jacket art as used for the 1965 D.M. Grant edition of "A Gent From Bear Creek", except with a change in the cover banner color from orange-red to green.

Contents: *Note*, by Glenn Lord; *The Riot at Cougar Paw; Pilgrims to the Pecos; High Horse Rampage; The Apache Mountain War; Pistol Politics; The Conquerin' Hero of the Humbolts; A Ring-Tailed Tornado.* $90/20.

B11b **The Pride of Bear Creek.** Donald M. Grant, West Kingston, Rhode Island, 1977. Orange-Brown cloth binding with gilt lettering. 12mo. 248 pp. Copies printed not stated. Cover price $7.00. Illustrated edition. Jacket art and three interior illustrations by Tim Kirk.

Contents: As B11a. $45/10.

B12a **Red Shadows.** Donald M. Grant, West Kingston, Rhode Island, 1968. Carmine cloth binding with gilt lettering. 12mo. 381 pp. 896 copies printed. Cover price $6.00. Jacket art, title page, frontispiece and four color interior plates by Jeff Jones. The plates are not in the sequence listed in front of the book.

Contents: *Introduction,* by Glenn Lord; *Skulls in the Stars; The Right Hand of Doom; Red Shadows; Rattle of Bones; The Castle of the Devil; The Moon of Skulls; The One Black Stain* (poem); *Blades of the Brotherhood; The Hills of the Dead; Hawk of Basti; The Return of Sir Richard Grenville* (poem); *Wings in the Night; The Footfalls Within; The Children of Asshur; Solomon Kane's Homecoming* (poem). $150/40.

B12b **Red Shadows.** Donald M. Grant, West Kingston, Rhode Island, 1971. Dark-gray cloth binding with gilt lettering. 12mo. 381 pp. 741 copies printed. Cover price $6.00. Jacket art, title page, frontispiece and four color interior

plates by Jeff Jones. The positions of the plates have been corrected to match the listing in front of the book.
Contents: As B12a. $150/40.

B12c   Red Shadows. Donald M. Grant, West Kingston, Rhode Island, 1978. Light brown leatherette binding with dark brown lettering. 8vo. 337 pp. 1,350 copies printed. Cover price $20.00. Jacket art, endpaper illustrations, title page and eight color interior plates by Jeff Jones. The format, size, jacket art and illustrations in this book are different from the two previous editions.
Contents: As B12a. $120/40.

B13a   Singers in the Shadows. Donald M. Grant, West Kingston, Rhode Island, 1970. Light-blue cloth binding with gilt lettering. 12mo. 55 pp. 549 copies printed. Cover price $3.00. Jacket art by Dave Karbonik. Eight interior illustrations by Robert B. Acheson. A slim collection of verse, first submitted in 1928 to Albert & Charles Boni, but rejected.
Contents: *Introduction*, by Glenn Lord; *Zukala's Hour; Night Mood; The Sea-Woman; The Bride of Cuchulain; The Stranger; Shadows; Rebel; White Thunder; The Men That Walk With Satan; Thus Spake Sven the Fool; Sacrifice; The Witch; The Lost Galley; Hadrian's Wall; Attila Rides No More; The Fear That Follows; Destination; The Tavern; The Road to Hell; The Twin Gates.* $150/40.

B13b   Singers in the Shadows. Science Fiction Graphics Inc., New York, 1977. Black cloth binding with gilt lettering. 8vo. 60 pp. 1,500 copies printed. Cover price $7.95. Jacket art and six interior illustrations by Marcus Boas. The format, size and illustrations in this book are different from the first edition and the poems have been rearranged.
Contents: *Introduction*, by Glenn Lord; *Zukala's Hour; The Sea-Woman; The Bride of Cuchulain; The Stranger; Rebel; White Thunder; The Men That Walk With Satan; Thus Spake Sven the Fool; The Witch; Sacrifice; Hadrian's Wall; Night Mood; Shadows; The Lost Galley; The Fear That Follows; The Tavern; Destination; The Road to Hell; Attila Rides No More; The Twin Gates.* $75/25.

B14a   Red Blades of Black Cathay. Donald M. Grant, West Kingston, Rhode Island, 1971. The stories in this volume were written in collaboration with Tevis Clyde Smith. Red cloth binding with gilt lettering. 12mo. 125 pp. 1,091 copies printed. Cover price $4.00. Jacket art and four interior illustrations by Dave Karbonik.
Contents: *How the Stories Came to Be*, by Tevis Clyde Smith; *Red Blades of Black Cathay; Diogenes of Today; Eighttoes Makes a Play.* $130/40.

B15a   Echoes from an Iron Harp. Donald M. Grant, West Kingston, Rhode Island, 1972. A volume of verse. Red cloth binding with gilt lettering. 8vo. 109 pp. 1,079 copies printed. Cover price $6.00. Jacket art, color frontispiece and ten interior illustrations by Alicia Austin.
Contents: *Introduction,* by Glenn Lord; *Age Comes to Rabelais; Belshazzar; But the Hills Were Ancient Then; Cimmeria; A Dawn in Flanders; The Day That I Die; Dreams of Nineveh; The Dust Dance* (Version 1)*; The Dust Dance* (Version 2)*; The Dweller in Dark Valley; Earth-Born; Fables for Little Folks; "Feach Air*

Muir Lionadhi Gealach Buidhe Mar Or"; Futility; Heritage; Illusion; John Ringold; Kid Lavigne is Dead; The Kissing of Sal Snooboo; A Lady's Chamber; The Last Day; Lost Altars; Memories; A Moment; Moonlight on a Skull; Not Only in Death They Die; Private Magrath of the A.E.F.; Reuben's Brethren; Roundelay of the Roughneck; The Sands of Time; The Sea; The Skull in the Clouds; Skulls and Dust; Skulls Over Judah; Slumber; A Song of Defeat; The Song of Horsa's Galley; A Song of the Legions; A Song for Men That Laugh; A Sonnet of Good Cheer; Sonora to Del Rio; Surrender; Tarantella; Thor's Son; Timur-lang; To Certain Orthodox Brethren; A Vision; A Warning; Where Are Your Knights, Donn Othna?; Who is Grandpa Theobold?; The Years Are as a Knife; Headings: *The Black Stone; The Blood of Belshazzar; Death's Black Riders; The Fearsome Touch of Death; The Grey God Passes; The Hour of the Dragon; Kelly the Conjure-Man; The Lion of Tiberias; Something About Eve; The Sowers of the Thunder; The Thing on the Roof.* $250/50.

B16a   Marchers of Valhalla. Donald M. Grant, West Kingston, Rhode Island, 1972. Red cloth binding with gilt lettering. 12mo. 121 pp. 1,654 copies printed. Cover price $4.50. Jacket art and six interior illustrations by Robert B. Acheson.

   Contents: *Introduction,* by Donald M. Grant; *Marchers of Valhalla; The Thunder-Rider.* $50/15.

B16b   Marchers of Valhalla. Donald M. Grant, West Kingston, Rhode Island, 1977. Blue cloth binding with gilt lettering. 4to. 191 pp. Copies printed not stated. Cover price $15.00. Jacket art, color frontispiece and ten interior color illustrations by Marcus Boas. This edition has been redesigned in a larger format, without an introduction and with one story added.

   Contents: *Marchers of Valhalla; The Grey God Passes; The Thunder-Rider.* $35/10.

B17a   The Sowers of the Thunder. Donald M. Grant, West Kingston, Rhode Island, 1973. Light-gray binding with black lettering and design. 8vo. 285 pp. 2,509 copies printed. Cover price $12.00. Jacket art and binding design, endpapers, color frontispiece, four full-page illustrations, 142 smaller illustrations and four illustrations, one for each story, repeated in the right-hand margin of odd-numbered pages by Roy G. Krenkel. Second printing (1973) 1,389 copies. Black binding with silver lettering.

   Contents: *Introduction,* by Roy G. Krenkel; *The Lion of Tiberias; The Sowers of the Thunder; Lord of Samarcand; The Shadow of the Vulture.* First printing $135/35. Second printing $75/25.

B18a   The Vultures. Fictioneer Books, Ltd., Lakemont, Georgia, 1973. Black leatherette binding with gilt lettering and design. 8vo. 190 pp. 1,100 copies printed. Cover price $5.95. Jacket art, binding design and six interior illustrations by Stephen Fabian. Second printing in 1975 with illustrated endpapers by Stephen Fabian. Maroon binding with silver lettering. Cover price $6.95, later increased to $8.50.

   Contents: *The Vultures; Afterword*, by Glenn Lord; *Showdown at Hell's Canyon.* First printing $75/15. Second printing $35/10.

B19a   Worms of the Earth. Donald M. Grant, West Kingston, Rhode Island, 1974. Dark red cloth binding with gilt lettering. 12mo. 233 pp. 2,500 copies printed. Cover price $6.00. Jacket art and four interior illustrations by David Ireland.
   Contents: *The Drums of Pictdom/Foreword; The Lost Race; Men of the Shadows; Kings of the Night; A Song of the Race* (poem); *Worms of the Earth; Fragment* (untitled); *The Dark Man.* $45/10

B19b   Worms of the Earth. Cross Plains Comics, New York and Wandering Star, London, England, 2000. Square bound soft cover. 4to. 63 pp. Copies printed not stated. Cover price $9.95. Comic book adaptation of Howard's story with art by Tim Conrad and Barry Windsor Smith. Cover art by Mark Schultz.
   Contents: *Worms of the Earth;* An interview with artist Tim Conrad; *Bran Mak Morn Destroyer,* by Fred Blosser; A Conversation with Gary Gianni; *The Adventures of Two-Gun Bob,* by Jim and Ruth Keegan; *Robert E. Howard, Bran Mak Morn, and the Picts,* by Rusty Burke; *Cross Plains, Texas, Project Pride,* by Rusty Burke. $15.

B20a   The Incredible Adventures of Dennis Dorgan. FAX Collector's Edition, West Linn, Oregon, 1974. Gray-green cloth binding with silver lettering and design. 8vo. 165 pp. Copies printed not stated. Cover price $11.95. Cover art, endpaper illustrations, frontispiece, story headings, and ten interior illustrations by Tom Foster.
   Contents: *Introduction,* by Darrell C. Richardson; *The Alleys of Singapore; The Jade Monkey; The Mandarin Ruby; The Yellow Cobra; In High Society; Playing Journalist; The Destiny Gorilla; A Knight of the Round Table; Playing Santa Claus; The Turkish Menace* (with Darrell C. Richardson). $45/10.

B21a   The Lost Valley of Iskander. FAX Collector's Edition, West Linn, Oregon, 1974. Dark green cloth binding with silver lettering and design. 8vo. 194 pp. Copies printed not stated. Cover price $12.95. Cover art, endpaper illustrations, title page decorations, chapter headings, three color plates and eight full-page illustrations by Michael W. Kaluta.
   Contents: *Introduction,* by Darrell C. Richardson; *The Daughter of Erlik Khan; The Lost Valley of Iskander; Hawk of the Hills.* $45/10.

B22a   The People of the Black Circle. Donald M. Grant, West Kingston, Rhode Island, 1974. Gray binding with maroon cloth spine and gilt lettering. 4to. 149 pp. 3,000 copies printed. Cover price $12.00. Jacket art, title page decoration, four color plates and eight interior illustrations by David Ireland.
   Contents: *The People of the Black Circle.* $50/15.

B22b   The People of the Black Circle. Berkley/Putnam, New York, 1977. Book club edition. Edited by Karl Edward Wagner. Light tan binding with brown lettering. 8vo. 215 pp. Copies printed not stated. Cover price not listed. Jacket art by Ken Kelly. Interior illustrations reprinted from *Weird Tales.* One of three matched volumes, which have the distinction of being the first collections of

Conan stories which were prepared from photocopies of the pages of *Weird Tales*. It is the first edition to present Conan as originally published.

Contents: *Foreword,* by Karl Edward Wagner; *The Devil in Iron; The People of the Black Circle; A Witch Shall be Born; Jewels of Gwahlur; Afterword,* by Karl Edward Wagner. $20/5.

B22c   The People of the Black Circle. Berkley Publishing Corporation, New York, 1978. Edited by Karl Edward Wagner. Beige binding with gilt lettering. 8vo. 215 pp. Copies printed not stated. Cover price 9.95. Jacket art by Ken Kelly. Interior illustrations reprinted from *Weird Tales.*

Contents: As B22b. $35/5.

B23a   Tigers of the Sea. Donald M. Grant, West Kingston, Rhode Island, 1974. Edited by Richard L. Tierney. Dark red cloth binding with gilt lettering. 12mo. 212 pp. Copies printed not stated. Cover price $6.00. Jacket art, endpaper illustrations, frontispiece and four interior illustrations by Tim Kirk.

Contents: *Introduction,* by Richard L. Tierney; *Tigers of the Sea* (with Richard L. Tierney); *Swords of the Northern Sea; The Night of the Wolf; The Temple of Abomination* (with Richard L. Tierney). $45/10.

B24a   Skull-Face Omnibus. Neville Spearman (Jersey), Limited, St. Helier, Jersey, 1974. Olive green binding with gilt lettering. 8vo. 475 pp. Copies printed not stated. Cover price £2.50. Jacket art by Reg Boorer. Second printing in 1975. Cover price £3.75.

Contents: *Foreword,* by August Derleth; *Which Will Scarcely Be Understood* (poem); *Robert E. Howard: A Memoriam,* by H.P. Lovecraft; *A Memory of Robert E. Howard,* by E. Hoffmann Price; *Wolfshead; The Black Stone; The Horror from the Mound; The Cairn on the Headland; Black Canaan; The Fire of Asshurbanipal; A Man-Eating Jeopard; Skull-Face; The Hyborian Age; Worms of the Earth; The Valley of the Worm; Skulls in the Stars; Rattle of Bones; The Hills of the Dead; Wings in the Night; The Shadow Kingdom; The Mirrors of Tuzun Thune; The Phoenix on the Sword; The Scarlet Citadel; The Tower of the Elephant; Rogues in the House; Shadows in Zamboula; Lines Written in the Realization That I Must Die* (poem). First printing $45/15. Second printing $25/8

B25a   Almuric. Donald M. Grant, West Kingston, Rhode Island, 1975. Dark red cloth binding with gilt lettering. 12mo. 217 pp. 3,500 copies printed. Cover price $7.00. Jacket art, frontispiece and seven interior illustrations by David Ireland.

Contents: *Almuric.* $40/10.

B26a   The Tower of the Elephant. Donald M. Grant, West Kingston, Rhode Island, 1975. Gray binding with maroon cloth spine and gilt lettering. 4to. 94 pp. 3,100 copies printed. Cover price $12.00. Jacket art, color frontispiece and eight color plates by Richard Robertson.

Contents: *The Tower of the Elephant; The God in the Bowl.* $55/15.

B26b   The Tower of the Elephant. Grosset & Dunlap Publishers, New York, 1978. Softcover edition. 4to. 94 pp. Copies printed not stated. Cover

price $6.95. Reprint of D.M. Grant's 1975 hardcover edition of the same title. Cover art, color frontispiece and eight color plates by Richard Robertson.
Contents: As B26a. $15.

B27a   A Witch Shall Be Born. Donald M. Grant, West Kingston, Rhode Island, 1975. Gray binding with maroon cloth spine and gilt lettering. 4to. 106 pp. 3,100 copies printed. Cover price $12.00. Jacket art, frontispiece, four color plates and six interior illustrations by Alicia Austin.
Contents: *A Witch Shall be Born.* $50/15.

B28a   Red Nails. Donald M. Grant, West Kingston, Rhode Island, 1975. Gray binding with maroon cloth spine and gilt lettering. 4to. 142 pp. 3,500 copies printed. Cover price $15.00. Jacket art, frontispiece, title page decoration, four color plates, chapter headings and four full-page, interior illustrations by George Barr.
Contents: *Red Nails.* $50/15.

B28b   Red Nails. Berkley/Putnam, New York, 1977. Book club edition. Edited by Karl Edward Wagner. Light tan binding with orange lettering. 8vo. 244 pp. Copies printed not stated. Cover price not listed. Jacket art by Ken Kelly. Interior illustrations reprinted from *Weird Tales.* One of three matched volumes, which have the distinction of being the first collections of Conan stories which were prepared from photocopies of the pages of *Weird Tales.* It is the first edition to present Conan as originally published.
Contents: *Foreword,* by Karl Edward Wagner; *Beyond the Black River; Shadows in Zamboula; Red Nails; The Hyborian Age; Afterword,* by Karl Edward Wagner. $20/5.

B28c   Red Nails. Berkley Publishing Corporation, New York, 1979. Edited by Karl Edward Wagner. Brown binding with gilt lettering. 8vo. 244 pp. Copies printed not stated. Cover price $9.95. Jacket art by Ken Kelly. Interior illustrations reprinted from *Weird Tales.*
Contents: As B28b. $35/5.

B29a   Rogues in the House. Donald M. Grant, West Kingston, Rhode Island, 1976. Gray binding with maroon cloth spine and gilt lettering. 4to. 91 pp. 3,500 copies printed. Cover price $15.00. Jacket art, color frontispiece, ten color plates and two interior illustrations by Marcus Boas.
Contents: *Rogues in the House; The Frost-Giant's Daughter.* $45/10.

B30a   Bloodstar. The Morning Star Press, New York, 1976. Edited by Armand Eisner and Gilbert Kane. Gray cloth binding with gilt lettering. 4to. 98 unnumbered pages. 1,000 numbered copies printed. Cover price $14.95. Cover art and interior illustrations by Richard Corben. This is a graphic novel adaptation and expansion by John Jakes of Robert E. Howard's story "The Valley of the Worm."
Contents: *Bloodstar and the Art of Richard Corben; Robert E. Howard; Bloodstar.* $135/20.

B30b Bloodstar. Ariel Books, New York, 1979. Ariel Books 25209. Softcover edition. 4to. 109 unnumbered pages. Copies printed not stated. Cover price $8.95. Cover art and interior illustrations by Richard Corben. Graphic novel adaptation and expansion by John Jakes and John Pocsik of Robert E. Howard's story "The Valley of the Worm."
 Contents: *Richard Corben; Robert E. Howard; Bloodstar.* $15.

B31a The Swords of Shahrazar. FAX Collector's Edition, West Linn, Oregon, 1976. Dark blue cloth binding with silver lettering and design. 8vo. 133 pp. Copies printed not stated. Cover price $12.95. Cover art, endpaper illustrations, title page decoration, chapter headings, three color plates and twelve full-page illustrations by Michael W. Kaluta.
 Contents: *Introduction,* by Frederick Cook; *The Curse of the Crimson God; The Treasures of Tartary; The Treasure of Shaibar Khan.* $50/15.

B32a The Devil in Iron. Donald M. Grant, West Kingston, Rhode Island, 1976. Gray binding with maroon cloth spine and gilt lettering. 4to. 153 pp. 3,500 copies printed. Cover price $15.00. Jacket art and six color plates by Dan Green.
 Contents: *Shadows in Zamboula; The Devil in Iron.* $45/10.

B32b The Devil in Iron. Grosset & Dunlap Publishers, New York, 1978. Softcover. 4to. 153 pp. 3,500 copies printed. Cover price $6.95. Reprint of D.M. Grant's 1976 hardcover edition of the same title. Cover art and six color plates by Dan Green.
 Contents: As B32a. $15.

B33a Black Vulmea's Vengeance. Donald M. Grant, West Kingston, Rhode Island, 1976. Blue cloth binding with silver lettering. 4to. 223 pp. 2,600 copies printed. Cover price $15.00. Jacket art and seven color plates by Robert J. Pailthorpe.
 Contents: *Swords of the Red Brotherhood; Black Vulmea's Vengeance; The Isle of Pirate's Doom.* $45/10.

B33b Black Vulmea's Vengeance. Baronet Books, New York, 1977. Soft cover. 4to. 219 pp. Reprint of D.M. Grant's 1976 hardcover edition of the same title. Copies printed not stated. Cover price $7.95. Cover art by Stephen Fabian. Seven interior color plates by Robert J. Pailthorpe.
 Contents: As B33a. $15.

B34a The Iron Man. Donald M. Grant, West Kingston, Rhode Island, 1976. Dark red cloth binding with gilt lettering. 12mo. 186 pp. Copies printed not stated. Cover price $7.00. Jacket art and three b/w interior illustrations by David Ireland.
 Contents: *Introduction,* by Donald M. Grant; *Men of Iron; The Iron Man; They Always Come Back; Fists of the Desert.* $35/8.

B35a Night Images. The Morning Star Press, New York, 1976. Edited by Armand Eisen and John Pocsik. A volume of verse. Black cloth binding with silver lettering. 4to. 102 pp. 750 unnumbered copies printed. Cover price $25.00. Jacket art by Frank Frazetta. Interior illustrations by Richard Corben.

Contents: *Foreword,* by John Pocsik; *Echoes from an Anvil: The Poetry of Howard,* by Armand Eisen; Of Dreams and of Visions: *The King and the Oak; The Cats of Anubis; Musings; No More the Serpent Prow; Haunting Columns; Black Dawn; Visions; Echoes from an Anvil; Altars and Jesters; The Ghost Kings.* Songs of Longing and of Love: *Egypt; The Heart of the Sea's Desire; The Day Breaks Over Simla; The Tide; A Song Out of East; Tiger Girl; Sea Girl.* Songs of War and Warriors: *A Thousand Years Ago; The Gold and the Grey; Marching Song of Connacht; Black Harps in the Hills; The Legacy of Tubal-Cain; Victory; Viking's Trail; The Phoenix on the Sword; Kings of the Night; The King and the Mallet; Song Before Clontarf; To Harry the Oliad Men; And Beowulf Rides Again.* Songs from the World: *Always Comes Evening; Solomon Kane's Homecoming; The Master-Drum; The Kiowa's Tale; Flight; Adventure; The Song of the Jackal; Empire; Singing Hemp; Days of Glory; Mark of the Beast; The Road to Rome; Roar, Silver Trumpets; The King of the Ages Comes; The Jackal; The Campus at Midnight; When the Gods Were Kings.* Songs of Death: *Oh Babylon, Lost Babylon; A Word from the Outer Dark; Age; Swamp Murder; To a Friend; The Dead Slaver's Tale; A Buccaneer Speaks; Hope Empty of Meaning; Hopes of Dreams.* $75/20.

B35b **Night Images.** The Morning Star Press, New York, 1976. Edited by Armand Eisen and John Pocsik. A volume of verse. Black cloth binding with silver lettering. 4to. 102 pp. 250 numbered copies printed. Cover price not listed. Jacket art by Frank Frazetta. Interior illustrations by Richard Corben.
Contents: As B35a. $125/40.

B36a **The Hour of the Dragon.** Berkley/Putnam, New York, 1977. Book club edition. Edited by Karl Edward Wagner. Dark-blue binding with orange lettering. 8vo. 212 pp. Copies printed not stated. Cover price not listed. Jacket art by Ken Kelly. Interior illustrations reprinted from *Weird Tales.* One of three matched volumes, which have the distinction of being the first collections of Conan stories which were prepared from photocopies of the pages of *Weird Tales.* It is the first edition to present Conan as originally published.
Contents: *Foreword,* by Karl Edward Wagner; *The Hour of the Dragon; Afterword,* by Karl Edward Wagner; Acknowledgments. $20/5.

B36b **The Hour of the Dragon.** Berkley Publishing Corporation, New York 1977. Edited by Karl Edward Wagner. Dark-blue binding with gilt lettering. 8vo. 212 pp. Copies printed not stated. Cover price 8.95. Jacket art by Ken Kelly. Interior illustrations reprinted from *Weird Tales.*
Contents: As B36a. $35/5.

B36c **The Hour of the Dragon.** Donald M. Grant, West Kingston, Rhode Island, 1989. Gray binding with maroon cloth spine and gilt lettering. 4to. 249 pp. 3,000 copies printed. Cover price $35.00. Jacket art, title page decoration and five color plates by Ezra Tucker. The first printing was missing 525 words at the end of chapter six. The books were recalled and replaced with a second printing which had the missing text restored.
Contents: *The Hour of the Dragon.* $45/10.

B37a **The Return of Skull-Face.** With Richard A. Lupoff. FAX Collector's Edition, West Linn, Oregon, 1977. Mottled tan cloth binding with black lettering. 8vo. 96 pp. Copies printed not stated. Cover price $9.95. Special edition. 215 copies signed by Richard A. Lupoff and Stephen E. Leialoha; 150 numbered copies for sale (cover price $17.00) and 65 non-numbered copies for presentation. Cover art, endpaper illustrations, title page decoration, and twelve full-page illustrations by Stephen E. Leialoha

Contents: *Introduction,* by Frank Belknap Long; *Is Collaboration a Crime,* by Richard A. Lupoff; *The Return of Skull-Face.* $40/10.

B38a **Son of the White Wolf.** FAX Collector's Edition, West Linn, Oregon, 1977. Dark red cloth binding with silver lettering and design. 8vo. 170 pp. Copies printed not stated. Cover price $12.95. Cover art, endpaper illustrations, chapter headings, title page decoration, three color plates and nine full-page illustrations by Marcus Boas.

Contents: *Introduction,* by Fred Cook; *Blood of the Gods; Country of the Knife; Son of the White Wolf.* $45/10.

B39a **Queen of the Black Coast.** Donald M. Grant, West Kingston, Rhode Island, 1978. Gray binding with maroon cloth spine and gilt lettering. 4to. 118 pp. 2,750 copies printed. Cover price $15.00. Jacket art, color frontispiece, six color plates, one color double-page, and five full-page interior illustrations by Michael R. Hague.

Contents: *Queen of the Black Coast; The Vale of Lost Women.* $50/15.

B40a **Mayhem at Bear Creek.** Donald M. Grant, West Kingston, Rhode Island, 1979. Brown cloth spine and gilt lettering. 12mo. 226 pp. Copies printed not stated. Cover price $7.00. Jacket art and three interior illustrations by Tim Kirk.

Contents: *"No Cowherders Wanted"; Mayhem and Taxes; Evil Deeds at Red Cougar; Sharp's Gun Serenade; The Peaceful Pilgrim; While Smoke Rolled; A Elkins Never Surrenders.* $40/10.

B41a **Black Colossus.** Donald M. Grant, West Kingston, Rhode Island, 1979. Gray binding with maroon cloth spine and gilt lettering. 4to. 184 pp. 3,000 copies printed. Cover price $20.00. Jacket art, color frontispiece, four double-page color plates, and 14 full or double-page interior illustrations by Ned Dameron.

Contents: *Black Colossus; Shadows in the Moonlight.* $50/10.

B42a **Jewels of Gwahlur.** Donald M. Grant, West Kingston, Rhode Island, 1979. Gray binding with maroon cloth spine and gilt lettering. 4to. 122 pp. 3,000 copies printed. Cover price $20.00. Jacket art, frontispiece and seven color plates by Dean Morrissey.

Contents: *Jewels of Gwahlur; The Snout in the Dark* (edited by L. Sprague de Camp and Lin Carter). $45/10.

B43a **The Road of Azrael.** Donald M. Grant, West Kingston, Rhode Island, 1979. Brown binding with gilt lettering and design. 8vo. 229 pp. Copies printed not stated. Cover price $20.00. Jacket art, endpaper illustrations, color frontispiece, story headings and five color plates by Roy G. Krenkel.

Contents: *The Road of Azrael; The Track of Bohemund; The Way of the Swords; Hawks over Egypt; Gates of Empire.* $75/20.

B43b   The Road of Azrael. Donald M. Grant, West Kingston, Rhode Island, 1979. Limited edition, signed by the artist. In slipcase. Leatherette binding with gilt lettering and design. 8vo. 229 pp. 310 numbered copies printed. Cover price $35.00. Jacket art, endpaper illustrations, color frontispiece, story headings and five color plates by Roy G. Krenkel.

Contents: As B43a. $125/25.

B44a   Hawks of Outremer. Donald M. Grant, West Kingston, Rhode Island, 1979. Edited by Richard L. Tierney. Red cloth binding with gilt lettering. 8vo. 153 pp. Copies printed not stated. Cover price $15.00. Jacket art, color frontispiece, one color, double-page plate, and six interior illustrations by Rob MacIntyre and Chris Pappas.

Contents: *Introduction,* by Richard L. Tierney; *Hawks of Outremer; The Blood of Belshazzar; The Slave-Princess* (with Richard L. Tierney). $50/20.

B45a   Lord of the Dead. Donald M. Grant, West Kingston, Rhode Island, 1981. Brown cloth binding with gilt lettering. 8vo. 186 pp. Copies printed not stated. Cover price $15.00. Jacket art, frontispiece, title page decoration and ten interior illustrations by G. Duncan Eagleson.

Contents: *Introduction—From Limehouse to River Street,* by Robert E. Briney; *The Lord of the Dead; The Mystery of Tannernoe Lodge* (with Fred Blosser); *Names in the Black Book.* $85/20

B46a   The Last Cat Book. Dodd, Mead & Company, New York, 1984. Softcover. 8vo. 60 unnumbered pages. Copies printed not stated. Cover price $ 5.95. Cover art and interior linoleum prints by Peter Kuper.

Contents: *The Last Cat Book.* $25.

B47a   Kull. Donald M. Grant, West Kingston, Rhode Island, 1985. Red binding with gilt lettering. 4to. 247 pp. Copies printed not stated. Cover price $25.00. Jacket art, title page illustration, seven double-page color plates and 14 color plates by Ned Dameron.

Contents: *Prolog; Exile of Atlantis; The Shadow Kingdom; The Altar and the Scorpion; Delcarde's Cat; The Skull of Silence; By This Axe I Rule; The Striking of the Gong; Swords of the Purple Kingdom; The King and the Oak* (poem); Untitled; *The Mirrors of Tuzun Thune; The Black City;* Untitled; *Epilog.* $100/25.

B47b   Kull. Donald M. Grant, West Kingston, Rhode Island, 1985. Limited edition, signed by the artist. In slipcase. Red leatherette binding with gilt lettering. 4to. 247 pp. 400 numbered copies printed. Cover price $50.00. Jacket art, title page illustration, seven double-page color plates and 14 color plates by Ned Dameron.

Contents: As B47a. $150/35.

B48a **The Pool of the Black One.** Donald M. Grant, West Kingston, Rhode Island, 1986. Gray binding with maroon cloth spine and gilt lettering. 4to. 134 pp. 3,000 copies printed. Cover price $20.00. Jacket art, title page decoration, six color plates and seven illustrations by Hank Jankus.
 Contents: *The Pool of the Black One; Drums of Tombalku;* $45/10.

B49a **Pigeons from Hell.** Eclipse Books, Forestville, California, 1988. Graphic novel adapted by Scott Hamilton. 4to. 51 pp. 1,000 numbered signed copies printed. Cover price $35.00. Cover art and interior color panels by Scott Hamilton.
 Contents: *Introduction,* by Ramsey Campbell; *Pigeons from Hell.* $35/5

B49b **Pigeons from Hell.** Eclipse Books, Forestville, California, 1988. Softcover. Graphic novel adapted by Scott Hampton. 4to. 51 pp. Copies printed not stated. Cover price $7.95. Cover art and interior color panels by Scott Hamilton.
 Contents: As B49a. $15.

B50a **Shadows of Dreams.** Donald M. Grant, West Kingston, Rhode Island, 1989. A volume of verse. Light Gray binding with silver lettering. 8vo. 94 pp. 750 signed copies printed. Cover price $25.00. Jacket art, endpaper illustrations, frontispiece and 22 interior illustrations by Richard Berry.
 Contents: *Introduction,* by Glenn Lord; *Shadows of Dreams; Flaming Marble; A Weird Ballad; A Warning to Orthodoxy; Whispers; A Riding Song; Castaway; Black Seas; Silence Falls on Mecca's Walls; Keresa, Keresa; Whispers on the Nightwinds; Nights to Both of Us Known; To Lyle Saxon; Symbols; A Stirring of Green Leaves; The Gladiator and the Lady; A Song of the Anchor Chain; The Path of the Strange Wanderers; I Praise My Nativity; Ballade; Destiny; Stay Not From Me; The Last Words He Heard; The Ecstacy of Desolation; Musings; Dreaming in Israel; The Dust Dance; A Challenge to Bast; The Odyssey of Israel; Romany Road; Twilight on Stonehenge; The Call of Pan; Samson's Broodings; The Road to Babel; The Dreams of Men; A Far Country; To a Nameless Woman; Song of a Fugitive Bard; A Poet's Skull; A Fable for Critics; Love; Song From an Ebony Heart; Love's Young Dream; A Ballad of Beer; John Brown; Abe Lincoln; Surrender.* $120/25.

B51a **Post Oaks and Sand Roughs.** Donald M. Grant, West Kingston, Rhode Island, 1990. Dark blue binding with gilt lettering. 8vo. 176 pp. Copies printed not stated. Cover price $25.00. Autobiographical novel. Jacket art by Phil Hale.
 Contents: *Introduction,* by Glenn Lord; *Post Oaks and Sand Rogues;* Index; Appendix. $40/10.

B52a **The Essential Conan.** The Science Fiction Book Club, New York, 1998. Book Club edition. Edited by Karl Edward Wagner. Black binding with silver lettering. 8vo. 643 pp. Copies printed not stated. Cover price not listed. Jacket art by Ken Kelly. Interior illustrations reprinted from *Weird Tales.* This is a one volume compilation of the three collections of Conan stories published by the Berkley/Putnam in 1977. The text has been cleaned up and the typographical errors which blemished the original three volumes have been corrected.

Contents: *Foreword*, by Karl Edward Wagner; *The Hour of the Dragon; Afterword*, by Karl Edward Wagner; *Foreword*, by Karl Edward Wagner; *The Devil in Iron; The People of the Black Circle; A Witch Shall Be Born; Jewels of Gwahlur; Afterword*, by Karl Edward Wagner; *Foreword*, by Karl Edward Wagner; *Beyond the Black River; Shadows in Zamboula; Red Nails; The Hyborian Age; Afterword*, by Karl Edward Wagner. $40/8.

B53a   The Savage Tales of Solomon Kane. Wandering Star, London, England, 1998. Limited edition. Dark blue cloth binding with gilt lettering and decorations. In slipcase. 4to. 389 pp + appendices. 1,050 signed/numbered copies printed. Cover price $160.00. Jacket art, endpaper illustrations, frontispiece, title page decoration, three color plates and numerous interior illustrations by Gary Gianni. Comes with a folio of six color plates and a CD with *The One Black Stain; The Return of Sir Richard Grenville,* and *Solomon Kane's Homecoming* read to music by Paul Blake.

Contents: *Foreword,* by Gary Gianni; *In Memoriam: Robert Ervin Howard,* by H.P. Lovecraft; *Skulls in the Stars; The Right Hand of Doom; Red Shadows; Rattle of Bones; The Castle of the Devil; Death's Black Riders; The Moon of Skulls; The One Black Stain* (poem); *The Blue Flame of Vengeance; The Hills of the Dead; Hawk of Basti; The Return of Sir Richard Grenville* (poem); *Wings in the Night; The Footfalls Within; The Children of Asshur; Solomon Kane's Homecoming* (poem); *Solomon Kane's Homecoming* (poem -variant). Appendices: *A Short Biography of Robert E. Howard,* by Rusty Burke; *Gary Gianni; Notes on the Original Howard Texts.* $600/100.

B53b   The Savage Tales of Solomon Kane. Wandering Star, London, England, 1998. Ultra limited edition. Bound in goat skin with gilt lettering and decorations. In slipcase. 4to. 389 pp + appendices. 100 signed/numbered copies printed. Cover price $265.00. Jacket art, endpaper illustrations, frontispiece, title page decoration, three color plates and numerous interior illustrations by Gary Gianni. Comes with a folio of six color plates and a CD with *The One Black Stain; The Return of Sir Richard Grenville,* and *Solomon Kane's Homecoming* read to music by Paul Blake.

Contents: As B53a. $600/150.

B53c   The Savage Tales of Solomon Kane. Del Rey/Ballantine Books, New York, 2005. Book club edition. 8vo. 414 pp. Black binding with gilt lettering. Copies printed not stated. Cover price not listed. Jacket art, frontispiece, title page decoration, three plates and numerous interior illustrations by Gary Gianni. A textually corrected, reprint of the 1998 Wandering Star limited edition hardcover.

Contents: As B53a. $15.

B53d   The Savage Tales of Solomon Kane. Del Rey/Ballantine Books, New York, 2004. 8vo. 414 pp. Softcover. Copies printed not stated. Cover price $15.95. Cover art, frontispiece, title page decoration, three plates and

numerous interior illustrations by Gary Gianni. A textually corrected, reprint of the 1998 Wandering Star limited edition hardcover.
Contents: As B53a. $15.

B54a   The Ultimate Triumph. Wandering Star, London, England, 1999. Classic edition. Medium brown cloth binding with red lettering and decorations. 4to. 259 pp + appendices. 2,300 copies printed. Cover price $50.00. Jacket art, endpaper illustrations, frontispiece, title page decoration, and 120 interior illustrations by Frank Frazetta.
Contents: *Foreword,* by Frank Frazetta; *Introduction,* by Rusty Burke; *Beyond the Black River; The House of Arabu; Spears of Clontarf; Lord of Samarcand; Night of the Wolf; Spear and Fang; Valley of the Worm; Poetry.* Appendices: *Barbarism vs Civilization* (Letters to Lovecraft); *Chronology; Waiting for the Barbarians,* by Patrice Louinet; *Frazetta and Robert E. Howard: The Power of Passion,* by Dr. David Winiewicz; *Notes on the Original Howard Texts.* $50/15.

B54b   The Ultimate Triumph. Wandering Star, London, England, 1999. Collector's edition. Medium brown cloth binding with red lettering and decorations. In slipcase. 4to. 259 pp + appendices. 1,500 numbered copies printed. Cover price $80.00. Jacket art, endpaper illustrations, frontispiece, title page decoration, four color plates and 120 interior illustrations by Frank Frazetta.
Contents: As B54a. $125/35.

B54c   The Ultimate Triumph. Wandering Star, London, England, 1999. Ultra deluxe edition. Bound in leather with red lettering and decorations. In leather slipcase. 4to. 259 pp + appendices. 100 numbered copies printed. Cover price $425.00. Jacket art, endpaper illustrations, frontispiece, title page decoration, five color plates and 120 interior illustrations by Frank Frazetta.
Contents: As B54a. $450/100.

B55a   The Conan Chronicles. Volume 1: The People of the Black Circle. Fantasy Masterworks Vol. 8, Victor Gollancz, London, 2000. Edited by Stephen Jones. Softcover edition. 12mo. 548 pp. Copies printed not stated. Cover price £7.99. Cover design and art by Richard Carr and John Howe. Frontispiece map of the Hyborian Age. This is the first volume of a two-volume set that collects all Robert E. Howard's Conan stories in the chronological order of Conan's biography as suggested by P. Schuyler Miller and John D. Clark, and not in the order that they were originally written and published. Contains a number of typographical errors, which may impact the readability of some stories.
Contents: *The Hyborian Age; The Tower of the Elephant; The Hall of the Dead* (Synopsis); *The God in the Bowl; Rogues in the House; The Hand of Nergal* (Fragment); *The Frost-Giant's Daughter; Queen of the Black Coast; The Vale of Lost Women; The Snout in the Dark* (Draft); *Black Colossus; Shadows in the Moonlight; A Witch Shall be Born; Shadows in Zamboula; The Devil in Iron; The People of the Black Circle; The Slithering Shadow; Drums of Tombalku* (Draft); *The Pool of the Black One; Afterword: Robert E. Howard and Conan: The Early Years,* by Stephen Jones. $25.

B56a The Conan Chronicles. Volume 2: The Hour of the Dragon. Fantasy Masterworks Vol. 16, Victor Gollancz, London, 2001. Edited by Stephen Jones. Softcover edition. 12mo. 575 pp. Copies printed not stated. Cover price £7.99. Cover design and art by Richard Carr and John Howe. Frontispiece map of the Hyborian Age. This is the second volume of a two-volume set that collects all Robert E. Howard's Conan stories in the chronological order of Conan's biography as suggested by P. Schuyler Miller and John D. Clark, and not in the order that they were originally written and published. As the first volume, this one contains a number of typographical errors, which makes some stories less enjoyable.

Contents: *Notes on Various Peoples of the Hyborian Age; Red Nails; Jewels of Gwahlur; Beyond the Black River; The Black Stranger; Wolves Beyond the Border* (Draft); *The Phoenix on the Sword; The Scarlet Citadel; The Hour of the Dragon; Cimmeria* (poem); *Afterword: Robert E. Howard and Conan: The Final Years,* by Stephen Jones. $25.

B57a Bran Mak Morn: The Last King. Wandering Star, London, England, 2001. Trade edition. Series editor Rusty Burke. Medium green cloth binding with gilt lettering and gilt and black decorations. 4to. 285 pp + appendices. Copies printed not stated. Cover price $50.00. Jacket art, endpaper illustrations, frontispiece, title page decoration, and numerous interior illustrations by Gary Gianni.

Contents: *Foreword,* by Gary Gianni; *Introduction,* by Rusty Burke; *Men of the Shadows; Kings of the Night; A Song of the Race* (poem)*; Worms of the Earth; The Dark Man; The Lost Race; Poem.* Miscellanea: *Notes on Miscellanea,* by Rusty Burke*; The Little People; The Little People* (Typescript); *The Children of the Night; Bran Mak Morn; Bran Mak Morn* (Manuscript); *Synopsis; Worms of the Earth* (Draft); *Fragment; Poem.* Appendices: *Robert E. Howard and the Picts: A Chronology; Robert E. Howard, Bran Mak Morn and the Picts,* by Rusty Burke and Patrice Louinet*; Notes on the Original Howard Texts.* $50/15.

B57b Bran Mak Morn: The Last King. Wandering Star, London, England, 2001. Limited edition. Series editor Rusty Burke. Medium green cloth binding with gilt lettering and gilt and black decorations. In slipcase. 4to. 285 pp + appendices. 850 signed/numbered copies printed. Cover price $125.00. Jacket art, endpaper illustrations, frontispiece, title page decoration, eight color plates and numerous interior illustrations by Gary Gianni. Comes with a CD with *The Worms of the Earth* read to music by Paul Blake, Andrew Hall and Tina Greatrex.

Contents: As B57a. $130/45.

B57c Bran Mak Morn: The Last King. Wandering Star, London, England, 2001. Ultra limited edition. Series editor Rusty Burke. Bound in leather with gilt lettering and gilt and black decorations. In leather slipcase. 4to. 285 pp + appendices. 50 signed/numbered copies printed. Cover price $250.00. Jacket art, endpaper illustrations, frontispiece, title page decoration, eight color plates and numerous interior illustrations by Gary Gianni. Comes

with a CD with *The Worms of the Earth* read to music by Paul Blake, Andrew Hall and Tina Greatrex.
Contents: As B57a. $250/75.

B57d **Bran Mak Morn: The Last King.** Del Rey/Ballantine Books, New York, 2005. Series editor Rusty Burke. Book club edition. 8vo. 367 pp. Black binding with gilt lettering. Copies printed not stated. Cover price not listed. Jacket art, title page decoration, three plates and numerous interior illustrations by Gary Gianni. This printing includes a newly discovered, unpublished, untitled story, and six additional pages of sketches by Gary Gianni. Reprint of the 2001 Wandering Star limited edition hardcover.
Contents: As B57a with additions. $15.

B57e **Bran Mak Morn: The Last King.** Del Rey/Ballantine Books, New York, 2005. Series editor Rusty Burke. Softcover. 8vo. 367 pp. Copies printed not stated. Cover price $15.95. Cover art, title page decoration, three plates and numerous interior illustrations by Gary Gianni. This printing includes a newly discovered, unpublished, untitled story, and six additional pages of sketches by Gary Gianni. Reprint of the 2001 Wandering Star limited edition hardcover.
Contents: As B57d. $15.

B58a **The Complete Action Stories.** Hermanthis Publications, 2001. Edited by Paul Herman. Softcover. 8vo. 361 pp. Copies printed not stated. Cover price not listed. Cover art and interior story headings from the original pulp magazine appearances. Reprinted in 2003 by Wildside Press in hardcover format.
Contents: *Introduction,* by Paul Herman; *The TNT Punch; The Sign of the Snake; Blow the Chinks Down; Breed of Battle; Dark Shanghai; Mountain Man; Guns of the Mountain; The Scalp Hunter; A Gent from Bear Creek; The Road to Bear Creek; The Haunted Mountain; War on Bear Creek; The Feud Buster; Cupid from Bear Creek; The Riot at Cougar Paw; The Apache Mountain War; Pilgrims to the Pecos; Pistol Politics; Evil Deeds at Red Cougar; High Horse Rampage; "No Cowherders Wanted"; The Conquerin' Hero of the Humbolts; Sharp's Gun Serenade;* Appendix. $35.

B58b **The Complete Action Stories.** Wildside Press, Holicong, Pennsylvania, 2003. Edited by Paul Herman. Dark blue cloth binding with gilt lettering. 8vo. 346 pp. Copies printed not stated. Cover price $39.95. Jacket artist not identified. Interior illustrations reprinted from *Action Stories.*
Contents: As B58a. $40/8.

B59a **Nameless Cults—The Cthulhu Mythos Fiction of Robert E. Howard.** Chaosium, Oakland, California, 2001. Edited by Robert M. Price. Softcover. 8vo. 353 pp. Copies printed not stated. Cover price not listed. Cover art by Harry Fassl. Interior art by Dave Carson.
Contents: *Introduction: Raven, Son of Morn,* by Robert M. Price; *The Black Stone; Worms of the Earth; The Little People; People of the Dark; The Children*

of the Night; The Thing on the Roof; The Abbey (with C.J. Henderson); *The Fire of Asshurbanipal; The Door to the World* (with Joseph S. Pulver); *The Hoofed Thing; Dig Me No Grave; The House in the Oaks* (with August Derleth); *The Black Bear Bites; The Shadow Kingdom; The Gods of Bal-Sagoth; Skull-Face; Black Eons* (with Robert M. Price); *The Challenge From Beyond* (with C.L. Moore, A Merritt, H.P. Lovecraft, and Frank Belknap Long). $15.

B60a   Conan of Cimmeria, Vol. I (1932–1933). Wandering Star, London, England, 2002. Limited edition. Edited by Patrice Louinet. Series editor Rusty Burke. Red cloth binding with gilt lettering and gilt and black decorations. In slipcase. 4to. 425 pp + appendices. 1,950 signed/numbered copies printed. Cover price $195.00. Jacket art, endpaper illustrations, color frontispiece, title page decorations, three color plates and numerous interior illustrations by Mark Schultz.

Contents: *Foreword*, by Mark Schultz; *Introduction*, by Patrice Louinet; *Cimmeria; The Phoenix on the Sword; The Frost-Giant's Daughter; The God in the Bowl; The Tower of the Elephant; The Scarlet Citadel; Queen of the Black Coast; Black Colossus; Iron Shadows in the Moon; Xuthal of the Dusk; The Pool of the Black One; Rogues in the House; The Vale of Lost Women; The Devil in Iron.* Miscellanea: *The Phoenix on the Sword* (first submitted draft); *Notes on the Various Peoples of the Hyborian Age; The Hyborean Age; Untitled Synopsis; Untitled Synopsis* (The Scarlet Citadel); *Untitled Synopsis* (Black Colossus); *Untitled Fragment; Untitled Synopsis; Untitled Draft; Hyborian Names and Countries; Hyborian Age Maps.* Appendices: *Hyborian Genesis*, by Patrice Louinet; *Notes on the Conan Typescripts and the Chronology*, by Patrice Louinet; *Notes on the Original Howard Texts.* $175/75.

B60b   Conan of Cimmeria, Vol. I (1932–1933). Wandering Star, London, England, 2002. Artist edition. Edited by Patrice Louinet. Series editor Rusty Burke. Red cloth binding with gilt lettering and gilt and black decorations. In slipcase. 4to. 425 pp + appendices. 100 signed/numbered copies printed. Cover price $270.00. Jacket art, endpaper illustrations, color frontispiece, title page decorations, three color plates, numerous interior illustrations and eight additional preliminary sketches by Mark Schultz.

Contents: As B60a. $200/75.

B60c   Conan of Cimmeria, Vol. I (1932–1933). Wandering Star, London, England, 2002. Ultra limited edition. Edited by Patrice Louinet. Series editor Rusty Burke. Leather binding with gilt lettering and gilt and black decorations. In leather slipcase. 4to. 425 pp + appendices. 100 signed/numbered copies printed. Cover price $390.00. Jacket art, endpaper illustrations, color frontispiece, title page decorations, four color plates, numerous interior illustrations, character studies and eight-page sketch book by Mark Schultz.

Contents: As B60a. $300/75.

B60d   The Coming of Conan the Cimmerian. Del Rey/ Ballantine, New York, 2003. Book club edition. Edited by Patrice Louinet. Series editor Rusty Burke. Black binding with gilt lettering. 8vo. 463 pp. Copies printed

not stated. Cover price not listed. Jacket art, frontispiece, title page decorations and numerous interior illustrations by Mark Schultz. Reprint of Wandering Star's 2002 limited edition of *Conan the Cimmerian. Vol. I (1932–1933).*
  Contents: As B60a. $15/5.

B60e   The Coming of Conan the Cimmerian. Del Rey/Ballantine Books, New York, 2003. Edited by Patrice Louinet. Softcover. 8vo. 463 pp. Copies printed not stated. Cover price $14.95. Cover art, frontispiece, title page decoration, three plates and numerous interior illustrations by Mark Schultz. Reprint of the 2002 Wandering Star limited edition hardcover.
  Contents: As B60a. $15.

B61a   Waterfront Fists and Others. Wildside Press, Holicong, Pennsylvania, 2003. Edited by Paul Herman. Dark blue cloth binding with gilt lettering. 8vo. 308 pp. Copies printed not stated. Cover price $39.95. Jacket artist not identified. Interior illustrations reprinted from the original magazine publications. This title was also published in a soft cover trade edition at $19.95
  Contents: *Bare Knuckles and Bulldogs: An Introduction to the Boxing Fiction of Robert E. Howard,* by Mark Finn; *Editor's Comments,* by Paul Herman; Letter to the Editor, *The Ring; Kid Lavigne is Dead* (poem)*; Dula Due to Be Champion; The Apparition in the Prize Ring; The Pit of the Serpent; The Bull Dog Breed; Sailor's Grudge; Fist and Fang; The Iron Man; Winner Take All; Waterfront Fists; Champ of the Forecastle; Alleys of Peril; Texas Fists; Circus Fists; Vikings of the Gloves; Night of the Battle; The Slugger's Game; General Ironfist; Sluggers of the Beach; Alleys of Darkness.* $40/8.

B62a   Graveyard Rats and Others. Wildside Press, Holicong, Pennsylvania, 2003. Edited by Paul Herman. Dark blue cloth binding with gilt lettering. 8vo. 194 pp. Copies printed not stated. Cover price $35.00. Jacket artist not identified. This title was also published in a soft cover trade edition at $16.95.
  Contents: *Introduction: A Black Wind off River Street,* by Don Herron; *Black Talons; Fangs of Gold; The Tomb's Secret; Names in the Black Book; Graveyard Rats; Black Wind Blowing.* $35/8.

B63a   Conan of Cimmeria, Vol. II (1934). Wandering Star, London, England, 2003. Limited edition. Edited by Patrice Louinet. Series editor Rusty Burke. Red cloth binding with gilt lettering and gilt and black decorations. In slipcase. 4to. 344 pp + appendices. 1,950 signed/numbered copies printed. Cover price $225.00. Jacket art, endpaper illustrations, color frontispiece, title page decorations, five color plates, and numerous interior illustrations by Gary Gianni.
  Contents: *Foreword,* by Gary Gianni; *Introduction,* by Rusty Burke; *The People of the Black Circle; The Hour of the Dragon; A Witch Shall Be Born.* Miscellanea: *Untitled Synopsis* (The People of the Black Circle); *The Story Thus Far...; Untitled Synopsis; Untitled Draft; Untitled Synopsis* (The Hour of the Dragon); *Notes on The Hour of the Dragon; Untitled Synopsis* (A Witch Shall Be Born). Appendices: *Hyborian Genesis, Part II,* by Patrice Louinet; *Notes on the Conan*

Graveyard Rats and Others. Wildside Press 2003. Jacket artist unknown. © 2003 Paul Herman.

Typescript and the Chronology, by Patrice Louinet; *Notes on the Original Howard Texts.* $175/75.

B63b Conan of Cimmeria, Vol. II (1934). Wandering Star, London, England, 2003. Ultra limited edition. Edited by Patrice Louinet. Series editor Rusty Burke. Red cloth binding with gilt lettering and gilt and black decorations. In slipcase. 4to. 344 pp + appendices. 100 signed/numbered copies printed. Cover price $400.00. Jacket art, endpaper illustrations, color frontispiece, title page decorations, three color plates, numerous interior illustrations and eight additional preliminary sketches by Gary Gianni.
    Contents: As B63a. $300/75.

B63c Conan of Cimmeria, Vol. II (1934). Wandering Star, London, England, 2003. Leather edition. Edited by Patrice Louinet. Series editor Rusty Burke. Leather binding with gilt lettering and gilt and black decorations. In leather slipcase. 4to. 344 pp + appendices. 100 signed/numbered copies printed. Cover price $600.00. Jacket art, endpaper illustrations, color frontispiece, title page decorations, four color plates, numerous interior illustrations, character studies and eight-page sketch book by Gary Gianni.
    Contents: As B63a. $400/75.

B63d The Bloody Crown of Conan. Del Rey/ Ballantine, New York, 2003. Book club edition. Edited by Patrice Louinet. Series editor Rusty Burke. Black binding with gilt lettering. 8vo. 366 pp. Copies printed not stated. Cover price not listed. Jacket art, frontispiece, title page decorations and numerous interior illustrations by Gary Gianni. Reprint of Wandering Star's 2003 limited edition of *Conan the Cimmerian. Vol. II (1934).*
    Contents: As B63a. $15/5.

B63e The Bloody Crown of Conan. Del Rey/Ballantine, New York, 2003. Edited by Patrice Louinet. Series editor Rusty Burke. Softcover. 8vo. 366 pp. Copies printed not stated. Cover price $15.95. Jacket art, frontispiece, title page decorations and numerous interior illustrations by Gary Gianni. Reprint of Wandering Star's 2003 limited edition of *Conan the Cimmerian. Vol. II (1934).*
    Contents: As B63a. $15.

B64a Gates of Empire. Wildside Press, Holicong, Pennsylvania, 2004. Edited by Paul Herman. Black cloth binding with gilt lettering. 8vo. 262 pp. 600 copies printed. Cover price $39.95. Jacket artist not identified.
    Contents: *Introduction,* by Fred Blosser; *Red Blades of Black Cathay; Hawks of Outremer; The Blood of Belshazzar; Lord of Samarcand; The Sowers of the Thunder; The Lion of Tiberias; The Shadow of the Vulture; Gates of Empire.* $40/8.

B65a Treasures of Tartary. Wildside Press, Holicong, Pennsylvania, 2004. Edited by Paul Herman. Black cloth binding with gilt lettering. 8vo. 218 pp. 600 copies printed. Cover price $35.00. Jacket artist not identified.

Gates of Empire. Wildside Press 2004. Jacket artist unknown. ©2004 Paul Herman.

Treasures of Tartary. Wildside Press 2004. Jacket artist unknown. © 2004 Paul Herman.

Contents: *Introduction—Far and Away: The Wandering Heroes of Robert E. Howard*, by James Reasoner; *Treasures of Tartary; Son of the White Wolf; Black Vulmea's Vengeance; Boot Hill Payoff; The Vultures of Whapeton.* $35/8.

B66a Shadow Kingdoms—The Weird Works of Robert E. Howard, Volume 1. Wildside Press, Holicong, Pennsylvania, 2004. Edited by Paul Herman. Black cloth binding with gilt lettering. 8vo. 206 pp. Copies printed not stated. Cover price $35.00. Jacket art by Stephen Fabian. This is the first volume of a planned 10-volume series of Robert E. Howard's *Weird Tales* stories, printed as originally written and in chronological order.

Contents: *Two-Gun Musketeer: Robert E. Howard's Weird Tales*, by Mark Finn; *Spear and Fang; In the Forest of Villefére; Wolfshead; The Lost Race; The Song of the Bats* (poem); *The Ride of Falume* (poem); *The Riders of Babylon* (poem); *The Dream Snake; The Hyena; Remembrance* (poem); *Sea Curse; The Gates of Nineveh* (poem); *Red Shadows; The Harp of Alfred* (poem); *Easter Island* (poem); *Skulls in the Stars; Crete* (poem); *Moon Mockery* (poem); *Rattle of Bones; Forbidden Magic* (poem); *The Shadow Kingdom; The Mirrors of Tuzun Thune; The Moor Ghost* (poem); *Red Thunder* (poem). $35/8.

B67a Moon of Skulls—The Weird Works of Robert E. Howard, Volume 2. Wildside Press, Holicong, Pennsylvania, 2005. Edited by Paul Herman. Black cloth binding with gilt lettering. 8vo. 216 pp. Copies printed not stated. Cover price $35.00. Jacket art by Stephen Fabian. This is the second volume of a planned 10-volume series of Robert E. Howard's *Weird Tales* stories, printed as originally written and in chronological order.

Contents: *The Gothic Orient,* by Mark Finn; *Skull-Face; Dead Man's Hate* (poem); *The Fearsome Touch of Death; A Song Out of Midian* (poem); *Shadows on the Road* (poem); *The Moon of Skulls; The Hills of the Dead; Black Chant Imperial* (poem); *The Voice of El-Lil.* $35/8.

B68a The Black Stranger and Other American Tales. University of Nebraska Press, Lincoln, Nebraska, 2005. Edited by Steven Tompkins. Blue cloth binding with silver lettering. 8vo. 351 pp. Copies printed not stated. Cover price $35.00. Also issued in a softcover edition. Cover price $17.95. Jacket art Mike Mignola.

Contents: *Introduction,* by Steve Tompkins; *The Black Stranger; Marchers of Valhalla; The Gods of Bal-Sagoth; Nekht Semerkeht; Black Vulmea's Vengeance; The Strange Case of Josiah Wilbarger; The Valley of the Lost; Kelly the Conjure-Man; Black Canaan; Pigeons from Hell; Old Garfield's Heart; The Horror from the Mound; The Thunder-Rider; "The Classic Tale of the Southwest"; The Grim Land* (poem). Source Acknowledgment. Hardcover $35/10. Softcover $18.

B69a Boxing Stories. University of Nebraska Press, Lincoln, Nebraska, 2005. Edited by Chris Gruber. Blue cloth binding with silver lettering. 8vo. 313 pp. Copies printed not stated. Cover price $35.00. Also issued in a softcover edition. Cover price 14.95. Jacket art by Gary Gianni.

Contents: *Introduction,* by Chris Gruber; *In the Ring* (poem); *The Pit of the Serpent; The Bull Dog Breed; The Champion of the Forecastle; Waterfront Law;*

Texas Fists; The Fightin'est Pair; Vikings of the Gloves; Cultured Cauliflowers; A New Game for Costigan; Hard-Fisted Sentiment; When You Were a Set-up and I was a Ham (poem); *The Spirit of Tom Molyneaux; Crowd-Horror; Iron Men; Kid Galahad; Fists of the Desert; They Always Come Back; Kid Lavigne is Dead* (poem). Note on the Texts. Hardcover $35/10. Softcover $15.

B70a **The End of the Trail.** University of Nebraska Press, Lincoln, Nebraska, 2005. Edited by Rusty Burke. Blue cloth binding with silver lettering. 8vo. 320 pp. Copies printed not stated. Cover price $35.00. Also issued in a softcover edition. Cover price 17.95. Jacket art by Jim and Ruth Keegan.

Contents: *Introduction,* by Rusty Burke; *"Golden Hope" Christmas; Drums of the Sunset; The Extermination of Yellow Donory; The Judgment of the Desert; Gunman's Debt; The Man on the Ground; The Sand-Hill's Crest* (poem); *The Devil's Joker*; *Knife, Bullet and Noose; Law-Shooters of Cowtown; The Last Ride* (with Robert Enders Allen); *John Ringold* (poem); *Vultures of Wahpeton; Vultures of Wahpeton*—Alternate Ending; *Vultures' Sanctuary; The Dead Remember; The Ghost Camp of Colorado; The Strange Case of Josiah Wilbarger; Beyond the Brazos River; Billy the Kid and the Lincoln County War; The Ballad of Bucksnort Roberts* (poem). Source Acknowledgment. Hardcover $35/10. Softcover $18.

B71a **Lord of Samarcand and Other Adventure Tales from the Old Orient.** University of Nebraska Press, Lincoln, Nebraska, 2005. Edited by Rusty Burke. Blue cloth binding with silver lettering. 8vo. 462 pp. Copies printed not stated. Cover price $35.00. Also issued in a softcover edition. Cover price 18.95. Jacket art by Sindy Bell.

Contents: *Introduction,* by Patrice Louinet; Tales: *Red Blades of Black Cathay* (with Tevis Clyde Smith); *Hawks of Outremer; The Blood of Belshazzar; The Sowers of the Thunder; Lord of Samarcand; Timur-lang* (poem); *The Lion of Tiberias; The Shadow of the Vulture; Gates of Empire; The Road of the Eagles; Hawks over Egypt; The Road of Azrael*. Miscellanea: *The Slave Princes* (Synopsis); *The Slave Princess* (Unfinished draft); *Two against Tyre* (Unfinished draft); *The Track of Bohemund* (Unfinished draft); *The Shadow of the Hun* (Unfinished draft); *"He Knew de Brazy..."* (Untitled fragment); *"The wind from the Mediterranean..."* (Untitled fragment); *Recap of Harold Lamb's "The Wolf Chaser"; "The Persians had all fled..."* (Untitled draft). Source Acknowledgment. Hardcover $35/10. Softcover $20.

B72a **The Riot at Bucksnort and Other Western Tales.** University of Nebraska Press, Lincoln, Nebraska, 2005. Edited by David Gentzel. Blue cloth binding with silver lettering. 8vo. 255 pp. Copies printed not stated. Cover price $35.00. Also issued in a softcover edition. Cover price 14.95. Jacket art by Scott Gustafson.

Contents: *Introduction* by David Gentzel; *Mountain Man; Meet Cap'n Kidd; Guns of the Mountain; The Peaceful Pilgrim; War on Bear Creek; The Haunted Mountain; The Feud Buster; The Riot at Cougar Paw; Pistol Politics; "No Cowherders Wanted"; The Conquerin' Hero of the Humbolts; A Gent from the Pecos; Gents on the Lynch; The Riot at Bucksnort; Knife River Prodigal; A Man-Eating Jeopard*. Source Acknowledgment. Hardcover $35/10. Softcover $15.

B73a **Blood of the Gods and Other Stories.** Girasol Collectables, Inc.,

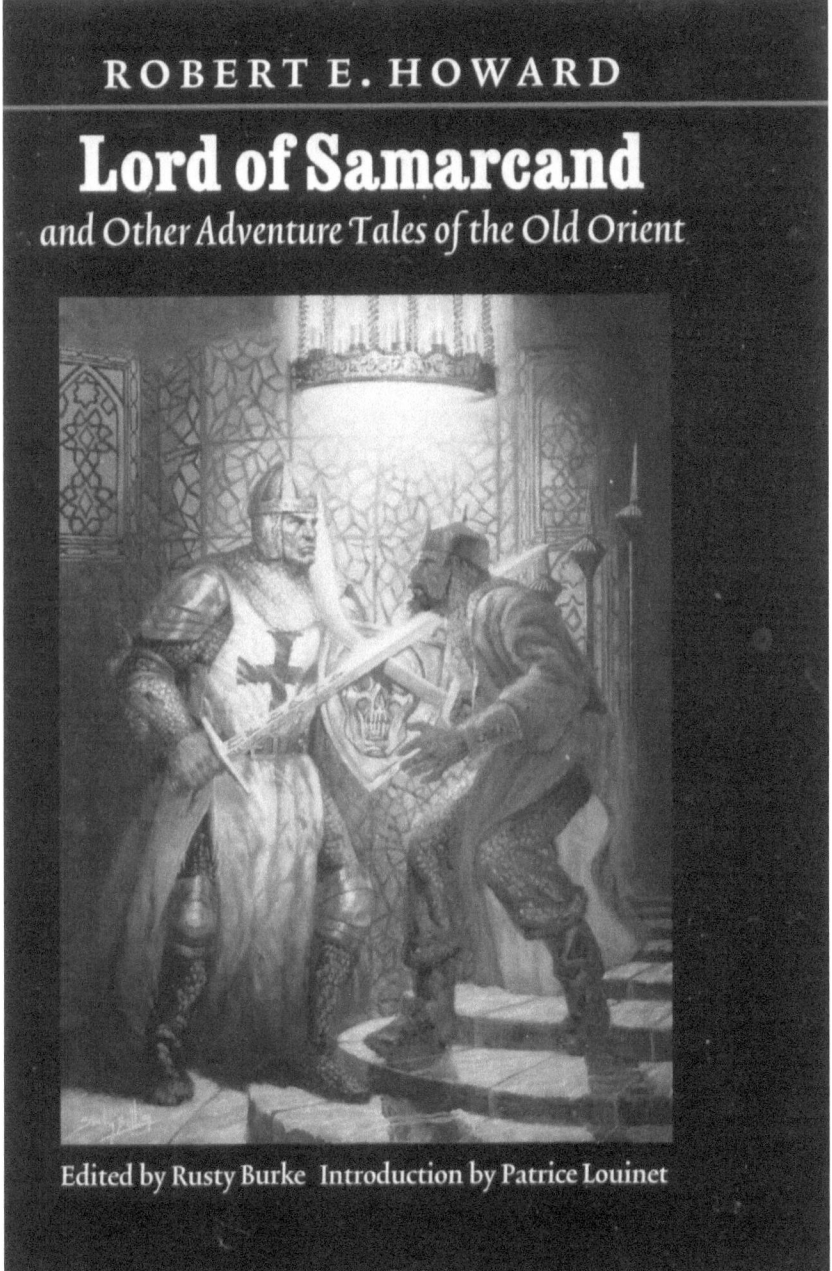

Lord of Samarcand and Other Adventure Tales from the Old Orient. University of Nebraska Press 2005. Jacket art by Sindy Bell. © 2005 REH Properties, Inc., and Sindy Bell.

The Riot at Bucksnort and Other Western Tales. University of Nebraska Press 2005. Jacket art by Scott Gustafson. © 2005 REH Properties, Inc., and Scott Gustafson.

Mississauga, Ontario, Canada, 2005. Edited by Paul Herman. Soft cover. 8vo. 221 pp. 1000 copies printed. Cover price $13.95. Cover art and illustrations by Joseph Clement Coll. Canadian copyright law differs from United States law. All of Howard's works published prior to 1954 are now in the public domain in Canada. For works published during Howard's lifetime, the copyrights expired 50 years after his death. For works published after his death, the copyrights expire 50 years after the first publication date. This would be all works published before Howard's death or prior to 01/01/1955. Since the five stories in this volume were first published between 1934 and 1936, they are all in the public domain in Canada.

Contents: *Introduction,* by Paul Herman; *The Country of the Knife; Hawk of the Hills; The Daughter of Erlik Khan; Blood of the Gods; Swords of Shahrazar; Afterword,* by Neil & Leigh Mechem. $15.

B74a   People of the Dark—The Weird Works of Robert E. Howard, Volume 3. Wildside Press, Holicong, Pennsylvania, 2005. Edited by Paul Herman. Black cloth binding with gilt lettering. 8vo. 214 pp. Copies printed not stated. Cover price $35.00. Jacket art by Stephen Fabian. This is the third volume of a planned 10-volume series of Robert E. Howard's *Weird Tales* stories, printed as originally written and in chronological order.

Contents: *Howard—The Texas Phoenix Flames in Darkness,* by Joe R. Lansdale; *Kings of the Night; The Song of a Mad Minstrel* (poem); *Children of the Night; The Footfalls Within; The Gods of Bal-Sagoth; The Black Stone; The Dark Man; The Thing on Roof; The Last Day* (poem); *Horror from the Mound; People of the Dark.* $35.

B75a   The Conquering Sword of Conan. Del Rey/ Ballantine, New York, 2005. Book club edition. Edited by Patrice Louinet. Series editor Rusty Burke. Black binding with gilt lettering. 8vo. 393 pp. Copies printed not stated. Cover price not listed. Jacket art, frontispiece, title page decorations and interior illustrations by Gregory Manchess. Reprint of Wandering Star's unpublished edition of *Conan the Cimmerian. Vol. III.*

Contents: *Foreword,* by Gregory Manchess; *Introduction,* by Patrice Louinet; *The Servants of Bit-Yakin; Beyond the Black River; The Black Stranger; The Man-Eaters of Zamboula; Red Nails;* Miscellanea: *Untitled Notes; Wolves Beyond the Border, Draft A; Wolves Beyond the Border, Draft B; The Black Stranger, Synopsis A; The Black Stranger, Synopsis B; The Man-Eaters of Zamboula, Synopsis; Red Nails, Draft.* Ephemera: *Letter to P. Schuyler Miller; Map of the Hyborian Age.* Appendices: *Hyborian Genesis Part III; Notes on the Conan Typescript and the Chronology; Notes on the Original Howard Texts.* $15.

B75b   The Conquering Sword of Conan. Del Rey/Ballantine, New York, 2005. Edited by Patrice Louinet. Series editor Rusty Burke. Softcover. 8vo. 393 pp. Copies printed not stated. Cover price $15.95. Jacket art, frontispiece, title page decorations and interior illustrations by Gregory Manchess. Reprint of Wandering Star's unpublished edition of *Conan the Cimmerian. Vol. III.* Published in November 2005, and prior to the release of the Wandering Star edition, which makes this the true first edition of the title.

Contents: As B75a. $20.

B76a   Wings in the Night—The Weird Works of Robert E. Howard, Volume 4. Wildside Press, Holicong, Pennsylvania, 2005. Edited by Paul Herman. Black cloth binding with gilt lettering. 8vo. 179 pp. Copies printed not stated. Cover price $35.00. Jacket art by Stephen Fabian. This is the fourth volume of a planned 10-volume series of Robert E. Howard's *Weird Tales* stories, printed as originally written and in chronological order.

Contents: *Revenge,* by Paul Herman; *Wings in the Night; Arkham* (poem); *An Open Window* (poem); *Worms of the Earth; The Phoenix on the Sword; The Scarlet Citadel; The Cairn on the Headland; The Tower of the Elephant; Autumn* (poem); *Moonlight on a Skull* (poem). $35.

Addendum

B77a   Savage Adventures. Wildcat Books, Lulu Enterprises, Inc, 2004. Omnibus edition. 321 pp. Cover price not listed. Cover art by David Burton. When the book was published in 2004, a copyright dispute arose. Since Wildcat Books is a small press publisher with limited resources, it did not have the financial means for proper legal representation. As a result, the book was withdrawn from publication after only 10 copies were printed. A copy sold recently on eBay for $43.00.

Contents: *Beyond the Black River; The Devil in Iron; Jewels of Gwahlur; Rogues in the House; Shadows in Zamboula; Skulls in the Stars; The Moon of Skulls; The Hills of the Dead; Wings in the Night; The Footfalls Within; The Valley of the Worm; Pigeons from Hell.* $50.

B. Mass Market Paperbacks

The first attempt to publish Robert E. Howard's work in the mass market paperback format was not successful. More than likely spurred by the sales of the hardcover Gnome Press Conan series in the early 1950s, Ace Books, Inc., published "Conan the Conqueror" in 1953 in a double edition paperback, back-to-back with Leigh Brackett's "The Sword of Rhiannon." It did not sell well. It has been suggested that the cover art, showing Conan in the outfit of a Roman legionnaire was offensive to Howard readers—who knew of his dislike for the Roman Empire—and refused to buy the book for that reason.

This does not seem to be a plausible explanation. In 1953, Howard's feelings for Rome was either unknown or forgotten by the majority of readers, besides the armor depicted on the cover is fairly generic. It has only sketchy resemblance to that of a Roman legionnaire. Apparently the market was not ready for Robert E. Howard in paperback, and not before 1964 was the next title published in this format. It was "Almuric," also published by Ace Books, Inc., along with its unauthorized Edgar Rice Burroughs science fiction titles.

The real boom for the Howard mass market paperback publishing came in 1966 when Lancer Books, Inc., launched an 11-volume paperback series based on the Conan stories with eight striking cover paintings by the distinguished fantasy artist Frank Frazetta. The series sold well and was reprinted numerous times. From 1966 and to the present, various mass market paperback publishers, including Lancer Books, Inc., Ace Books, Inc., Zebra Books (Kensington Publishing Company), Prestige, Centaur Press, Berkley Publishing Corporation, Bantam Books, and Baen Publishing Enterprises have published and reprinted Howard's works in a variety of editions. In the United Kingdom, a number of Robert E. Howard's books—including the original Lancer Conan series—were published in paperback editions by Orbit/Futura, Sphere and Panther books.

The books are listed chronologically, in the order of publication. Reprints of a title are not listed individually, unless they varies from the first edition by publisher, format or contents. In that case, the reprint will be listed under the original title as a, b, or c, as may be appropriate. The suggested values indicated are for titles in "fine" condition. Books in better condition will demand higher prices, and books in lower grades may sell for less. Because of their inexpensive material and binding, there is a noticeable difference in the value of a "fine" copy and the average used mass market paperback. The majority of used paperbacks grade no higher than "good" or "very good" at best. There is a tendency to over-grade paperback books. Please refer to Chapter 4 for paperback grading criteria.

P1a   Conan the Conqueror. Ace Books, Inc., New York, 1953. Ace D-36. Original title: "The Hour of the Dragon." This is an Ace double novel book, back to back with Leigh Brackett's "The Sword of Rhiannon." 187 pp. Cover price $.35. Cover art by Norman Saunders.
   Contents: *Conan the Conqueror.* $35.

P2a   Almuric. Ace Books, Inc., New York, 1964. Ace F-305. 157 pp. Cover price $.40. Cover art and foreword illustration by Jack Gaughan.
   Contents: *Almuric.* $20.

P2b   Almuric. Ace Books, Inc, New York, 1970. Ace 01750. 157 pp. Cover price $.60. Cover art by Jeff Jones. Foreword heading illustration by Jack Gaughan.
   Contents: As P2a. $12.

P2c Almuric. New English Library, London, England, 1971. New English Library 2864. 125 pp. Cover price 25p. Cover art by Richard Clifton-Dey.
Contents: As P2a. $10

P2d Almuric. Sphere Books Limited, London, England, 1977. Sphere 4717–1. 155 pp. Cover price 65p. Cover art by Chris Achilleos.
Contents: As P2a. $12.

P2e Almuric. Berkley Publishing Corporation, New York, 1977. Berkley 03483–6. 202 pp. Cover price $1.95. Cover art and color fold-out poster by Ken Kelly.
Contents: As P2a. $12.

P3a Conan the Adventurer. With L. Sprague de Camp. Lancer Books, Inc., New York, 1966. Lancer 73–526. 224 pp. Cover price $.60. Cover art by Frank Frazetta. Frontispiece map of the Hyborian Age. Reprinted in 1967, 1968, 1969, 1970, 1971, 1972, 1972, and 1973.
    Contents: *Introduction,* by L. Sprague de Camp; *The People of the Black Circle; The Slithering Shadow; Drums of Tombalku* (with L. Sprague de Camp); *The Pool of the Black One.* $12.

P3b Conan the Adventurer. With L. Sprague de Camp. Sphere Books Limited, London, England, 1973. Sphere 4688–4. 192 pp. Cover price 30p. Cover art by Frank Frazetta. Frontispiece map of the Hyborian Age. Reprinted in 13 printings 'til 1988. The 1988 printing has cover art by Blas Gallego.
    Contents: As P3a. $10.

P3c Conan the Adventurer. With L. Sprague de Camp. Ace Books, New York, 1977. Ace 11675–2. 224 pp. Cover price $1.95. Cover art by Frank Frazetta. Frontispiece map of the Hyborian Age. Reprinted in 20 printings 'til 1986. Ace Books reprinted the 12-volume Conan series in both white spine/cover and black spine/cover printings.
    Contents: As P3a. $8.

P4a Conan the Warrior. Lancer Books, Inc., New York, 1967. Lancer 73–549. Edited by L. Sprague de Camp. 222 pp. Cover price $.60. Cover art by Frank Frazetta. Frontispiece map of the Hyborian Age. Reprinted in 1968, 1969, 1970, 1971, 1972, 1972, and 1973.
    Contents: *Introduction* , by L. Sprague de Camp; *Red Nails; Jewels of Gwahlur; Beyond the Black River.* $12.

P4b Conan The Warrior. Sphere Books Limited, London, England, 1973. Sphere 4689–2. Edited by L. Sprague de Camp. 192 pp. Cover price 30p. Cover art by Frank Frazetta. Frontispiece map of the Hyborian Age. Reprinted in 11 printings 'til 1988. The 1988 printing has cover art by Blas Gallego.
    Contents: As P4a. $10.

P4c Conan the Warrior. Ace Books, New York, 1977. Ace 11677–9. Edited by L. Sprague de Camp. 222 pp. Cover price $1.95. Cover art by Frank

Frazetta. Frontispiece map of the Hyborian Age. Reprinted in 20 printings 'til 1986.
Contents: As P4a. $8.

P5a   Conan the Conqueror. Lancer Books. Inc., New York, 1967. Lancer 73–572. Edited by L. Sprague de Camp. 224 pp. Cover price $.60. Cover art by Frank Frazetta. Frontispiece map of the Hyborian Age. Reprinted in 1969, 1970, 1971, 1972, 1972, and 1973.
Contents: *Introduction,* by L. Sprague de Camp; *Conan the Conqueror.* $12.

P5b   Conan the Conqueror. Sphere Books Limited, London, England, 1974. Sphere 4692–2. Edited by L. Sprague de Camp. 191 pp. Cover price 30p. Cover art by Frank Frazetta. Frontispiece map of the Hyborian Age. Reprinted in 13 printings 'til 1988. The 1988 printing has cover art by Blas Gallego.
Contents: As P5a. $10.

P5c   Conan the Conqueror. Ace Books, New York, 1977. Ace 11679–5. Edited by L. Sprague de Camp. 224 pp. Cover price $1.95. Cover art by Frank Frazetta. Frontispiece map of the Hyborian Age. Reprinted in 20 printings 'til 1986.
Contents: As P5a. $8.

P6a   Conan the Usurper. With L. Sprague de Camp. Lancer Books, Inc., New York, 1967. Lancer 73–599. 256 pp. Cover price $.60. Cover art by Frank Frazetta. Frontispiece map of the Hyborian Age. Reprinted in 1968, 1969, 1970, 1971, 1972, 1972, and 1973.
Contents: *Introduction* , by L. Sprague de Camp; *The Treasure of Tranicos* (edited by L. Sprague de Camp); *Wolves Beyond the Border* (edited by L. Sprague de Camp); *The Phoenix on the Sword; The Scarlet Citadel.* $12.

P6b   Conan the Usurper. With L. Sprague de Camp. Sphere Books Limited, London, England, 1974. Sphere 4697–3. 203 pp. Cover price 35p. Cover art by Frank Frazetta. Frontispiece map of the Hyborian Age. Reprinted in 10 printings 'til 1989. The 1989 printing has cover art by Kirk Reinert.
Contents: As P6a. $10.

P6c   Conan the Usurper. With L. Sprague de Camp. Ace Books, New York, 1977. Ace 11678–7. 256 pp. Cover price $1.95. Cover art by Frank Frazetta. Frontispiece map of the Hyborian Age. Reprinted in 20 printings 'til 1986.
Contents: As P6a. $8.

P7a   King Kull. With Lin Carter. Lancer Books, Inc., New York, 1967. Lancer 73–650. Edited by Glenn Lord. 223 pp. Cover price $.60. Cover art by Roy G. Krenkel. Frontispiece map of Kull's World by Lin Carter. Reprinted in 1969 and 1972.
Contents: *Prolog; Exile of Atlantis; The Shadow Kingdom; The Altar and the Scorpion; Black Abyss* (with Lin Carter); *Delcardes' Cat; The Skull of Silence; Riders Beyond the Sunrise* (with Lin Carter); *By This Axe I Rule; The Striking of*

the Gong (edited by Lin Carter); *Swords of the Purple Kingdom; Wizard and Warrior* (with Lin Carter); *The Mirrors of Tuzun Thune; The King and the Oak; Epilog.* $12.

P7b **King Kull.** Sphere Books Limited, London, England, 1976. Sphere 4716-3. Edited by Glenn Lord. 187 pp. Cover price 60p. Editing changes made by Lin Carter for the Lancer edition have been removed. Cover art by Chris Achilleos. Frontispiece map of Kull's world by Lin Carter.

Contents: As P7a. $12.

P7c **Kull.** Bantam Books, Inc., New York, 1978. Bantam 12019-0. 190 pp. Cover price $1.95. Fold-out cover art by Lou Feck. Frontispiece map by Kirk.

Contents: *Introduction,* by Andrew J. Ouffutt; *Prolog; Exile of Atlantis; The Shadow Kingdom; The Altar and the Scorpion; Delcardes' Cat; The Skull of Silence; By This Axe I Rule; The Striking of the Gong* (edited by Lin Carter); *Swords of the Purple Kingdom; The Mirrors of Tuzun Thune; The King and the Oak; The Black City* (fragment); *Untitled* (fragment); *Untitled* (fragment); *Epilog.* $10.

P7d **Kull.** Baen Publishing Enterprises, New York, 1995. Baen 87673. 207 pp. Cover price $5.99. Cover art by Ken Kelly.

Contents: *Introduction: The Human Side,* by David Drake; *Prolog; Exile of Atlantis; The Shadow Kingdom; The Altar and the Scorpion; Delcarde's Cat; The Skull of Silence; By This Axe I Rule!; The Striking of the Gong; Swords of the Purple Kingdom; The Mirrors of Tuzun Thune; The King and the Oak; The Black City* (fragment); *Untitled* (fragment); *Untitled* (fragment); *The Curse of the Golden Skull; Epilog.* $12.

P8a **Conan.** With L. Sprague de Camp and Lin Carter. Lancer Books, Inc., New York, 1968. Lancer 73-685. 221 pp. Cover price $.60. Cover art by Frank Frazetta. Frontispiece map of the Hyborian Age. Reprinted in 1968, 1969, 1970, 1970, 1971, 1972, 1972, and 1973.

Contents: *Introduction ,* by L. Sprague de Camp; Letter from Robert E. Howard to P.S. Miller; *The Hyborian Age,* Part I; *The Thing in the Crypt,* by L. Sprague de Camp and Lin Carter; *The Tower of the Elephant; The Hall of the Dead* (with L. Sprague de Camp); *The God in the Bowl* (edited by L. Sprague de Camp); *Rogues in the House; The Hand of Nergal* (with Lin Carter); *The City of Skulls,* by L. Sprague de Camp and Lin Carter. $12.

P8b **Conan.** With L. Sprague de Camp and Lin Carter. Sphere Books Limited, London, England, 1974. Sphere 4691-4. 187 pp. Cover price 30p. Cover art by Frank Frazetta. Frontispiece map of the Hyborian Age. Reprinted in 13 printings 'til 1989. The 1989 printing has cover art by Blas Gallego.

Contents: As P8a. $10.

P8c **Conan.** With L. Sprague de Camp and Lin Carter. Ace Books, New York, 1977. Ace 11671-X. 221 pp. Cover price $1.95. Cover art by Frank Frazetta. Frontispiece map of the Hyborian Age. Reprinted in 20 printings 'til 1986.

Contents: As P8a. $8.

P9a Wolfshead. Lancer Books, Inc., New York, 1968. Lancer 73–721. Edited by Glenn Lord. 190 pp. Cover price $.60. Cover art by Frank Frazetta.
  Contents: *Introduction,* by Robert E. Howard; *The Black Stone; The Valley of the Worm; Wolfshead; The Fire of Asshurbanipal; The House of Arabu; The Horror from the Mound; The Cairn on the Headland.* $12.

P9b Wolfshead. Lancer Books, Inc., New York, 1972. Lancer 75299–095. Edited by Glen Lord. 190 pp. Cover price $.95. Cover art by Frank Frazetta. Same cover art as 9a, but with a different cover design.
  Contents: As 9a. $10.00

P9c Wolfshead. Bantam Books, Inc., New York, 1979. Bantam 12353-X. 147 pp. Cover price $1.95. Cover artist not identified.
  Contents: *Introduction,* by Robert Bloch; *The Black Stone; The Valley of the Worm; Wolfshead; The Fire of Asshurbanipal; The House of Arabu; The Horror from the Mound.* $10.

P10a Conan the Avenger. With Björn Nyberg and L. Sprague de Camp. Lancer Books, Inc., New York, 1968. Lancer 73–780. 192 pp. Cover price $.60. Cover art by Frank Frazetta. Frontispiece map of the Hyborian Age. Reprinted in 1969, 1970, 1970, 1971, 1972, 1972, and 1973.
  Contents: *Introduction*, by L. Sprague de Camp; *The Return of Conan,* by Björn Nyberg and L. Sprague de Camp; *The Hyborian Age,* Part II. $12.

P10b Conan the Avenger. With Björn Nyberg and L. Sprague de Camp. Sphere Books Limited, London, England, 1974. Sphere 4703–1. 192 pp. Cover price 35p. Cover art by Frank Frazetta. Frontispiece map of the Hyborian Age. Reprinted in 8 printings 'til 1989. The 1989 printing has cover art by Blas Gallego.
  Contents: As P10a. $10.

P10c Conan the Avenger. With Björn Nyberg and L. Sprague de Camp. Ace Books, New York, 1977. Ace 11680–9. 192 pp. Cover price $1.95. Cover art by Frank Frazetta. Frontispiece map of the Hyborian Age. Reprinted in 20 printings 'til 1986.
  Contents: As P10a. $8.

P11a Conan the Freebooter. With L. Sprague de Camp. Lancer Books, Inc., New York, 1968. Lancer 74–963. 223 pp. Cover price $.75. Cover art by John Duillo. Frontispiece map of the Hyborian Age. Reprinted in 1969, 1970, 1971, and 1973.
  Contents: *Introduction*, by L. Sprague de Camp; *Hawks Over Shem* (with L. Sprague de Camp); *Black Colossus; Shadows in the Moonlight; The Road of the Eagles* (with L. Sprague de Camp); *A Witch Shall Be Born.* $12.

P11b Conan the Freebooter. With L. Sprague de Camp. Sphere Books Limited, London, England, 1974. Sphere 4696–5. 205 pp. Cover price 30p. Cover art by John Duillo. Frontispiece map of the Hyborian Age. Reprinted in 9 printings 'til 1988. The 1988 printing has cover art by Kirk Reinert.
  Contents: As P11a. $10.

P11c Conan the Freebooter. With L. Sprague de Camp. Ace Books, New York, 1977. Ace 11673–6. 223 pp. Cover price $1.95. Cover art by John Duillo. Frontispiece map of the Hyborian Age. Reprinted in 20 printings 'til 1986. John Duillo's cover art was replaced by Boris Vallejo.
Contents: As P11a. $8.

P12a Conan the Wanderer. With L. Sprague de Camp and Lin Carter. Lancer Books, Inc., New York, 1968. Lancer 74–976. 222 pp. Cover price $.95. Cover art by John Duillo. Frontispiece map of the Hyborian Age. Reprinted in 1969, 1970, 1971, 1972, 1972, and 1973.
Contents: *Introduction* , by L. Sprague de Camp; *Black Tears,* by L. Sprague de Camp and Lin Carter; *Shadows in Zamboula; The Devil in Iron; The Flame Knife* (with L. Sprague de Camp). $12.

P12b Conan the Wanderer. With L. Sprague de Camp and Lin Carter. Sphere Books Limited, London, England, 1974. Sphere 4698–1. 186 pp. Cover price 35p. Cover art by John Duillo. Frontispiece map of the Hyborian Age. Reprinted in 9 printings 'til 1988.
Contents: As P12a. $10.

P12c Conan the Wanderer. With L. Sprague de Camp and Lin Carter. Ace Books, New York, 1977. Ace 11674–4. 222 pp. Cover price $1.95. Cover art by John Duillo. Frontispiece map of the Hyborian Age. Reprinted in 20 printings 'til 1986. John Duillo's cover art was replaced by Boris Vallejo.
Contents: As P12a. $8.

P13a Conan of Cimmeria. With L. Sprague de Camp and Lin Carter. Lancer Books, Inc., New York, 1969. Lancer 75–072. 189 pp. Cover price $.95. Cover art by Frank Frazetta. Frontispiece map of the Hyborian Age. Reprinted in 1970, 1971, 1972, 1972, and 1973.
Contents: *Introduction* , by L. Sprague de Camp; *The Curse of the Monolith,* by L. Sprague de Camp and Lin Carter; *The Bloodstained God* (with L. Sprague de Camp); *The Frost Giant's Daughter* (edited by L. Sprague de Camp); *The Lair of the Ice Worm,* by L. Sprague de Camp and Lin Carter; *Queen of the Black Coast; The Vale of Lost Women; The Castle of Terror,* by L. Sprague de Camp and Lin Carter; *The Snout in the Dark* (with L. Sprague de Camp and Lin Carter. $12.

P13b Conan of Cimmeria. With L. Sprague de Camp and Lin Carter. Sphere Books Limited, London, England, 1974. Sphere 4695–7. 192 pp. Cover price 30p. Cover art by Frank Frazetta. Frontispiece map of the Hyborian Age. Reprinted in 10 printings 'til 1989. The 1987–89 printings have cover art by Kirk Reinert.
Contents: As P13a. $10.

P13b Conan of Cimmeria. With L. Sprague de Camp and Lin Carter. Ace Books, New York, 1977. Ace 11672–8. 189 pp. Cover price $1.95. Cover art by Frank Frazetta. Frontispiece map of the Hyborian Age. Reprinted in 20 printings 'til 1986.
Contents: As P13a. $8.

P14a   Bran Mak Morn. Dell Publishing Co., Inc., New York, 1969. Dell 0774. 192 pp. Cover Price $.60. Cover art by Frank Frazetta.
   Contents: *The Drums of Pictdom/Foreword; The Lost Race; Men of the Shadows; Kings of the Night; A Song of the Race; Worms of the Earth; Fragment* (untitled); *Night of the Wolf; The Dark Man.* $15.

P14b   Bran Mak Morn. Baen Publishing Enterprises, New York, 1996. Baen 87705. 234 pp. Cover price $5.99. Cover art by Ken Kelly.
   Contents: Acknowledgments; *Introduction,* by David Weber; *Foreword; The Lost Race; Men of the Shadows; Kings of the Night; A Song of the Race; Worms of the Earth; Fragment; The Dark Man; The Gods of Bal-Sagoth.* $12.

P15a   The Moon of Skulls. Centaur Press, New York, 1969. 127 pp. Cover price $.60. Cover art by Jeff Jones. Second printing 1974. Cover price $1.25. Third printing 1976. Cover price $1.50. Seven interior illustrations by Marcus Boas. Peter Haddock from England pirated a number of Centaur Press books, including the three Solomon Kane books and had them printed in Hungary. Except for the imprint these books are identical to the Centaur Press' first printings. All three were issued in 1972.
   Contents: *Introduction; The Moon of Skulls; Skulls in the Stars; The Footfalls Within.* $12.

P16a   The Hand of Kane. Centaur Press, New York, 1970. 127 pp. Cover price $.75. Cover art by Jeff Jones. Second printing 1976. Cover price $1.50. Frontispiece and six interior illustrations by Ned Dameron.
   Contents: *The Hills of the Dead; Hawk of Basti; Wings in the Night; The Children of Asshur.* $12.

P17a   Solomon Kane. Centaur Press, New York, 1971. 126 pp. Cover price $.75. Cover art by Jeff Jones. Second printing 1974. Cover price $1.25. Third printing 1976. Cover price $1.50. Seven interior illustrations by David Wenzel.
   Contents: *Introduction,* by Albert E. Gechter; *The Right Hand of Doom; Red Shadows; Rattle of Bones; The Castle of the Devil; Blades of the Brotherhood; The Return of Sir Richard Grenville; Solomon Kane's Homecoming.* $12.

P17b   Solomon Kane. Baen Publishing Enterprises, New York, 1995. Baen 87695. 311 pp.Cover price $5.99. Cover art by Ken Kelly.
   Contents: *Introduction,* by Ramsey Campbell; *Skulls in the Stars; The Right Hand of Doom; Red Shadows; Rattle of Bones; The Castle of the Devil; Death's Black Riders; The Moon of Skulls; The One Black Stain; Blades of the Brotherhood; The Hills of the Dead; Hawk of Basti; The Return of Sir Richard Grenville; Wings in the Night; The Footfalls Within; The Children of Asshur; Solomon Kane's Homecoming.* $20.

P18a   The Dark Man and Others. Lancer Books, Inc., New York, 1972. Lancer 75265–095. 254 pp. Cover price $.95. Cover art by Victor Valla. Reprint of Arkham House Publishers' 1963 first edition.
   Contents: *Introduction,* by August Derleth; *The Voice of El-Lil; Pigeons from Hell; The Dark Man; The Gods of Bal-Sagoth; People of the Dark; The Children*

of the Night; The Dead Remember; The Man on the Ground; The Garden of Fear; The Thing on the Roof; The Hyena; Dig Me No Grave; The Dream Snake; In the Forest of Villefére; Old Garfield's Heart. $12.

P19a The Sowers of the Thunder. Zebra Books, New York,1975. Zebra 89083–113. 285 pp. Cover price $1.50. Cover art by Jeff Jones. Interior illustrations by Roy G. Krenkel. Reprint of D.M. Grant's 1973 hardcover edition of the same title. Reprinted in 1975 and 1976.

Contents: *Introduction,* by Roy G. Krenkel; *The Lion of Tiberias, The Sowers of the Thunder, Lord of Samarcand; The Shadow of the Vulture.* $12.

P19b The Sowers of the Thunder. Sphere Books Limited, London, England, 1977. Sphere 4727–9. 172 pp. Cover price 65p. Cover art by Melvyn.

Contents: As P19a. $12.

P19c The Sowers of the Thunder. Ace Books, New York,1979. Ace 77620–5. 285 pp. Cover price $1.95. Cover art by Esteban Maroto. Interior illustrations by Roy G. Krenkel. Reprint of D.M. Grant's 1973 hardcover edition of the same title.

Contents: As P19a. $12.

P20a Tigers of the Sea. Zebra Books, New York, 1975. Zebra 89083–119. Edited by Richard L. Tierney. 188 pp. Cover price $1.50. Cover art by Jeff Jones. Illustrated by Tim Kirk. Reprint of D.M. Grant's 1974 hardcover edition of the same title.

Contents: *Introduction,* by Richard L. Tierney; *Tigers of the Sea* (with Richard L. Tierney); *Swords of the Northern Sea; The Night of the Wolf; The Temple of Abomination* (with Richard L. Tierney). $12.

P20b Tigers of the Sea. Sphere Books Limited, London, England, 1977. Sphere 4726–0. Edited by Richard Tierney. 159 pp. Cover price 65p. Cover art by Melvyn.

Contents: As P20a. $12.

P20c Tigers of the Sea. Ace Books, New York, 1979. Ace 80705–4. Edited by Richard L. Tierney. 212 pp. Cover price $1.95. Cover art by Sanjulian. Illustrated by Tim Kirk. Reprint of D.M. Grant's 1974 hardcover edition of the same title.

Contents: As P20a. $10.

P20d Cormac Mac Art—Tigers of the Sea. Ace Books, New York, 1984. Ace 80706–2. 190 pp. Cover price $2.50. Cover art by Sanjulian. Illustrated by Tim Kirk. Reprint of D.M. Grant's 1974 hardcover edition of the same title.

Contents: As P20a. $10.

P21a Worms of the Earth. Zebra Books, New York, 1975. Zebra 89083–126. 188 pp. Cover price $1.50. Cover art by Jeff Jones. Four interior illustrations by David Ireland. Reprint of D.M. Grant's 1974 hardcover edition of the same title.

Tigers of the Sea. Zebra Books 1975. Cover art by Jeff Jones. © 1974 Glenn Lord.

Contents: *The Drums of Pictdom/Foreword; The Lost Race; Men of the Shadows; Kings of the Night; A Song of the Race; Worms of the Earth; Fragment* (untitled); *The Dark Man*. $10.

P21b **Worms of the Earth.** Orbit/Futura, London, England, 1976. Orbit 8600-7879. 188 pp. Cover price 60p. Four interior illustrations by David Ireland. Cover art by Chris Achilleos.
Contents: As 21a. $15.

P21c **Worms of the Earth.** Ace Books, New York, 1979. Ace 91770-4. 233 pp. Cover price $1.95. Cover art by Sanjulian. Four interior illustrations by David Ireland.
Contents: As P21a. $10.

P22a **A Gent from Bear Creek.** Zebra Books, New York, 1975. Zebra 89083-132. 223 pp. Cover price $1.50. Cover art by Jeff Jones. Three interior illustrations by Tim Kirk. Reprint of D.M. Grant's 1965 hardcover edition of the same title.
Contents: *Striped Shirts and Busted Hearts; Mountain Man; Meet Cap'n Kidd; Guns of the Mountains; A Gent from Bear Creek; The Feud Buster; The Road to Bear Creek; The Scalp Hunter; Cupid from Bear Creek; The Haunted Mountain; Educate or Bust; War on Bear Creek; When Bear Creek came to Chawed Ear*. $10.00

P23a **The Vultures of Whapeton.** Zebra Books, New York, 1975. Zebra 09083-144. 191 pp. Cover price $1.50. Cover art by Jeff Jones.
Contents: *The Vultures of Whapeton; Afterword,* by Glenn Lord; *Showdown at Hell's Canyon; Drums of the Sunset; Wild Water*. $10.

P23b **The Vultures of Whapeton.** Berkley Books, New York, 1980. Berkley 425-04435. 216 pp. Cover price $1.95. Cover art by Ken Kelly.
Contents: *The Vultures of Whapeton; Showdown at Hell's Canyon; Drums of the Sunset; Wild Water; Afterword,* by Glenn Lord. $10.

P24a **The Incredible Adventures of Dennis Dorgan.** Zebra Books, New York, 1975. Zebra 89083-149. 192 pp. Cover price $1.50. Cover art by Jeff Jones. Reprint of FAX's 1974 hardcover edition of the same title.
Contents: *Introduction; The Alleys of Singapore; The Jade Monkey; The Mandarin Ruby; The Yellow Cobra; In High Society; Playing Journalist; The Destiny Gorilla; A Knight of the Round Table; Playing Santa Claus; The Turkish Menace* (with Darrell C. Richardson). $10.

P25a **The Lost Valley of Iskander.** Zebra Books, New York, 1976. Zebra 89083-157. 195 pp. Cover price $1.50. Cover art by Jeff Jones. Story, chapter headings and nine interior illustrations by Michael W. Kaluta. Reprint of FAX's 1974 hardcover edition of the same title.
Contents: *Introduction,* by Darrell C. Richardson; *The Daughter of Erlik Khan; The Lost Valley of Iskander; Hawk of the Hills*. $10.

P25b **The Lost Valley of Iskander.** Orbit/Futura, London, England,

1976. Orbit 8600 7880. 194 pp. Cover price 60p. Cover art by Chris Achilleos. Story, chapter headings and interior illustrations by Michael W. Kaluta.
Contents: As P25a. $15.

P25c   The Lost Valley of Iskander. Berkley Books, New York, 1979. Berkley 425–04243. 207 pp. Cover price $1.95. Cover art by Ken Kelly.
Contents: As P25a. $10.

P25d   The Lost Valley of Iskander. Ace Books, New York, 1986. Ace 49515. 207 PP. Cover price $2.95 Cover art by Ken Kelly, same cover art as P25c.
Contents: As P25a. $10.

P26a   The Iron Man. Zebra Books, New York, 1976. Zebra 89083–171. 186 pp. Cover price $1.50. Cover art by Jeff Jones. Three interior illustrations by David Ireland. Reprint of the D.M. Grant 1976 hardcover edition of the same title, however, the paperback edition was published prior to the release of the hardcover title.
Contents: *Introduction,* by Donald M. Grant; *Men of Iron; The Iron Man; They Always Come Back; Fists of the Desert.* $10.

P26b   The Iron Man with the Adventures of Dennis Dorgan. Ace Books, 1983. Ace 37365-8. 232 pp. Cover price $2.50. Cover artist not identified. Reprint of D.M. Grant's 1976 hardcover edition and Fax Collector's Edition 1974 hardcover edition, with the same titles, but without the illustrations.
Contents: The Iron Man: *Introduction,* by Donald M. Grant; *Men of Iron; The Iron Man; They Always Come Back; Fists of the Desert.* The Incredible Adventures of Dennis Dorgan: *Introduction,* by Darrell C. Richardson; *The Alleys of Singapore; The Jade Monkey; The Mandarin Ruby; The Yellow Cobra; In High Society; Playing Journalist; The Destiny Gorilla; A Knight of the Round Table; Playing Santa Claus; The Turkish Menace* (with Darrell C. Richardson). $25.

P27a   The Book of Robert E. Howard. Zebra Books, New York 1976. Zebra 89083–163. Edited by Glenn Lord. 345 pp. Cover price $1.95. Cover art and interior illustrations by Jeff Jones.
Contents: *Introduction,* by Glenn Lord; *Pigeons from Hell; Recompense; The Pit of the Serpent; Empire; Etchings in Ivory: Flaming Marble; Skulls and Orchids; Medallions in the Moon; The Gods That Men Forget; Bloodstones and Ebony. Thor's Son; Cimmeria; A Sonnet of Good Cheer; Red Blades of Black Cathay; The Dust Dance; The Bar by the Side of the Road; Knife, Bullet and Noose; The Gold and the Grey; Gents on the Lynch; A Song Out of Midian; She Devil; The Day That I Die; The Voice of El-Lil; Black Wind Blowing; The Curse of the Golden Skull; Black Talons.* $15.

P27b   The Book of Robert E. Howard. Berkley Books, New York, 1980. Berkley 425–04449. 240 pp. Cover price $1.95. Cover art by Ken Kelly.
Contents: As P27a. $12.

P28a   The Second Book of Robert E. Howard. Zebra Books, New York 1976. Zebra 89083–183. Edited by Glenn Lord. 368 pp. Cover price $1.95. Cover art and interior illustrations by Jeff Jones.

The Iron Man, Zebra Books 1976. Cover art by Jeff Jones. © 1976 Donald M. Grant and Glenn Lord.

Contents: *Introduction,* by Glenn Lord; *Letter* to Wilfred B. Talman; *Sword Woman; Which Will Scarcely Be Understood; The Striking of the Gong; The Song of Horsa's Galley; The Good Knight; A Word from the Outer Dark; Black Canaan; The Song of a Mad Minstrel; Kelly the Conjure-Man; Surrender; The Footfalls Within; Knife-River Prodigal; Musings; Life; The House of Suspicion; Reuben's Brethren; Two Against Tyre; The Guise of Youth; "For the Love of Barbara Allen"; Guns of Khartum; Lines Written in the Realization That I Must Die.* $15.

P28b   The Second Book of Robert E. Howard. Berkley Books, New York, 1980. Berkley 425–04455. 239 pp. Cover price $1.95. Cover art by Ken Kelly.
Contents: As P28a. $12.

P29a   Swords of Shahrazar. Orbit/Futura, London, England, 1976. Orbit 8600 7881. 122 pp. Cover price 50p. Cover artist not identified.
Contents: *Swords of Shahrazar; The Treasures of Tartary; The Curse of the Crimson God.* $15.

P29b   Swords of Shahrazar. Berkley Books, New York, 1978. Berkley 425–03709. 165 pp. Cover price $1.95. Cover art and fold-out color poster by Ken Kelly.
Contents: *The Treasures of Tartary; Swords of Shahrazar; The Curse of the Crimson God; The Brazen Peacock; The Black Bear Bites.* $12.

P29c   Swords of Shahrazar. Ace Books, New York, 1987. Ace 79237–5. 165 pp. Cover price $2.95. Cover art by Ken Kelly, same cover art as P29b.
Contents: As P29b. $10.

P30a   Pigeons from Hell. Zebra Books, New York, 1976. Zebra 89083–189. Edited by Glenn Lord. 315 pp. Cover price $1.95. Cover art by Jeff Jones.
Contents: *Introduction,* by Glenn Lord; *Pigeons from Hell; The Gods of Bal-Sagoth; People of the Dark; The Children of the Night; The Dead Remember; The Man on the Ground; The Garden of Fear; The Hyena; Dig Me No Grave; The Dream Snake; In the Forest of Villefère; Old Garfield's Heart; The Voice of El-Lil.* $12.

P30b   Pigeons from Hell. Ace Books, New York, 1979. Ace 66320. 315 pp. Cover price $1.95. Cover art by Esteban Maroto.
Contents: *Introduction; Pigeons from Hell; The Gods of Bal-Sagoth; People of the Dark; The Children of the Night; The Dead Remember; The Man on the Ground; The Garden of Fear; The Hyena; Dig Me No Grave; The Dream Snake; In the Forest of Villefère; Old Garfield's Heart; The Voice of El-Lil.* $10.

P31a   Skull-Face Omnibus Vol. 1.: Skull-Face and Others. Panther Books, London, England, 1976. Panther 04220–2. 250 pp. Cover price 60p. Cover art by Chris Achilleos.
Contents: *Foreword,* by August Derleth; *Which Will Scarcely Be Understood; Robert Ervin Howard: A Memoriam,* by H.P. Lovecraft; *A Memory of Robert E. Howard,* by E. Hoffmann Price; *Skull-Face; Wolfshead; The Black Stone; The Horror from the Mound; The Cairn on the Headland; Black Canaan.* $25.

Skull-Face Omnibus. Vol. 1. Panther Books 1976. Cover art by Chris Achilleos. © 1946 August Derleth.

P32a Skull-Face Omnibus Vol. 2.: The Valley of the Worm. Panther Books, London, England, 1976. Panther 04374–8. 236 pp. Cover price 60p. Cover art by Chris Achilleos.

Contents: *Foreword,* by August Derleth; *Which Will Scarcely Be Understood; Robert Ervin Howard: A Memoriam,* by H.P. Lovecraft; *The Fire of Asshurbanipal; A Man-Eating Jeopard; Worms of the Earth; Kings of the Night; The Valley of the Worm; Skulls in the Stars; Rattle of Bones; The Hills of the Dead; Wings in the Night.* $25.

P33a Skull-Face Omnibus Vol. 3.: The Shadow Kingdom and Others. Panther Books, London, England, 1976. Panther 04372–1. 248 pp. Cover price 60p. Cover art by Chris Achilleos.

Contents: *Foreword,* by August Derleth; *Which Will Scarcely Be Understood; Robert Ervin Howard: A Memoriam,* by H.P. Lovecraft; *The Hyborian Age; The Shadow Kingdom; The Mirrors of Tuzun Thune. The Phoenix on the Sword; The Scarlet Citadel; The Tower of the Elephant; Rogues in the House; Shadows in Zamboula; Lines Written in Realization That I Must Die.* $25.

P34a Black Vulmea's Vengeance. Zebra Books, New York, 1977. Zebra 89083–244. 207 pp. Cover price $1.50. Cover art by Barber. Reprint of D.M. Grant's 1976 hardcover edition of the same title.

Contents: *Swords of the Red Brotherhood; Black Vulmea's Vengeance; The Isle of Pirate's Doom.* $12.

P34b Black Vulmea's Vengeance. Berkley Books, New York, 1979. Berkley 425–04296. 183 pp. Cover price $1.95. Cover art by Ken Kelly.
Contents: As P34a. $10.

P34c Black Vulmea's Vengeance. Ace Books, New York, 1987. Ace 06661–5. 183 pp. Copies printed not stated. Cover price $2.95. Cover art by Ken Kelly, same cover art as P34b.
Contents: As P34a. $12.

P35a The Sword Woman. Zebra Books, New York, 1977. Zebra 89083–261. 176 pp. Cover price $1.50. Cover art and five interior illustrations by Stephen Fabian.

Contents: *Introduction,* by Leigh Brackett; *Res Adventura; Blades for France; Mistress of Death* (with Gerald W. Page); *The King's Service; The Shadow of the Hun.* $12.

P35b Sword Woman. Berkley Books, New York, 1979. Berkley 425–04445. 169 pp. Cover price $1.95. Cover art by Ken Kelly.
Contents: As P35a. $10.

P35c Sword Woman. Ace Books, New York, 1986. Ace 79279–0. 169 pp. Cover price $2.95. Same cover art as P35b.
Contents: As P35a. $8.

P36a Three-Bladed Doom. Zebra Books, New York, 1977. Zebra 89083–277. 315 pp. Cover price $1.50. Howard wrote two different length versions of

Skull-Face Omnibus. Vol. 2. Panther Books 1976. Cover art by Chris Achilleos. © 1946 August Derleth.

Skull-Face Omnibus. Vol. 3. Panther Books 1976. Cover art by Chris Achilleos. © 1946 August Derleth.

Black Vulmea's Vengeance. Zebra Books 1977. Cover art by Tom Barber. © 1976 Glenn Lord.

this oriental adventure story, featuring Francis X. Gordon (El Borak). The longer version was rewritten as a Conan story by L. Sprague de Camp with the title *The Flame Knife.* Cover art by Enrich.
Contents: *Three-Bladed Doom.* $12.

P36b   Three-Bladed Doom. Orbit/Futura, London, England, 1977. Orbit 8600 7954. 128 pp. Cover price 65p. Cover art by Peter Jones.
Contents: As P36a. $15.

P36c   Three-Bladed Doom. Ace Books, New York, 1979. Ace 80780–1. 154 pp. Cover price $1.95. Cover art by Sanjulian. Reprinted in 1987 with same cover art. Cover price $2.95.
Contents: As P36a. $12.

P37a   The Hour of the Dragon. Berkley Books, New York, 1977. Berkley 425–03608. Edited by Karl Edward Wagner. 296 pp. Cover price $1.95. Cover art and color fold-out poster by Ken Kelly. Frontispiece reprinted from *Weird Tales.*
Contents: *Foreword,* by Karl Edward Wagner; *The Hour of the Dragon; Afterword,* by Karl Edward Wagner; Acknowledgments. $12.

P38a   The People of the Black Circle. Berkley Books, New York, 1977. Berkley 425–03609. Edited by Karl Edward Wagner. 293 pp. Cover price $1.95. Cover art and color fold-out poster by Ken Kelly. Frontispiece reprinted from *Weird Tales.*
Contents: *Foreword,* by Karl Edward Wagner; *The Devil in Iron; The People of the Black Circle; A Witch Shall be Born; Jewels of Gwahlur; Afterword,* by Karl Edward Wagner. $12.

P39a   Red Nails. Berkley Books, New York, 1977. Berkley 425–03610. Edited by Karl Edward Wagner. 295 pp. Cover price $1.95. Cover art and color fold-out poster by Ken Kelly. Frontispiece and end illustration reprinted from *Weird Tales.*
Contents: *Foreword,* by Karl Edward Wagner; *Beyond the Black River; Shadows in Zamboula; Red Nails; The Hyborian Age; Afterword,* by Karl Edward Wagner. $12.

P40a   The Last Celt. Berkley Windhover Book, New York, 1977. Edited by Glenn Lord. 12mo. 416 pp. Cover price $5.95. Cover art by Ken Kelly. Reprint of D.M. Grant's 1976 hardcover edition of the same title. Includes magazine covers, photographs, and other illustrations as the original.
Contents: *Introduction,* by E. Hoffmann Price; *Foreword,* by Glenn Lord; Autobiography: *The Wandering Years; An Autobiography; A Touch of Trivia; Letter; On Reading—and Writing;* Biography*: Facts of Biography; A Biographical Sketch of Robert E. Howard,* by Alvin Earl Perry*; Robert E. Howard: A Memoriam,* by H.P. Lovecraft*; Lone Star Fictioneer,* by Glenn Lord*; A Memory of R.E. Howard,* by E. Hoffmann Price*; The Last Celt,* by Harold Preece*;* Bibliography*: The Bibliography; Books; Fiction; Verse:* Title Index; First Line Index; Headings; *Articles; Letters; Index by Periodicals; Translations:* Books; Fiction; Verse; Headings; Articles; Letters*; Unpublished Fiction; Unpublished Verse:* Title Index; Headings; *Unpublished*

Articles; Series Index; Lost Manuscripts; Unborn Books; Comics; Television Adaptation; The Junto; About the Author: Books; Amateur Publications; Robert E. Howard United Press Association; Articles; Conan Pastiches; Miscellanea: *The Hand of Nergal; The Battle that Ended the Century; Pictures in the Fire; The Hall of the Dead; The Robert E. Howard Memorial Collection; Iron Shadows in the Moon; Letters; The Golden Caliph; R.E.H. as Mythical Dane; Cartoon from the Junto; Map of the Hyborian Age; A Robert E. Howard Photograph Album; A Gent from Bear Creek* (dust jacket); *Magazine Covers; Obituaries.* $20.

P41a   Robert E. Howard Omnibus. Orbit/Futura, London, England, 1977. Orbit 8600 7955. 336 pp. Cover price 90p. Cover art by Peter Jones. Reprinted in 1978.
   Contents: *The Footfalls Within; The Pool of the Black One; The Good Knight; Hawks of Outremer; Gates of Empire; The Grey God Passes; The Secret of Lost Valley; Dermod's Bane; Knife River Prodigal; Drums of the Sunset; Black Vulmea's Vengeance; The House of Arabu.* $25.

P42a   Marchers of Valhalla. Sphere Books Limited, London, England, 1977. Sphere 4728–7. 156 pp. Cover price 65p. Cover art by Melvyn.
   Contents: *The Grey God Passes; A Thunder of Trumpets; Marchers of Valhalla; Sea Curse; Out of the Deep; The Thunder-Rider; "For the Love of Barbara Allen"; The Valley of the Lost.* $12.

P42b   Marchers of Valhalla. Berkley Books, New York, 1978. Berkley 425–03702. 215 pp. Cover price $1.95. Cover art and fold-out color poster by Ken Kelly.
   Contents: *Birthpangs of Hyboria,* by Fritz Leiber; *The Grey God Passes; A Thunder of Trumpets; Marchers of Valhalla; Sea Curse; Out of the Deep; The Thunder-Rider; "For the Love of Barbara Allen"; The Valley of the Lost.* $12.

P43a   Skull-Face. Berkley Books, New York, 1978. Berkley 425–03708. 248 pp. Cover price $1.95. Cover art and fold-out color poster by Ken Kelly. Frontispiece and one story heading from *Weird Tales.*
   Contents: *Pictures in the Flames—An Introduction,* by Richard A. Lupoff; *Skull-Face; Lord of the Dead; Names in the Black Book; Taverel Manor* (with Richard A. Lupoff). $12.

P44a   Son of the White Wolf. Orbit/Futura, London, England, 1977. Orbit 8600 7953. 144 pp. Cover price 65p. Cover art by Peter Jones.
   Contents: *Blood of the Gods; The Country of the Knife; Son of the White Wolf.* $15.

P44b   Son of the White Wolf. Berkley Books, New York, 1978. Berkley 425–03710. 184 pp. Cover price $1.95. Cover art and fold-out color poster by Ken Kelly.
   Contents: As P44a. $12.

P44c   Son of the White Wolf. Ace Books, New York, 1987. Ace 77521–7. 184 pp. Cover price $2.95. Cover art by Ken Kelly, same cover art as P44b.
   Contents: Same as P44a. $12.

Robert E. Howard Omnibus. Orbit Books 1977. Cover art by Peter Jones. © 1977 Glenn Lord.

Son of the White Wolf. Orbit Books 1977. Cover art by Peter Jones. © 1977 Glenn Lord.

P45a   Black Canaan. Berkley Books, New York, 1978. Berkley 425–03711. 181 pp. Cover price $1.95. Cover art and fold-out color poster by Ken Kelly.
   Contents: *Introduction,* by Gahan Wilson; *Black Canaan; Delenda Est; The Haunter of the Ring; The House in the Oaks; The Cobra in the Dream; Dermod's Bane; People of the Black Coast; The Dwellers under the Tombs; The Noseless Horror; Moon of Zambebwei.* $15.

P46a   The Last Ride. Berkley Books, New York, 1978. Berkley 425–03754. 181 pp. Cover price $1.95. Cover art and fold-out color poster by Ken Kelly.
   Contents: *The Last Ride; The Extermination of Yellow Donory; Knife, Bullet and Noose; The Devil's Joker; Vultures' Sanctuary; Law-Shooters of Cowtown; Gunman's Debt.* $15.

P47a   Solomon Kane—Skulls in the Stars. Bantam Books, Inc., New York, 1978. Bantam 12031-X. 173 pp. Cover price $1.95. Cover artist not identified. Frontispiece map by Tim Kirk.
   Contents: *Introduction,* by J. Ramsey Campbell; *Skulls in the Stars; The Right Hand of Doom; Red Shadows; Rattle of Bones; The Castle of the Devil; The Moon of Skulls; The One Black Stain; Blades of the Brotherhood.* $12.

P48a   Solomon Kane—The Hills of the Dead. Bantam Books, Inc., New York, 1979. Bantam 12166–9. 141 pp. Cover price $1.95. Cover artist not identified. Frontispiece map by Tim Kirk.
   Contents: *The Mystery of Solomon Kane,* by J. Ramsey Campbell; *The Hills of the Dead; Hawk of Basti; The Return of Sir Richard Grenville; Wings in the Night; The Footfalls Within; The Children of Asshur; Solomon Kane's Homecoming.* $12.

P49a   The Dark Man Omnibus Vol. 1. Panther Books, London, England, 1978. Panther 04293–8. 148 pp. Cover price 85p. Cover art by Peter Jones.
   Contents: *Introduction,* by August Derleth; *The Voice of El-Lil; Pigeons From Hell; The Dark Man; The Gods of Bal-Sagoth; The Man on the Ground; In the Forest of Villefère.* $25.

P50a   The Dark Man Omnibus Vol 2.: The Dead Remember. Panther Books, London, England 1979. Panther 04808–1. 128 pp. Cover price 80p. Cover artist Joe Petagno.
   Contents: *People of the Dark; The Children of the Night; The Dead Remember; The Garden of Fear; The Thing on the Roof; The Hyena; Dig Me No Grave; The Dream Snake; Old Garfield's Heart.* $35.

P51a   The Gods of Bal-Sagoth. Ace Books, New York, 1979. Ace 29525–8. 235 pp. Cover price $1.95. Cover artist not identified.
   Contents: *The Gods of Bal-Sagoth; Casonetto's Last Song; King of the Forgotten People; Usurp the Night; The Curse of the Golden Skull; The Shadow of the Beast; Nekht Semerkeht; Restless Waters; The Isle of the Eons; Afterword,* by Glenn Lord. $10.

P52a   The Howard Collector. Ace Books, New York, 1979. Ace 34458–5. Edited by Glenn Lord. 267 pp. Cover price $1.95. Cover artist not identified.

The Last Ride. Berkley Books 1978. Cover art by Ken Kelly. © 1978 Alla Ray Kuykendall and Alla Ray Morris.

Contents: *Preface*, by Glenn Lord; Part I: *Two Against Tyre; Sea Curse; The Curse of the Golden Skull; Death's Black Riders; Untitled Fragment; Spanish Gold on Devil Horse; The Heathen; The Thessalians; Ye College Days; Cupid vs. Pollux; Musings of a Moron; Sunday in a Small Town; West is West; Knife, Bullet and Noose; Sentiment; Midnight; Kelly the Conjure-Man; With a Set of Rattlesnake Rattles; The Beast from the Abyss; Hope Empty of Meaning; Life; Solomon Kane's Homecoming* (Variant Version); *Visions; Harvest; On With the Play; Roads; The Bar by the Side of the Road; Marching Song of Connacht; The Legacy of Tubal-Cain; Letters*. Part II: *Robert Ervin Howard*, by E. Hoffman Price; *Burkett News*, by Mrs. T.A. Burns; *Perhaps for Howard*, by W. Fraser Sandercombe; *Letter*, E. Hoffmann Price to H.P. Lovecraft; *Letter*, Dr. I.M. Howard to H.P. Lovecraft; *Around the Supper Table*, by James C. White; *Letter*, Dr. I.M. Howard to E. Hoffmann Price; *The Warrior*, by Emil Petaja; *R.E.H.*, by R.H. Barlow; *I Speak of Shattered Spring*, by Dale Harding Exum; *Letter*, E. Hoffmann Price to *The Acolyte; To Robert Ervin Howard*, by Wade Wellman; *Letter*, Harold Preece to Lenore Preece; *Letter*, Harold Preece to Glenn Lord. Part III: *Acheron—A Revisionary Theory*, by Robert Yaple; *Arenjun*, by Ed Lesko, Jr.; *Howard's Cannibalizing*, by Fred Blosser; *Dust*, by Bryce D. Thompson; *Conan's Parents*, by Fred Blosser; *Nameless Cults: A History*, by Charles O. Gray; *After "Recompense"*, by Wade Wellman. $15.

P53a   The Road of Azrael. Bantam Books, Inc., New York, 1980. Bantam 13326-8. 175 pp. Cover price $2.25. Cover artist not identified.
    Contents: *Introduction*, by Gordon R. Dickson; *Hawks over Egypt; The Track of Bohemund; Gates of Empire; The Road of Azrael; The Way of the Swords*. $10.

P54a   The Treasure of Tranicos. Ace Books, New York, 1980. Ace 82245-2. Revised and rewritten by L. Sprague de Camp from an original R.E. Howard story "The Black Stranger." 191 pp. Cover price $2.50. Cover art by Sanjulian. Interior illustrations by Esteban Maroto.
    Contents: *Introduction*, by L. Sprague de Camp; *The Treasure of Tranicos* (revised by L. Sprague de Camp); *The Trail of Tranicos*, by L. Sprague de Camp; *Skald in the Post Oaks*, by L. Sprague de Camp. $8.

P55a   The Flame Knife. Ace Books, New York, 1981. Ace 11666-3. Conan story revised and rewritten by L. Sprague de Camp from the original R.E. Howard oriental adventure story "Three-Bladed Doom." 158 pp. Cover price $2.50. Cover art by Sanjulian. Interior illustrations by Esteban Maroto.
    Contents: *The Flame Knife*. $8.

P56a   Heroes of Bear Creek. Ace Books, New York, 1983. Ace 32815-6. 423 pp. Cover price $3.95. Cover art by James Warhola. Reprint of D.M. Grant's hardcover editions, with the same titles.
    Contents: Part One: A Gent From Bear Creek: *Striped Shirts and Busted Hearts; Mountain Man; Meet Cap'n Kidd; Guns of the Mountains; A Gent from Bear Creek; The Feud Buster; The Road to Bear Creek; The Scalp Hunter; Cupid from Bear Creek; The Haunted Mountain; Educate or Bust; War on Bear Creek; When Bear Creek came to Chawed Ear*. Part Two: The Pride of Bear Creek: *The Riot at Cougar Paw; Pilgrims to the Pecos; High Horse Rampage; The Apache*

Mountain War; Pistol Politics; The Conquerin' Hero of the Humbolts; A Ring-Tailed Tornado. Part Three: Mayhem on Bear Creek: *"No Cowherders Wanted"; Mayhem and Taxes; Evil Deeds at Red Cougar; Sharp's Gun Serenade; The Peaceful Pilgrim; While Smoke Rolled; A Elkins Never Surrenders.* $75.

P57a   The She Devil. Ace Books, New York, 1983. Ace 76099–6. 167 pp. Cover price $2.50. Cover art by Jodi Penalva.

Contents: *She Devil; Ship in Mutiny; The Purple Heart of Erlik; The Dragon of Kao Tsu; Murderer's Grog; Desert Blood; Guns of Khartum; Daughters of Feud.* $15.

P58a   Cthulhu—The Mythos and Kindred Horrors. Baen Books, New York, 1987. Ace 65641–4. Edited by David Drake. 247 pp. Cover price $4.99. Cover art by Steve Hickman. Reprinted in 1989 and 1992.

Contents: *Introduction,* by David Drake; *Arkham; The Black Stone; The Fire of Asshurbanipal; The Thing on the Roof; Dig Me No Grave; Silence Falls on Mecca's Walls; The Valley of the Worm; The Shadow of the Beast; Old Garfield's Heart; People of the Dark; Worms of the Earth; Pigeons from Hell; An Open Window.* $12.

P59a   Robert E. Howard's World of Heroes. Robinson Publishing, London, England, 1989. Robinson 85487–001. Edited by Mike Ashley. 424 pp. Cover price £3.95. Cover art by Chris Achilleos.

Contents: *From Conan to Indiana Jones,* by Mike Ashley; *The Valley of the Worm; The Shadow Kingdom; Jewels of Gwahlur; Worms of the Earth; Kings of the Night; The Gods of Bal-Sagoth; Hawks of Outremer; Wings in the Night; Swords of Shahrazar; The Daughter of Erlik Khan.* $40.

P60a   Cormac Mac Art. Baen Publishing Enterprises, New York, 1995. Baen 87651. 209 pp. Cover price $5.99. Cover art by Ken Kelly.

Contents: *Introduction: Ancient History,* by David Drake; *A Note on the Text,* by David Drake; *The Land Toward Sunset,* by David Drake; *Tigers of the Sea,* with David Drake; *Swords of the Northern Sea; Night of the Wolf; The Temple of Abomination; The Temple of Abomination* (Outline). $12.

P61a   Eons of the Night. Baen Publishing Enterprises, New York, 1996. Baen 87717. 238 pp. Cover price $5.99. Cover art by Ken Kelly.

Contents: *Robert E. Howard,* by S.M. Stirling; *Introduction; The House of Arabu; The Garden of Fear; The Twilight of the Grey Gods; Spear and Fang; Delenda Est; Marchers of Valhalla; Sea Curse; Out of the Deep; In the Forest of Villefére; Wolfshead.* $12.

P62a   Trails in Darkness. Baen Publishing Enterprises, New York, 1996. Baen 87726. 231 pp. Cover price $5.99. Cover art by Ken Kelly.

Contents: *Introduction,* by S.M. Stirling; *The Dead Remember; Black Canaan; Kelly the Conjure-Man; The Valley of the Lost; The Man on the Ground; Black Hound of Death; "For the Love of Barbara Allen"; The Hoofed Thing; Moon of Zambebwei; The Horror from the Mound.* $12.

P63a   Beyond the Borders. Baen Publishing Enterprises, New York, 1996. Baen 87742. 245 pp. Cover price $5.99. Cover art by Ken Kelly.

The She-Devil. Ace Books 1983. Cover art by Jodi Penalva. © 1983 Alla Ray Kuykendall and Alla Ray Morris.

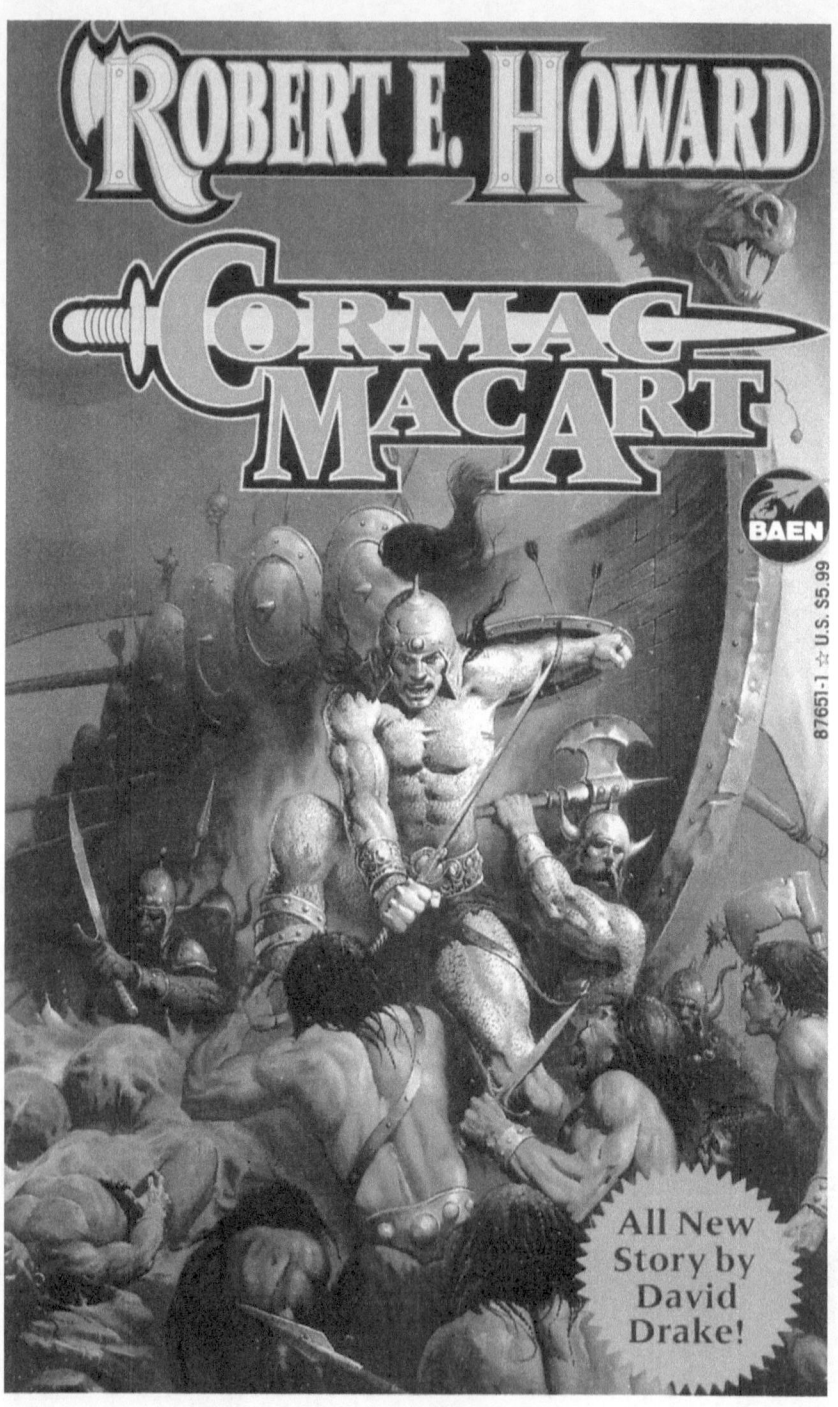

Cormac Mac Art. Baen Publishing Enterprises 1995. Cover art by Ken Kelly. © 1995 Baen Books, Glenn Lord and Alla Ray Morris.

Eons of the Night. Baen Publishing Enterprises 1996. Cover art by Ken Kelly. © 1996 Alla Ray Morris.

Trails in Darkness. Baen Publishing Enterprises 1996. Cover art by Ken Kelly. © 1996 Alla Ray Morris.

Beyond the Borders. Baen Publishing Enterprises 1996. Cover art by Ken Kelly. © 1996 Alla Ray Morris.

Contents: *Introduction,* by T.K.F. Weisskopf; *The Voice of El-Lil; The Cairn on the Headland; Casonetto's Last Song; The Cobra in the Dream; Dig Me No Grave; The Haunter of the Ring; Dermod's Bane; King of the Forgotten People; The Children of the Night; The Dream Snake; The Hyena; People of the Black Coast; The Fire of Asshurbanipal.* $12.

Addendum

P64a Echoes of Valor. TOR Fantasy Book, New York, 1987. TOR 55750-6. Edited by Karl Edward Wagner. 286 pp. Cover price $2.95. Cover art by Ken Kelly. This volume includes the first complete, unedited publication of "The Black Stranger" as Robert E. Howard wrote it.

Contents: Acknowledgments; Editor's Introduction to *The Black Stranger,* by Karl Edward Wagner; *The Black Stranger,* by Robert E. Howard; *Adept's Gambit,* by Fritz Leiber; *Wet Magic,* by Henry Kuttner. $20.

C. Magazines

The pulp magazines of the 1920s and 1930s was the media that first introduced the American reader to the fiction of Robert E. Howard. His first story "Spear and Fang" appeared in the July 25 issue of the magazine *Weird Tales*, followed by many other stories and verse, some published well beyond his untimely death. But *Weird Tales* was not the only magazine that Howard wrote for and his stories were published in a variety of adventure, action, fantasy, science fiction and sports magazines.

The following listing is presented in alphabetical order, while individual issues under a magazine heading are listed in chronological order. The inclusion of the word 'cover' following the year, indicates that the cover art illustrates the Howard contribution to that issue. The suggested values listed are for magazines in "very good" condition. Magazines in better condition will demand higher prices, and those in lower grades may sell for less. Because of their inexpensive material and binding, there is a prominent difference in the value of a "fine" copy and the average used and well-read pulp magazine. The majority of issues on the market today grades no higher than "good" or "very good" at best. There is a common tendency to over-grade pulp magazines. Please refer to Chapter 4 for grading criteria.

The listing includes only commercially produced, mass market magazines. Limited by volume restriction, it does not include Howard material published in amateur press journals or fanzines, newspapers, school papers, privately printed publications or limited edition specialty magazines.

M1 Action Stories (Fiction House)

Jan.	1931	The TNT Punch	$125
Jun.	1931	The Sign of the Snake	$125
Oct.	1931	Blow the Chinks Down	$125
Nov.	1931	Breed of Battle	$125
Jan.	1932	Dark Shanghai	$125
Mar.	1934	Mountain Man	$125
May.	1934	Guns of the Mountain	$125
Aug.	1934	The Scalp Hunter	$125
Oct.	1934 cover	A Gent from Bear Creek	$150
Dec.	1934	The Road to Bear Creek	$125
Feb.	1935	The Haunted Mountain	$125
Apr.	1935	War on Bear Creek	$125
Jun.	1935	The Feud Buster	$125
Aug.	1935	Cupid from Bear Creek	$125
Oct.	1935 cover	The Riot at Cougar Paw	$150
Dec.	1935	The Apache Mountain War	$125
Feb.	1936 cover	Pilgrims to the Pecos	$150
Apr.	1936	Pistol Politics	$125
Jun.	1936	Evil Deeds at Red Cougar	$125
Aug.	1936	High Horse Rampage	$100
Sep.	1936 cover	"No Cowherders Wanted"	$125
Oct.	1936	The Conquerin' Hero of the Humbolts	$100
Jan.	1937 cover	Sharp's Gun Serenade	$125

M2 Argosy All-Story Weekly (Munsey)

Jul.	1929	Crowd-Horror	$150

M3 Argosy (Munsey)

Aug.	1936	The Dead Remember	$100
Oct.	1936	A Gent from the Pecos	$100
Oct.	1936	Gents on the Lynch	$100
Oct.	1936	The Riot at Bucksnort	$100
Nov.	1936	Vultures' Sanctuary	$100

M4 Avon Fantasy Reader (Avon)

# 2	1947	The Mirrors of Tuzun Thune	$35
# 7	1948	The Cairn on the Headland	$25
# 8	1948 cover	Queen of the Black Coast	$25
# 10	1949 cover	A Witch Shall Be Born	$25
# 12	1950 cover	The Blonde Goddess of Bal-Sagoth	$25
# 14	1950 cover	The Temptress of the Tower of Torture and Sin	$25
# 18	1952 cover	The Witch From Hell's Kitchen	$25

M5 Complete Stories (Street & Smith)

Aug.	1936 cover	The Country of the Knife	$100

M6 Cowboy Stories (Street & Smith)

Jun.	1936	A Man-Eating Jeopard	$175
Jul.	1937	Knife-River Prodigal	$150

M7	**Dime Sports Magazine** (Popular)		
Apr.	1936	*Iron Jaw*	$100
M8	**Double-Action Western Magazine** (Columbia)		
Dec.	1956	*While Smoke Rolled*	$50
M9	**Famous Fantastic Mysteries** (Popular)		
Dec.	1952 cover	*Skull-Face*	$20
Jun.	1953	*Worms of the Earth*	$30
M10	**Fantastic** (Ziff-Davis)		
May.	1961	*The Garden of Fear*	$35
Dec.	1961	*The Dead Remember*	$35
Jan.	1967	*The People of the Black Circle*	$40
M11	**Fantastic Universe** (King-Size Publishing)		
Oct.	1955	*Hawks over Shem* (w/de Camp)	$10
Dec.	1955	*Conan, Man of Destiny* (w/de Camp)	$10
Apr.	1956	*The Blood-Stained God* (w/de Camp)	$10
Dec.	1956	*Gods of the North*	$10
M12	**Fantasy Fiction** (Future)		
Aug.	1953	*The Frost Giant's Daughter* (de Camp)	$25
M13	**Fantasy Magazine** (Future)		
Mar.	1953	*The Black Stranger* (w/de Camp)	$20
M14	**Fight Stories** (Fiction House)		
Jul.	1929	*The Pit of the Serpent*	$250
Feb.	1930	*The Bull Dog Breed*	$250
Mar.	1930	*Sailor's Grudge*	$250
May.	1930	*Fist and Fang*	$250
Jun.	1930	*The Iron Man*	$250
Jul.	1930	*Winner Take All*	$250
Sep.	1930	*Waterfront Fists*	$200
Nov.	1930	*Champ of the Forecastle*	$200
Jan.	1931	*Alleys of Peril*	$125
May.	1931	*Texas Fists*	$125
Dec.	1931	*Circus Fists*	$125
Feb.	1932	*Vikings of the Gloves*	$125
Mar.	1932	*Night of Battle*	$125
Fal.	1937	*Manila Manslaughter*	$125
Win.	1937	*You Got to Kill a Bulldog*	$125
Spr.	1938	*Costigan vs. Kid Camera*	$100
Jun.	1938	*Champ of the Seven Seas*	$100
Win.	1938	*Cannibal Fists*	$100
Sum.	1939	*Shanghaied Mitts*	$100
Win.	1939	*Sucker*	$100
Sum.	1940	*Stand Up and Slug!*	$75
Fal.	1940	*"...Includin' the Scandinavian"*	$75
Win.	1940	*Leather Lightning*	$75
Fal.	1941	*The Waterfront Wallop*	$75

Spr.	1942	*Sampson Had a Soft Spot*	$75
Sum.	1942	*Slugger Bait*	$75
Fal.	1942	*Shore Leave for a Slugger*	$75

M15 Ghost Stories (Macfadden)
Apr.	1929	*The Apparition in the Prize Ring*	$150

M16 Golden Fleece (Sun)
Nov.	1938 cover	*Black Vulmea's Vengeance*	$125
Jan.	1939	*Gates of Empire*	$100

M17 Hopalong Cassidy's Western Magazine (Standard)
Fal.	1950	*Texas John Alden*	$175

M18 Jack Dempsey's Fight Magazine (Fiction House)
May.	1934 cover	*The Slugger's Game*	$200
Jun.	1934 cover	*General Ironfist*	$150
Aug.	1934 cover	*Sluggers of the Beach*	$150

M19 The Magazine of Fantasy and Science Fiction (Mercury)
Aug.	1966	*"For the Love of Barbara Allen"*	$25
Feb.	1967	*The Hall of the Dead*	$25

M20 Magazine of Horror (Robert Lowndes)
Jun.	1965	*Skulls in the Stars*	$25
Nov.	1965	*The Dweller in Dark Valley*	$20
Nov.	1965	*Rattle of Bones*	$20
Win.	1966	*Destination*	$10
Sum.	1966	*Valley of the Lost*	$20
Spr.	1967	*The Vale of Lost Women*	$15
Sum.	1967	*A Song for Men That Laugh*	$10
Fal.	1967	*Dermod's Bane*	$10
Nov.	1967	*Out of the Deep*	$15
Jan.	1968	*The Years are as a Knife*	$10
May.	1968	*Kings of the Night*	$20
Jul.	1968	*Worms of the Earth*	$20
Jul.	1969	*Not Only in Death They Die*	$10
Dec.	1969	*Slumber*	$10
Feb.	1970	*The Noseless Horror*	$15
Fal.	1970	*A Song of Defeat*	$10
Apr.	1971	*The Grisly Horror*	$15

M21 Masked Rider Western (Standard)
May.	1944	*Texas John Alden*	$150

M22 Max Brand's Western Magazine (Popular)
Jan.	1950	*Shave That Hawg!*	$35
Jun.	1950	*Vultures' Sanctuary*	$35

M23 Oriental Stories (Popular)
Oct.	1930	*The Voice of El-Lil*	$250
Feb.	1931 cover	*Red Blades of Black Cathay*	$250

Apr.	1931	*Hawks of Outremer*	$250
Aut.	1931	*The Blood of Belshazzar*	$250
Win.	1932	*The Sowers of the Thunder*	$500
Spr.	1932	*Lord of Samarkand*	$500

M24 The Magic Carpet Magazine (Popular)
Jul.	1933	*The Lion of Tiberias*	$225
Jan.	1934	*Alleys of Darkness*	$225
Jan.	1934	*The Shadow of the Vulture*	$225

M25 Smashing Novels Magazine (Columbia)
Dec.	1936	*The Vultures of Whapeton*	$100

M26 Space Science Fiction (Space)
Sep.	1952	*The God in the Bowl*	$50

M27 Spaceway Science Fiction (Fantasy Pub.)
Sep.	1969	*People of the Black Coast*	$50

M28 Spicy-Adventure Stories (Culture)
Apr.	1936 cover	*She Devil*	$200
Jun.	1936	*Desert Blood*	$200
Sep.	1936	*The Dragon of Kao Tsu*	$200
Nov.	1936	*The Purple Heart of Erlik*	$200
Jan.	1937	*Murderer's Grog*	$200
Sep.	1942	*Revenge by Proxy*	$100
Oct.	1942	*Nothing to Lose*	$125
Nov.	1942	*Outlaw Working*	$100

M29 Sports Story Magazine (Street & Smith)
Sep.	1931	*College Socks*	$50
Oct.	1931	*Man With the Mystery Mitts*	$50
Dec.	1931	*The Good Knight*	$50

M30 Startling Mystery Stories (Popular)
Spr.	1967	*Secret of the Lost Valley*	$25
Fal.	1967	*A Vision*	$25
Win.	1968	*The Haunter of the Ring*	$25

M31 Star Western (Popular)
Sep.	1936	*The Curly Wolf of Sawtooth*	$75

M32 Stirring Science Stories (Albing)
Feb.	1941	*Always Comes Evening*	$20

M33 Strange Detective Stories (Metropolitan)
Dec.	1933	*Black Talons*	$150
Feb.	1934	*Fangs of Gold*	$150
Feb.	1934	*The Tomb's Secret*	$150

M34 Strange Tales (Clayton)
Jun.	1932	*People of the Dark*	$250
Jan.	1933	*The Cairn on the Headland*	$250

M35	**Super-Detective Stories** (Culture)		
May.	1934	Names in the Black Book	$150
M36	**Thrilling Adventures** (Standard)		
Jan.	1935	The Treasures of Tartary	$150
Dec.	1936	Son of the White Wolf	$100
M37	**Thrilling Mystery** (Standard)		
Feb.	1936	Graveyard Rats	$200
Jun.	1936	Black Wind Blowing	$200
M38	**Top-Notch** (Street & Smith)		
Oct.	1934	Swords of Shahrazar	$150
Dec.	1934	The Daughter of Erlik Khan	$150
Jun.	1935 cover	Hawk of the Hills	$150
Jul.	1935 cover	Blood of the Gods	$150
M39	**Weird Tales** (Popular)		
Jul.	1925	Spear and Fang	$1,500
Aug.	1925	In the Forest of Villefére	$600
Apr.	1926 cover	Wolfshead	$600
Jan.	1927	The Lost Race	$200
May.	1927	The Song of the Bats	$150
Oct.	1927	The Ride of Falume	$200
Jan.	1928	The Riders of Babylon	$150
Feb.	1928	The Dream Snake	$300
Mar.	1928	The Hyena	$200
Apr.	1928	Remembrance	$150
May.	1928	Sea Curse	$175
Jul.	1928	The Gates of Nineveh	$150
Aug.	1928 cover	Red Shadows	$350
Sep.	1928	The Harp of Alfred	$175
Dec.	1928	Easter Island	$150
Jan.	1929	Skulls in the Stars	$150
Feb.	1929	Crete	$125
Apr.	1929	Moon Mockery	$150
Jun.	1929	Rattle of Bones	$200
Jul.	1929	Forbidden Magic	$100
Aug.	1929	The Shadow Kingdom	$200
Sep.	1929	The Mirrors of Tuzun Thune	$150
Sep.	1929	The Moor Ghost	$150
Oct.	1929	Skull-Face I	$150
Nov.	1929	Skull-Face II	$150
Dec.	1929	Skull-Face III	$150
Jan.	1930	Dead Man's Hate	$100
Feb.	1930	The Fearsome Touch of Death	$125
Apr.	1930	A Song out of Midian	$100
May.	1930	Shadows on the Road	$100
Jun.	1930 cover	The Moon of Skulls I	$250
Jul.	1930	The Moon of Skulls II	$125
Aug.	1930	The Hills of the Dead	$125

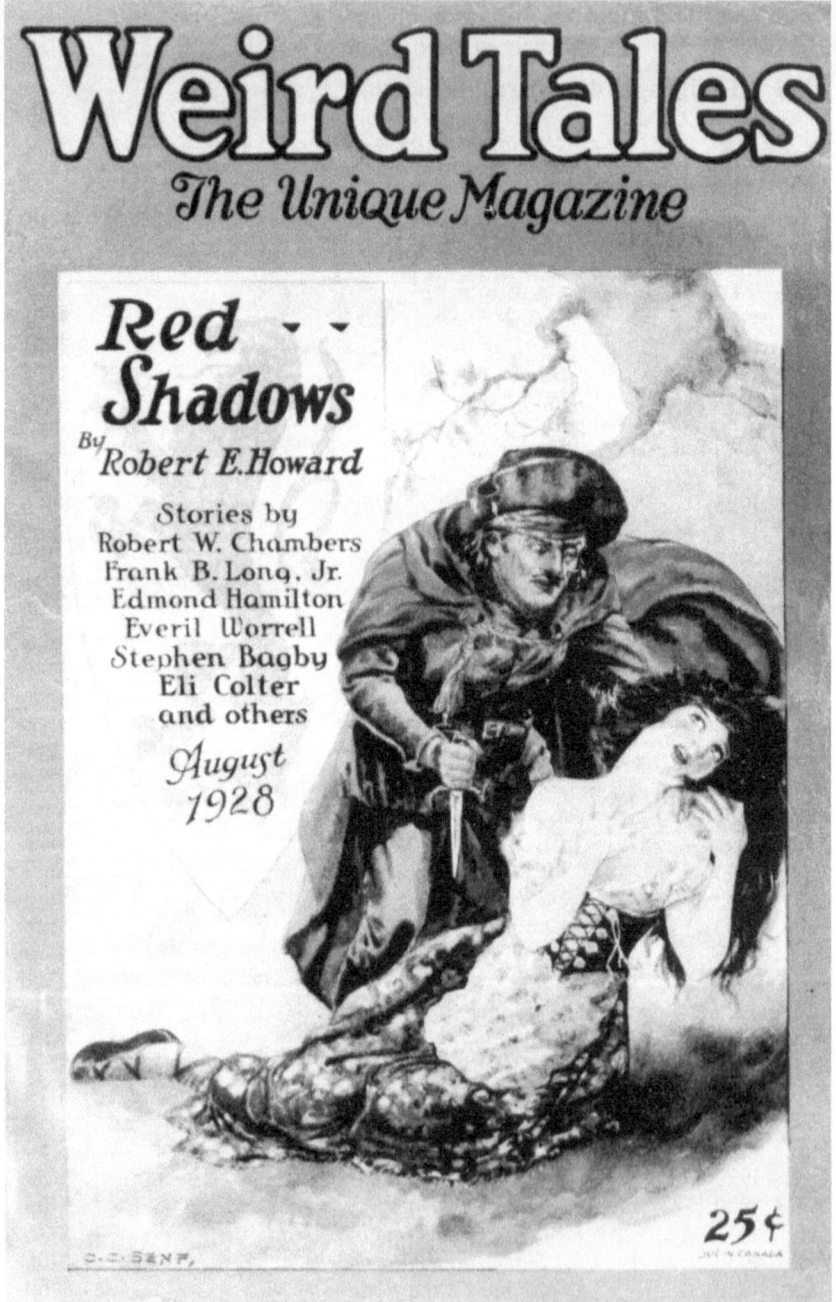

Red Shadows. Cover art by C.C. Senf. *Weird Tales*, August 1928. © 1976 Glenn Lord.

Sep.	1930	Black Chant Imperial	$125
Nov.	1930	Kings of the Night	$150
Feb.	1931	The Song of a Mad Minstrel	$100
Apr.	1931	The Children of the Night	$125
Sep.	1931	The Footfalls Within	$125
Oct.	1931	The Gods of Bal-Sagoth	$125
Nov.	1931	The Black Stone	$125
Dec.	1931 cover	The Dark Man	$200
Feb.	1932	The Thing on the Roof	$125
Mar.	1932	The Last Day	$100
May.	1932	The Horror from the Mound	$125
Jul.	1932	Wings in the Night	$125
Aug.	1932	Arkham	$100
Sep.	1932	An Open Window	$125
Nov.	1932	Worms of the Earth	$150
Dec.	1932	The Phoenix on the Sword	$500
Jan.	1933	The Scarlet Citadel	$175
Mar.	1933	The Tower of the Elephant	$125
Apr.	1933	Autumn	$100
May.	1933	Moonlight on a Skull	$100
Jun.	1933 cover	Black Colossus	$300
Jul.	1933	The Man on the Ground	$125
Sep.	1933 cover	The Slithering Shadow	$400
Oct.	1933	The Pool of the Black One	$250
Dec.	1933	Old Garfield's Heart	$100
Jan.	1934	Rogues in the House	$350
Feb.	1934	The Valley of the Worm	$125
Apr.	1934	Shadows in the Moonlight	$125
May.	1934 cover	Queen of the Black Coast	$400
Jun.	1934	The Haunter of the Ring	$100
Aug.	1934 cover	The Devil in Iron	$350
Sep.	1934 cover	The People of the Black Circle I	$350
Oct.	1934	The People of the Black Circle II	$250
Dec.	1934 cover	A Witch Shall Be Born	$600
Feb.	1935	The Grisly Horror	$175
Mar.	1935	Jewels of Gwahlur	$300
May.	1935	Beyond the Black River I	$300
Jun.	1935	Beyond the Black River II	$150
Nov.	1935 cover	Shadows in Zamboula	$400
Dec.	1935 cover	The Hour of the Dragon I	$500
Jan.	1936	The Hour of the Dragon II	$150
Feb.	1936	The Hour of the Dragon III	$150
Mar.	1936	The Hour of the Dragon IV	$100
Apr.	1936	The Hour of the Dragon V	$100
Jun.	1936	Black Canaan	$100
Jul.	1936 cover	Red Nails I	$350
Aug.	1936	Red Nails II	$225
Oct.	1936	Red Nails III	$200
Nov.	1936	Black Hound of Death	$100

The Dark Man. Cover art by C.C. Senf. *Weird Tales,* December 1931. © 1976 Glenn Lord.

A Witch Shall Be Born. Cover art by Margaret Brundage. *Weird Tales,* December 1934. © 1976 Glenn Lord.

Shadows in Zamboula. Cover art by Margaret Brundage. *Weird Tales*, November 1935. © 1976 Glenn Lord.

Dec.	1936 cover	The Fire of Asshurbanipal	$400
Feb.	1937	Dig Me No Grave	$100
Aug.	1937	The Soul-Eater	$75
Sep.	1937	The Dream and the Shadow	$75
Oct.	1937	Which Will Scarcely Be Understood	$75
Nov.	1937	Futility	$75
Dec.	1937	Fragment	$75
Feb.	1938	Haunting Columns	$75
Mar.	1938	The Poets	$75
Apr.	1938	The Singer in the Mist	$75
May.	1938	Pigeons from Hell	$100
Jun.	1938	The Last Hour	$75
Jul.	1938	Ships	$75
Aug.	1938	Lines Written in the Realization That I Must Die	$75
Sep.	1938	A Thunder of Trumpets	$75
Nov.	1938	Recompense	$75
Dec.	1938	The Ghost Kings	$75
Feb.	1939	The King and the Oak	$50
Mar.	1939	Desert Dawn	$50
May.	1939	Almuric I	$75
Jun.	1939	Almuric II	$50
Aug.	1939	Almuric III	$50
Jun.	1939	The Hills of Kandahar	$50
Oct.	1939	Worms of the Earth	$50
Nov.	1951	Pigeons from Hell	$35
Nov.	1953	The Black Stone	$20
Sep.	1954	The Dark Man	$20
Sum.	1973	Spear and Fang	$30
Fal.	1973	The Man on the Ground	$10
Win.	1973	Sea Curse	$10

M40 Western Aces (Ace)
| Oct. | 1935 | Boot-Hill Payoff | $75 |

M41 Zane Grey Western Magazine (Margulies)
| Jun. | 1970 | The Extermination of Yellow Donory | $25 |

D. Special Publications

With a few exceptions, the private printings of Robert E. Howard's work began with Glenn Lord's "Etchings in Ivory" in 1968, followed by Roy A. Squires limited printings of a few of Howard's poems beginning in 1972. From then and to the present, individuals and small publishing enterprises have released a multitude of Robert E. Howard publications. These printings are usually in the format of pamphlets or chapbooks bound in wraps, limited in the number of copies printed and containing a single or a few poems or stories. Because of their small numbers and usually high quality of material and craftsmanship, they have increased substantially in value since they were first released. Along with high grade, key pulp magazines and some amateur press publications, they are showing the fastest escalating value of Robert E. Howard collectibles.

The publications are listed chronologically, in the order they were published in. Reprints of a title are not listed individually, unless they varies from the first edition by publisher, format or contents. Reprints and variants of a title are listed under the original title as a, b, c, or d as may be appropriate. The suggested values indicated are for titles in "fine" condition. Specimens in better condition will demand higher prices and copies in lower grades may sell for less.

S1a **The Hyborian Age.** LANY Cooperative Publishers, Los Angeles, 1938. 22 pp. Wraps. Copies printed not stated. Cover price $.35. Interior map of the Hyborian Age by Robert E. Howard and linoleum cut of Howard by Duane W. Rimel.
  Contents: *Dedication and Foreword; Introduction,* A Letter from H.P. Lovecraft to Donald A. Wollheim; *The Hyborian Age; A Probable Outline of Conan's Career,* by P. Schuyler Miller and John D. Clark. $800.

S2a **The Garden of Fear.** Crawford Publishing House, Los Angeles, California, 1945. 12mo. 79 pp. Wraps. Copies printed not stated. Cover price $.25. Cover art by Alva Rogers. Exists in three cover color variants, blue, green and yellow. Poor quality paper. Hard to find in collectable condition.
  Contents: *The Garden of Fear,* by Robert E. Howard; *The Man with the Hour Glass,* by L.A. Eshbach; *Celephais,* by H.P. Lovecraft; *Mars Colonizes,* by Miles J. Breuer; *The Golden Bough,* by David H. Keller. $35.

S3a **The Challenge from Beyond.** The Pennsylvania Dutch Cheese Press, 1954. 11 pp. Wraps. Copies printed not stated. Published by William H. Evans for distribution through the Fantasy Amateur Press Association.
  Contents: *The Challenge From Beyond,* with C.L. Moore, A Merritt, H.P. Lovecraft and Frank Belknap Long. $500.

S3b **The Illustrated Challenge from Beyond.** Necronomicon Press, West Warwick, Rhode Island, 1978. 8 vol. 28 pp. Wraps. 750 numbered copies printed. Cover price $5.95. Cover art and three interior illustrations by David Ireland.
  Contents: As S3a. $40.

S3c **The Challenge from Beyond.** Necronomicon Press, West Warwick, Rhode Island, 1990. 8vo. 32 pp. Wraps. Copies printed not stated. Cover price $4.50. Cover art by Robert H. Knox. Contains two back-to-back versions of the same story written by different authors. Reprinted in 1997.
  Contents: *The Challenge From Beyond,* by C.L. Moore, A. Merritt, H.P. Lovecraft, Robert E. Howard and Frank Belknap Long. *The Challenge From Beyond,*

by Stanley G. Weinbaum, Donald Wandrei, Edward E. Smith, Harl Vincent and Murray Leinster. $20.

S4a Etchings in Ivory. Glenn Lord, Pasadena, Texas, 1968. 12mo. 26 pp. Poems in Prose. Wraps. 268 copies printed. Cover price $1.25. A pirated edition exists with Robert E. Howard's name on the front cover set in upper and lower case. On the original printing, the name appears in all upper case.

  Contents: *Introduction,* by Donald S. Fryer; *Proem; Flaming Marble; Skulls and Orchids; Medallions in the Moon; The Gods That Men Forget; Bloodstones and Ebony.* $200.

S4b Etchings in Ivory. Hall Publications, Aberdeen, Maryland, 1975. 8vo. 18 pp. Wraps. Copies printed not stated. Cover price $3.95. Title page decoration and seven interior illustrations by John Stewart.

  Contents: *Introduction,* by Wayne Warfield; *Proem; Flaming Marble; Skulls and Orchids; Medallions in the Moon; The Gods That Men Forget; Bloodstones and Ebony.* $35.

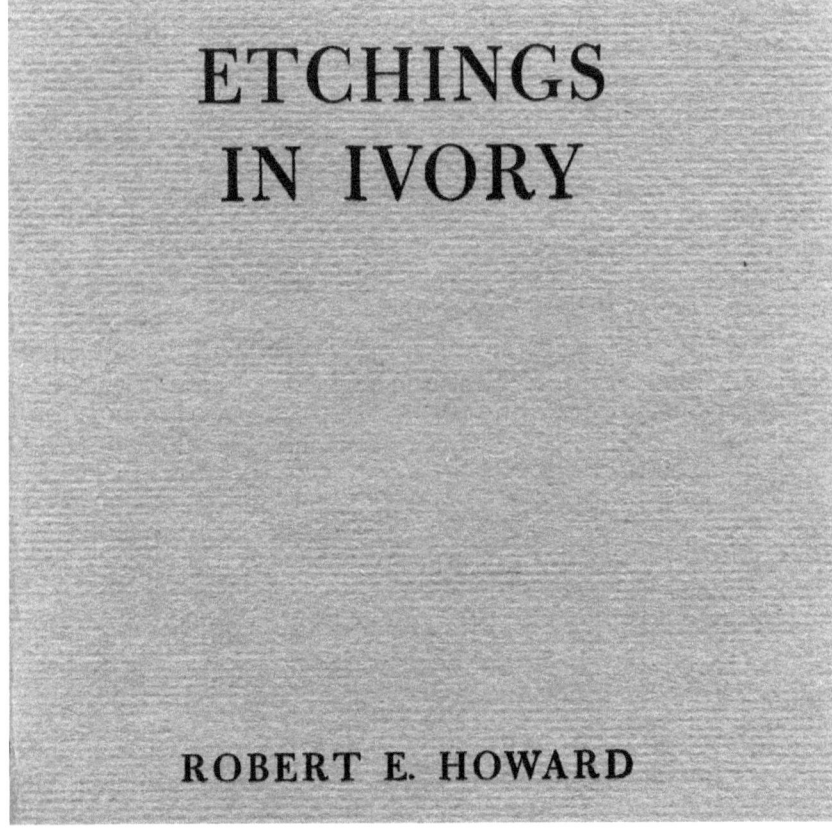

Etchings in Ivory. Glenn Lord 1968. No cover art. © 1968 Glenn Lord.

S5a Black Dawn. Roy A Squires, Glendale, California 1972. 7 unnumbered pages. Poem. Wraps. 234 numbered copies printed. Cover price $5.00.
 Contents: *Black Dawn.* $75.

S6a The Road to Rome. Roy A. Squires, Glendale, California, 1972. 6 unnumbered pages. Poem. Wraps. 217 numbered copies printed. Cover price $5.00.
 Contents: *The Road to Rome.* $75.

S7a A Song of the Naked Lands. Roy A. Squires, Glendale, California, 1973. 6 unnumbered pages. Poem. Wraps. 230 numbered copies printed. Cover price $5.00.
 Contents: *A Song of the Naked Lands.* $75.

S8a The Gold and the Grey. Roy A. Squires, Glendale, California, 1974. Poem. Wraps. 218 numbered copies printed. Cover price $5.00.
 Contents: *The Gold and the Grey.* $75.

S9a Altars and Jesters: An Opium Dream. Roy A. Squires, Glendale, California, 1974. Poem. Wraps. 218 numbered copies printed. Cover price $5.00.
 Contents: *Altars and Jesters.* $75.

S10a Verses in Ebony. George T. Hamilton, Yorba Linda, California, 1974. 16mo. 28 unnumbered pages. Wrappers with color prints by Kirwan. Comes in a decorated envelope. 50 copies printed. Cover price not listed. Unauthorized mock-up for approval for projected publication, which was eventually released in 1975 with authorization, but with a different contents.
 Contents: *Black Dawn; The Road to Rome; The Gold and the Grey; A Song of the Naked Lands.* $200.

S11a Verses in Ebony. George T. Hamilton, Yorba Linda, California, 1975. 16mo. 18 unnumbered pages. Wraps with dust jacket. Comes in a decorated envelope. 263 copies printed. Cover price not listed. Black and white jacket art by Kirwan. There exists a 1974 mock-up of this publication with colored jacket art, which was printed in 50 copies.
 Contents: *Empire; A Legend of Faring Town; Echoes from an Anvil; The Night Winds; Men Build Them Houses; Viking's Trail; Swamp Murder; Alien; Singing Hemp; The Outgoing of Sigurd the Jerusalem-Farer; To a Friend; Revolt Pagan; To All the Lords of Commerce.* $100.

S12a Valley of the Lost. Charles Miller, Columbia, Pennsylvania, 1975. 8vo. 21pp. Wraps. 777 numbered copies printed. Cover price $3.00. Title page illustration and five interior illustrations by Bot Roda.
 Contents: *Valley of the Lost.* $35.

S13a The Grey God Passes. Charles Miller, Columbia, Pennsylvania, 1975. 8vo. 36 pp. Wraps. Copies printed not stated. Cover price $4.00. Title page illustration and five interior illustrations by Walt Simonson.
 Contents: *The Grey God Passes.* $40.

VALLEY OF THE LOST

ROBERT E. HOWARD

Valley of the Lost. Charles Miller 1975. No cover art. © 1975 Glenn Lord.

S14a Rhymes of Death. Dennis McHaney, Memphis, Tennessee, 1975. 8vo. 29 pp. Wraps with dust jacket. 600 numbered copies printed. Cover price not listed. Frontispiece, title page decoration and ten interior illustrations by Tom Foster.
    Contents: *An Open Window; Arkham; Which Will Scarcely Be Understood; Fragment; The Tempter; Niflheim; Emancipation; Ecstacy; A Hairy Chested Idealist Sings; The Ballad of Bucksnort Roberts; Futility; The End of the Glory Trail.* $40.

S15a **Two Against Tyre.** Dennis McHaney, Memphis, Tennessee, 1975. 8vo. 26 pp. Wraps. 900 unnumbered copies printed. Cover price $3.00. Cover art and three b/w interior illustrations by Stephen Fabian.
  Contents: *Two Against Tyre.* $20.

S15b **Two Against Tyre.** Dennis McHaney, Memphis, Tennessee, 1975. 8vo. 26 pp. Wraps with double, differently colored covers. 600 numbered copies printed on 70 lb paper. Cover price $4.00. Cover art and three b/w interior illustrations by Stephen Fabian.
  Contents: *Two Against Tyre.* $40.

S16a **Blades for France.** George T. Hamilton, Yorba Linda, California, 1975. 8vo. 22 pp. Wraps with dust jacket. 300 copies printed. Cover price $5.45. Cover art and interior illustrations by Stephen Fabian.
  Contents: *Introduction,* by E. Hoffmann Price; *Blades for France.* $70.

S17a **Shadow of the Hun.** George T. Hamilton, Yorba Linda, California, 1975. 8vo. 22 pp. Wraps with dust jacket. 318 copies printed. Cover price $5.45. Jacket art and interior illustrations by Stephen Fabian.
  Contents: *Foreword,* by Tevis Clyde Smith; *Shadow of the Hun.* $70.

S18a **Isle of Pirate's Doom.** George T. Hamilton, Yorba Linda, California, 1975. 8vo. 35 pp. Wraps with dust jacket. 302 copies printed. Cover price $5.45. Jacket art and interior illustrations by Stephen Fabian.
  Contents: *Introduction,* by Fred Blosser; *Isle of Pirate's Doom.* $50.

S19a **The King's Service.** George T. Hamilton, Yorba Linda, California, 1976. 8vo. 18 pp. Wraps with dust jacket. 310 copies printed. Cover price $5.45. Jacket art, frontispiece and interior illustrations by Stephen Fabian.
  Contents: *Introduction,* by Richard L. Tierney; *The King's Service.* $75.

S20a **Runes of Ahrh-Eih-Eche.** Jonathan Bacon, Lamoni, Iowa, 1976. 4to. 38 pp. Wraps. 1,000 numbered and signed copies printed. Cover price not listed. Cover art by Randall Spurgin.
  Contents: *Acknowledgments; Introduction,* by Jonathan Bacon; *Letters; Howardian Alphabet,* by Randall Spurgin. Appendix: *Ghost Camp of Colorado.* $50.

S21a **The Grim Land and Others.** Jonathan Bacon, Stygian Isle Press, Lamoni, Iowa, 1976. 8vo. 36 unnumbered pages. 450 numbered and signed copies printed. Cover price not listed. Cover Art by Lee Brown Coye. Interior illustrations by various artists.
  Contents: *Introduction,* by Tevis Clyde Smith; *The Devils Woodchopper* (fragment completed by Tevis Clyde Smith); *Ballade of Some Howard Heroes,* by Tevis Clyde Smith; *Nectar; The Grim Land; The Gods of the Jungle Drums; De Ole River Ox; The Road to Yesterday; The Adventurer; To An Earthbound Soul; The Outcast; Today; A Pirate Remembers.* $75.

S22a **Bicentennial Tribute to Robert E. Howard.** George T. Hamilton, Yorba Linda, California, 1976. 8vo. 37 pp. Wraps with dust jacket. 194 copies printed. Cover price $5.95. Jacket art, frontispiece and interior illustrations by Stephen Fabian. Photos of Glenn Lord, Stephen E. Fabian and Fred Blosser.

Two Against Tyre. Dennis McHaney 1975. Cover art by Stephen Fabian. © 1975 Glenn Lord and Stephen Fabian.

Blades for Frances. George T. Hamilton 1975. Cover art by Stephen Fabian. © 1975 Glenn Lord and George T. Hamilton.

HAMILTON

Bicentennial Tribute to Robert E. Howard. George T. Hamilton 1976. Cover art by Stephen Fabian. © 1976 George T. Hamilton.

Contents: *Howard's Atlantis,* by Fred Blosser; *Three from Grant,* by Fred Blosser; *Interview with Steve Fabian,* by George T. Hamilton; *Some Notes on Publishing REH,* by Donald M. Grant; *The Return of the Sorcerer,* by Robert E. Howard; *Ultima Thule, Number 2,* by Glenn Lord; *Ultima Thule, Number 3,* by Glenn Lord. $100.

S23a   Voices of the Night and Other Poems. Necronomicon Press, West Warwick, Rhode Island, 1976. 8 pp. Wraps. 500 copies printed. Cover price $1.00. No cover art.

   Contents: *Voices of the Night; Song at Midnight; Always Comes Evening.* $100.

S24a   The Shadow of the Beast. George T. Hamilton, Yorba Linda, California, 1977. 8vo. 27 pp. Wraps with dust jacket. 280 copies printed. Cover price $5.95. Cover art and interior illustrations by Stephen Fabian.

   Contents: *The Shadow of the Beast; Tomb of the Dragon.* $50.

S25a   Up, John Kane! and Other Poems. Roy A. Squires, Glendale, California, 1977. 8vo. 8 unnumbered pages. Poems. Wraps. 353 numbered copies printed. Cover price not listed.

   Contents: *Up John Kane!; When Death Drops Her Veil; A Dying Pirate Speaks of Treasure; Mad Meg Gill; Dreams.* $75.

S26a   The Illustrated Gods of the North. Necronomicon Press, West Warwick, Rhode Island, 1977. 8vo. 16 unnumbered pages. Wraps. 750 numbered copies printed. Cover price not listed. Interior illustrations by Mark King.

   Contents: *Gods of the North.* $35.

S27a   Spears of Clontarf. George T. Hamilton, Placentia, California, 1978. 8vo. 38 pp. Wraps with dust jacket. 152 copies printed. Cover price $5.95. Cover art and interior illustrations by Stephen Fabian.

   Contents: *Letter,* to Mr. Bates from Robert E. Howard; *Spears of Clontarf.* $70.

S27b   Spears of Clontarf. Thomas Kovacs, Dark Carnival Press, Zurich, Switzerland, 1986. 4to. 30 pp. Wraps. Swiss publication printed in English. 80 numbered copies printed. Cover art and illustrations by Bodo Schafer.

   Contents: *Spears of Clontarf.* $50.

S28a   The Ghost Ocean. Gibbelins Gazette, Knoxville, Tennessee, 1982. Compiled by Vernon Clark and Rusty Burke. 46 pp. Wraps. 360 numbered copies printed (50 hardcover copies). Cover price not listed. Cover art and interior illustrations by Rick McCollum, Steven R. Trout and Charles Williams, Jr.

   Contents: *The Isle of Hy-Brasil; The One Black Stain; Viking's Vision; To All Sophisticates; Man Am I; Never Beyond the Beast; Shadows from Yesterday; The Ghost Ocean; The Song of the Last Briton; The Gates of Babylon; Lilith; Two Men; Memories of Alfred; To a Woman; When the Glaciers Rumbled South; Candles; Shadow Thing; Song of the Pict; The Flood; The Adventurer's Mistress.* $115.

S29a   Bran Mak Morn: A Play and Others. Cryptic Publications, Bloomfield, New Jersey, 1983. 80 pp. Wraps. 425 copies printed (25 signed by Glenn Lord). Cover price $4.50. Cover art by Stephen Fabian.

   Contents: *Introduction,* by Marc A. Cerasini and Charles Hoffman; *Bran Mak Morn; Double Cross; The Black Moon; Hand of the Black Goddess; The Diablos Trail; Ship in Mutiny.* $100.

S30a   The Rhyme of the Three Slavers. Thomas Kovacs, Zurich, Switzerland, 1983. Broadside sheet. 250 copies printed. Numbered and signed by publisher. Published for the Raven Club.
  Contents: *The Rhyme of the Three Slavers.* $25.

S31a   Two-Fisted Detective Stories. Cryptic Publications, Bloomfield, New Jersey, 1984. Edited by Robert M. Price. 8 vo. 71 pp. Wraps. 500 copies printed (50 numbered copies signed by Price and Fabian; 26 lettered copies and 20 presentation copies). Cover price $4.50. Cover art and interior illustrations by Stephen Fabian.
  Contents: *Introduction,* by Marc A. Cerasini and Charles Hoffmen; *The Silver Heel; The Voice of Death; Untitled Synopsis; Sons of Hate.* $45.

S32a   The Adventures of Lal Singh. Cryptic Publications, Mount Olive, North Carolina, 1985. 8 vo. 20 pp. Wraps. Copies printed not stated. Cover price $3.00. Cover art by Stephen Fabian.
  Contents: *Introduction,* by Robert M. Price; *The Tale of the Rajah's Ring; The Further Adventures of Lal Singh; Lal Singh, Oriental Gentleman.* $75.

S33a   Pay Day. Cryptic Publications, Mount Olive, North Carolina, 1986. 20 pp. Wraps. Copies printed not stated. Cover price $3.50. Cover art by Stephen Fabian.
  Contents; *Introduction,* by Robert M. Price; *A Touch of Color; The Loser; A Horror in the Night; Nerve; The Sophisticate; The Block; The Nut's Shell; Pay Day.* $75.

S34a   Writer of the Dark. Thomas Kovacs, Dark Carnival Press, Zurich, Switzerland, 1986. 180 pp. Wraps. Swiss publication printed in English. 500 numbered copies printed. 200 were bound in a red cover with illustration of a rat, 300 were bound in undecorated tan covers. Cover price not listed. Cover art and illustrations by Bodo Schafer.
  Contents: *Foreword,* by Thomas Kovacs; *Introduction,* by Glenn Lord; *Letter*: Robert E. Howard to Tevis Clyde Smith; Poems: *Skulls; Ghost Dancers; Long Ago; Tiger Girl; Let the Gods Die; Swamp Murder; The Cooling of Spike McRue; A Legend; The Song of the Gallows Tree; Song Before Clontarf.* Stories: *The Ghost with the Silk Hat; Graveyard Rats; Teeth of Doom; The Mark of the Bloody Hand; Spears of Clontarf; A Gent from the Pecos.* Red cover $125, tan cover $75.

S35a   Lurid Confession # 1. Cryptic Publications, Mount Olive, North Carolina, 1986. 8 vo. 41 pp. Wraps. Copies printed not stated. Cover price $4.00. Cover art by Stephen Fabian.
  Contents: *Scandal Sheet,* by Robert M. Price; *I Model My Soul,* by Carl Jacobi; *The Curse of Greed; A Matter of Age; The Voice of the Mob; The Devil in His Brain; I Wore the Brassiere of Doom,* by Sally Theobald; *True Ghostly Confessions,* by Will Murray. $45.

S36a   Lewd Tales. Cryptic Publications, Mount Olive, North Carolina, 1987. 8 vo. 22 pp. Wraps. Copies printed not stated. Cover price $4.00. Cover art by Stephen Fabian.

Contents: *Introduction,* by Robert M. Price; *Songs of Bastards* (play); *Bastards All* (play); *Ancient Englishe Ballad.* $50.

S37a   North of Khyber. Cryptic Publications, Mount Olive, North Carolina, 1987. 8 vo. 44 pp. Wraps. Copies printed not stated. Cover price $5.00. Cover art by Stephen Fabian.

Contents: *Introduction,* by Robert M. Price; *North of Khyber; The Land of Mystery; El Borak; The Shunned Castle; A Power Among the Islands.* $50.

S38a   The Coming of El Borak. Cryptic Publications, Mount Olive, North Carolina, 1987. 8 vo. 60 pp. Wraps. Copies printed not stated. Cover price $5.00. Cover art by Stephen Fabian.

Contents: *Introduction,* by Robert M. Price; *The Coming of El Borak; Khoda Khan's Tale; The Iron Terror;* Untitled fragment; *El Borak.* $50.

S39a   Neolithic Love Song. Thomas Kovacs, Zurich, Switzerland, 1987. Broadside sheet. 36 copies printed. Numbered and signed by publisher. Art by Thomas Geissmann.

Contents: *Neolithic Love Song.* $25.

S40a   The Sonora Kid. Cryptic Publications, Mount Olive, North Carolina, 1988. 8 vo. 40 pp. Wraps. Copies printed not stated. Cover price $5.00. Cover art by Stephen Fabian.

Contents: *The West Tower; Brotherly Advice; Desert Rendezvous; Red Curls and Bobbed Hair; The Sonora Kid-Cowhand; The Sonora Kid's Winning Hand* (fragment); Untitled/unfinished (*A blazing sun...*); Untitled/unfinished (*The Hades Saloon...*); Untitled/unfinished (*The hot Arizona sun...*); Untitled/unfinished (*Madge Meraldson set...*); Untitled/unfinished (*Steve Allison settled...*); Untitled/unfinished (*The way it came...*). $50.

S41a   The Ballad of King Geraint. Gibbelins Gazette, Knoxville, Tennessee, 1989. 70 copies printed. Wraps.

Contents: *The Ballad of King Geraint.* $75.

S42a   Desire and Other Erotic Poems. Charles Hoffman, New York, 1989. REHupa mailing "Adequate Adventure Stories #4."

Contents: *Prelude; Desire; Lilith; The Dust Dance* (Version 1, lines 53–720); *The Palace of Bast; A Negro Girl; The Harlot; The Ballad of Singapore Nell; Good Mistress Brown; The Myth; A Song for All Women; Strange Passion; Lesbia; Daughter of Evil.* $75.

S43a   No Refuge. Rusty Burke, Houston, Texas, 1989. 30 numbered copies printed.

Contents: Letter from Robert E. Howard to H.P. Lovecraft, December 1930. $50.

S44a   Selected Letters 1923–30. Necronomicon Press, West Warwick, Rhode Island, 1989. Edited by Glenn Lord with Rusty Burke and S.T. Joshi. 8vo. 84 pp. Wraps. Copies printed not stated. Cover price $9.95. Cover art by Robert H. Knox.

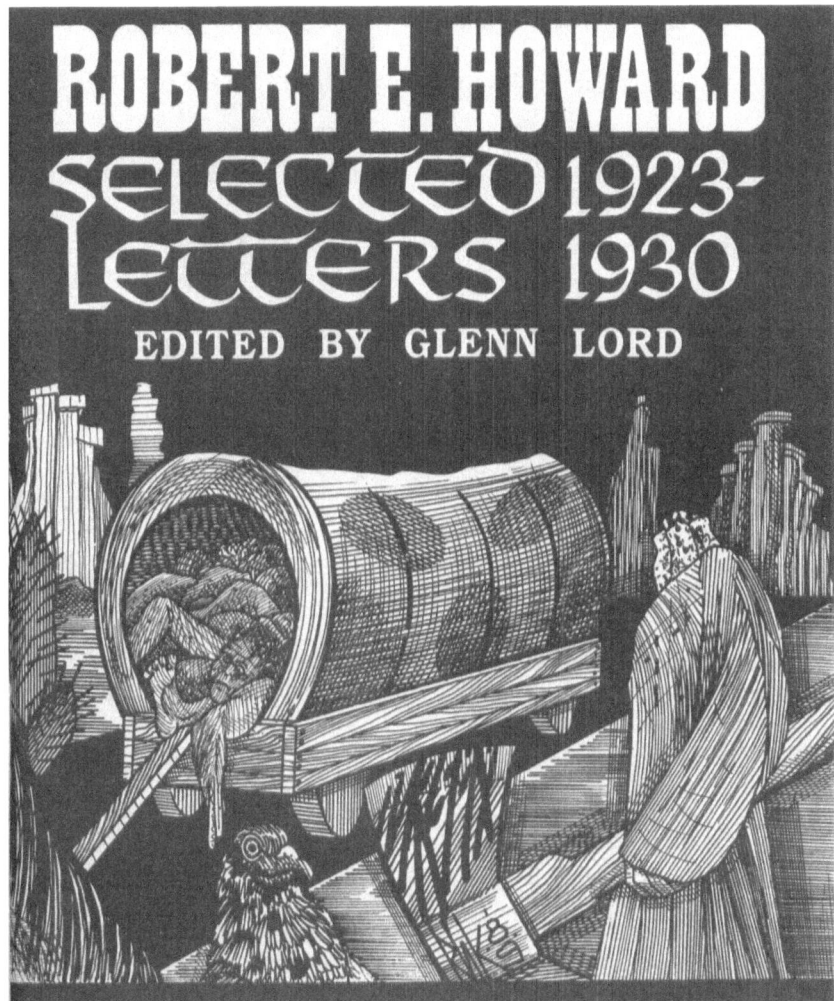

Selected Letters 1923–1930. **Necronomicon Press 1989. Cover art by Robert H. Knox. © 1989 Alla Ray Morris.**

Contents: *Introduction,* by Glenn Lord. *Letters,* from Robert E. Howard to Tevis Clyde Smith, Harold Preece, Farnsworth Wright, and H.P. Lovecraft. $50.

S45a   Robert E. Howard's Fight Magazine No. 1. Necronomicon Press, West Warwick, Rhode Island, 1990. Edited by Robert M. Price. 8vo. 48 pp. Wraps. Copies printed not stated. Cover price $4.50. Cover art by Robert H. Knox.
Contents: *In the Editor's Corner,* by Robert M. Price; *The Pit of the Serpent; The Bull Dog Breed; Sailor's Grudge; Fist and Fang; Winner Take All; Waterfront Fists.* $30.

S46a   Robert E. Howard's Fight Magazine No. 2. Necronomicon Press, West Warwick, Rhode Island, 1990. Edited by Robert M. Price. 8vo. 40 pp. Wraps. Copies printed not stated. Cover price $4.50. Cover art by Robert H. Knox.
   Contents: *The Champion of the Forecastle; Alleys of Peril; Waterfront Law; Texas Fists; The Fightin'est Pair; The Champ*(poem)*; When you Were a Set-up and I Was a Ham* (poem). $30.

S47a   Robert E. Howard's Fight Magazine No. 3. Necronomicon Press, West Warwick, Rhode Island, 1991. Edited by Robert M. Price. 8vo. 45 pp. Wraps. Copies printed not stated. Cover price $4.50. Cover art by Robert H. Knox.
   Contents: *Circus Fists; Vikings of the Gloves; Night of the Battle; The Slugger's Game; General Ironfist; Sluggers of the Beach.* $25.

S48a   Selected Letters 1931–36. Necronomicon Press, West Warwick, Rhode Island, 1991. Edited by Glenn Lord with Rusty Burke, S.T. Joshi and Steve Behrends. 8vo. 79 pp. Wraps. Copies printed not stated. Cover price $9.95. Cover art by Robert H. Knox.
   Contents: *Introduction,* by Robert M. Price; *Letters,* from Robert E. Howard to Tevis Clyde Smith, H.P. Lovecraft, Farnsworth Wright, Wilfred Blanch Talman, August Derleth, Clark Ashton Smith, and Thurston Torbett. $45.

S49a   Flight. Stolte, Reno, Nevada, 1992. Brown binding, quarter bound in black with silver lettering. 20 copies printed. Not for sale but trade.
   Contents: *Flight; Flint's Passing.* $200.

S50a   A Man-Eating Jeopard. Alla Ray Morris, Cross Plains, Texas, 1994. 8vo. 12 pp. Wraps. Copies printed not stated. Cover price not listed. Cover art and title page art from original story in *Cowboy Stories,* June 1936. Reprinted in 1998.
   Contents: *A Man-Eating Jeopard.* $40.

S51a   The Black Reaper. Millennium Publications, Kingston, Rhode Island, 1995. 4to. 32 unnumbered pages. Comic book format. Copies printed not stated. Cover price $4.95. Cover art by Terry Pavlet. Interior panels by Terry Pavlet, Carlos Phoenix Jimenez, Mark A.W. Jackson and Charles Lang.
   Contents: *Introduction,* by Terry Pavlet; *Destiny; Black Seas; Empire; A Call of Pan; A Far Country; Flaming Marble; Symbols; Musings; Love.* $25.

S52a   Robert E. Howard's Fight Magazine No. 4. Necronomicon Press, West Warwick, Rhode Island, 1996. Edited by Robert M. Price. 8vo. 40 pp. Wraps. Copies printed not stated. Cover price $5.00. Cover art and interior illustrations by Jason Eckhardt and Robert H. Knox.
   Contents: *Sailor Costigan and the Swami; By the Law of the Shark; Flying Knuckles; Hard-Fisted Sentiment; The Honor of the Ship; Two "Sailor Steve" Fragments; In the Ring* (poem)*; Slugger's Wow* (poem). $25.

S53a   Ghor, Kin-Slayer, The Saga of Genserics's Fifth-Born Son. Necronomicon Press, West Warwick, Rhode Island, 1997. 8vo. 176 pp. Wraps.

Selected Letters 1931–1936. Necronomicon Press 1991. Cover art by Robert H. Knox. © 1991 Alla Ray Morris.

Copies printed not stated. Cover price $8.95. Cover art by Robert H. Knox. Conceived in the late 1970s by Jonathan Bacon, this novel-length text is based on a single chapter by Robert E. Howard and completed by 17 noted fantasy writers. Originally intended for serialization in the amateur press journal *Fantasy Crossroads*—which was discontinued in 1979, this is the first full length edition of the entire project.

Contents: *Genseric's Son,* by Robert E. Howard; *The Coming of Ghor,* by Karl

Robert E. **HOWARD**
Karl Edward **WAGNER**
Joseph Payne **BRENNAN**
Richard L. **TIERNEY**
Michael **MOORCOCK**
Charles R. **SAUNDERS**
andrew j. **OFFUTT**
Manly Wade **WELLMAN**
Darrell **SCHWEITZER**
A. E. **VAN VOGT**
Brian **LUMLEY**
Frank Belknap **LONG**
Adrian **COLE**
Ramsey **CAMPBELL**
H. Warner **MUNN**
Marion Zimmer **BRADLEY**
Richard A. **LUPOFF**

GHOR Kin-Slayer

The Saga of Generic's Fifth-Born Son

Ghor, Kin-Slayer. Necronomicon Press 1997. Cover art by Robert H. Knox. © 1997 Necronomicon Press.

Edward Wagner; *Ghor's Revenge,* by Joseph Payne Brennan; *The Ice Woman's Prophecy,* by Richard L. Tierney; *The Nemedians,* by Michael Moorcock; *Betrayal in Belverus,* by Charles R. Saunders; *Lord General of Nemedia,* by Andrew J. Offutt; *The Oath of Agha Junghaz,* by Manly Wade Wellman; *The Mouth of the Earth,* by Darrel Schweitzer; *The Gods Defied,* by A.E. Van Vogt; *Swordsmith and Sorcerer,* by Brian Lumley; *The Gift of Lycanthrophy,* by Frank Belknap Long; *The War Among the Gods,* by Adrian Cole; *The Ways of Chaos,* by Ramsey Campbell; *The Caves of Stygia,* by H. Warner Munn; *Doom of the Trice-Cursed,* by Marion Zimmer Bradley; *The River of Fog,* by Richard Lupoff; Publisher's Note. $25.

S54a   The Complete Yellow Jacket. Paul Herman, Plano, Texas, 1999. Edited by Paul Herman. 42 pp. 100 numbered copies printed. Eight additional lettered presentation copies. Wraps. Cover price not listed. No cover art. Early Robert E. Howard writings in the Howard Payne College's school paper. Reprinted 2001.
   Contents: *Introduction,* by Paul Herman; *Halt, Who Goes There!; After the Game; Sleeping Beauty; Weekly Short Story; Private Magrath of the A.E.F.; The Thessalians; Ye College Days; Cupid V. Pollux; The Reformation of a Dream.* $40.

S55a   The Black Stranger. Wandering Star, London, England, 2002. Original Howard typescript facsimile. 4to. 98 pp. 250 numbered copies printed. An additional 26 lettered copies were available at the Cross Plains Public Library. Comes in a four-flapped folder. The folder is illustrated and signed by Gary Gianni.
   Contents: *Introduction,* by Steve Tompkins; *The Black Stranger.* $125.

S56a   Robert E. Howard's Strange Tales. Dennis McHaney, Memphis, Tennessee, 2005. Edited by Dennis McHaney. 8vo. 176 pp. Wraps. A print-on-demand publication. Cover price $13.95. Cover art by Lawrence.
   Contents: *Introduction: Howard's Strange Tales,* by Dennis McHaney; *People of the Dark; The Cairn on the Headland; The Garden of Fear; Gods of the North; The Voice of El-Lil; The Fearsome Touch of Death; Black Canaan; A Thunder of Trumpets* (with Frank Thurston Torbett). $15.

E. AMATEUR PRESS JOURNALS

With the revival of public interest in the works of Robert E. Howard in the late 1960s and culminating in the 1970s, a number of privately printed publications or amateur press journals, also know as fanzines appeared. The quality of production and contents varied widely from simple pieces of little interest and ineptly illustrated by Krenkel or Frazetta imitators to high quality printing and selective, worthwhile and interesting material. Some of these publications lasted only a few issues, while others stood the test of time and gained enough subscriber support to sustain a longer run. By the early 1980s, most of them had disappeared. Some were revived later, concurrent with the appearance of new publications.

As a source of information on the unpublished and more obscure material and lesser known facts on Robert E. Howard, the amateur press publications are without equal. In some cases, however, the reader needs to look beyond the egocentric accounts with which some writers and editors take up space that could have been put to better use. A less hubristic approach by featured contributors, and more factual, scholarly and well-researched information, would assure a wider public interest and enhance the chances for the continued survival of the current Howard amateur press journals.

A1   AMRA. George H. Scithers, Philadelphia, Pennsylvania. The first volume was edited and published by George R. Heap. Second volume, which began with issue 7 in November of 1959, was edited and published by George Scithers. *AMRA* lasted for 72 issues and ceased publication in 1982. Except for the early issues, *AMRA* was not a publication entirely dedicated to Robert E. Howard and his work, but provided a general forum for fantasy writers. Cover art and interior illustrations by Roy G. Krenkel and other prominent artists of the time. A number of articles and essays from *AMRA*, were reprinted in the books *The Conan Reader* (Mirage Press, 1968), *The Conan Sword Book* (Mirage Press, 1969), and *The Conan Grimoire* (Mirage Press, 1972). $10 to $80 per issue.

A2   The Howard Collector. Glenn Lord, Pasadena, Texas, 1961. Edited by Glenn Lord. First two issues printed in 250 copies. Issues No. 3 to No. 9 printed in 150 copies. Later issues printed in 300 to 500 copies. Issues No. 3 through No. 11 were printed by Donald M. Grant. Contained fiction, poems, letters and writings by Robert E. Howard, plus relevant reviews and essays. Skillfully edited and professionally printed, the magazine was discontinued in 1973 after 18 issues. Cover price $.60 to $1.00. Only issue no. 9 was reprinted. It is the amateur press publication that has set the standard for its many successors. $35 to $100 per issue.

Contents: No. 1 (1961): *Midnight; The Sands of Time* (poem); *Sonora to Del Rio* (poem); *With a Set of Rattlesnake Rattles.* No. 2 (1962): Letter to Harold Preece; *The One Black Stain* (poem); *The Skull in the Clouds* (poem). No. 3 (1962): *West is West; Surrender* (poem); Letter to Harold Preece. No. 4 (1962): *Skulls and Dust* (poem); *Aha! Or the Mystery of the Queen's Necklace; Sea Curse; Futility* (poem). No. 5 (1964): *Kelly the Conjure-Man; The Last White Man; Belshazzar* (poem); *A Dawn in Flanders* (poem); *Timur-lang* (poem); *John Ringold* (poem); Letter to Clark Ashton Smith; Letter to August Derleth; *A Warning* (poem). No 6. (1965): *Knife, Bullet, and Noose; The Thessalians; Who is Grandpa Theobold?* (poem); Letter to Tevis Clyde Smith. No. 7 (1965): *Spear and Fang; The Dust Dance* (ver.1) (poem); *Cupid vs. Pollux; Cimmeria* (poem); Two letters to Harold Preece; Letter to Kirk Mashburn; Letter to Emil Petaja. No. 8 (1966): *Alleys of Treachery; The Shadow of Doom; Age Comes to Rabelais* (poem); *Roundelay of the Roughneck* (poem); Letter to Harold Preece. No. 9 (1967): *The Curse of the Golden Skull; The Day That I Die* (poem); *A Sonnet of Good Cheer* (poem); Letter to Farnsworth Wright; *Untitled Story; Sentiment* (poem); Letter to Harold

AMRA—*1959.* Vol. 2. No. 48. © Terminus, Owlswick, & Ft. Mudge Electrick Street Railway Gazette.

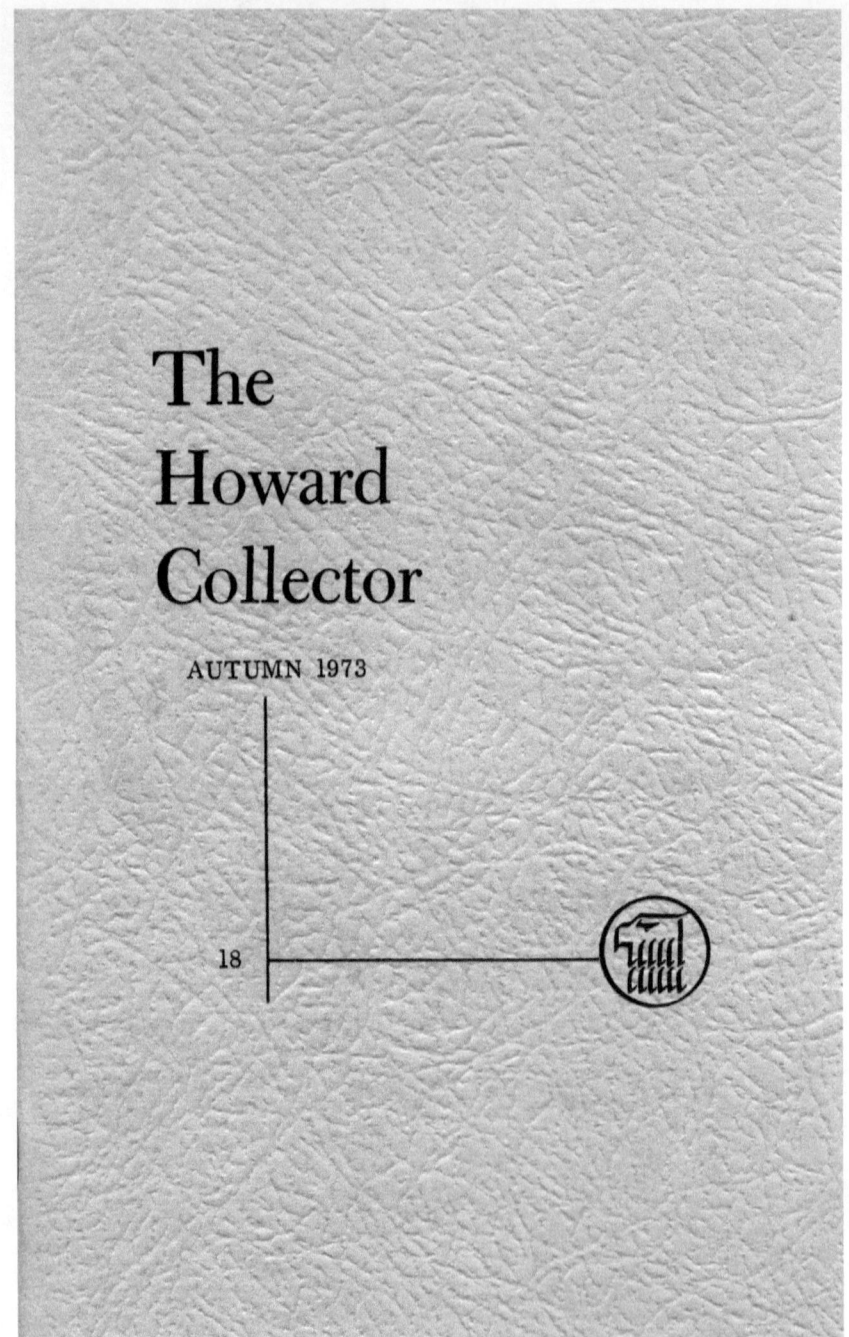

The Howard Collector—1961. © Glenn Lord.

Preece; *Skulls Over Judah* (poem). No. 10 (1968): *Heritage* (poem); *Musings of a Moron; Death's Black Riders;* Letter to Harold Preece; *The Dust Dance* (ver.2)(poem). No. 11 (1969): *Ghost in the Doorway; Thor's Son* (poem); *Reuben's Brethren* (poem); *Sunday in a Small Town; Ye College Days; Where are Your Knights, Donn Othna?* (poem); Heading: *Hour of the Dragon;* Letter to Farnsworth Wright; Two letters to Clark Ashton Smith. No 12 (1970): *Two Against Tyre; To Certain Orthodox Brethren* (poem); *A Song of the Legions* (poem); Letter to Carl Jacobi; Letter to Harold Preece. No. 13 (1970): *The Heathen; The Song of Horsa's Galley* (poem); *A Moment* (poem); Two letters to Harold Preece; Letter to Wilfred B. Talman. No. 14 (1971): *Sailor Dorgan and the Jade Monkey; Singing in the Wind* (poem); *A Dream; No More the Serpent Prow* (poem); *A Pledge* (poem); *Age* (poem). No. 15 (1971): *The Beast From the Abyss; Solomon Kane's Homecoming* (poem); Letter to H.P. Lovecraft; Letter to August Derleth; *Eighttoes Makes a Play; Hope Empty of Meaning* (poem). No. 16 (1972): *The Fire of Asshurbanipal;* Letter to Harold Preece; *Visions* (poem); *Marching Song of Connacht* (poem). No. 17 (1972): *Roads* (poem); *The Bar by the Side of the Road* (poem); *Harvest* (poem); *On With the Play* (poem); *Spanish Gold on Devil Horse* (Pt.1). No. 18 (1973): *Spanish Gold on Devil Horse* (Pt.2); Two letters to R.H. Barlow; *Life* (poem); *The Legacy of Tubal-Cain* (poem).

A3   Deeper Than You Think—A Literary Glimpse of Robert E. Howard. *A Literary Glimpse of Robert E. Howard.* Joel Frieman, 1968. Edited by Joel Frieman. A handsomely printed publication, containing a mixture of reprinted Howard material, essays, articles, letters, and reviews. Published in January 1968.

Contents: *Editorial,* by Robert E. Howard (introduction to *Wolfshead*); *One of Joel's Idols,* by Ranjee Shahani; Letter by L. Sprague de Camp; *The Celtica Notes of Robert E. Howard; The Writing of Conan of the Isles,* by Lin Carter; *About King Kull,* by Roy G. Krenkel; *On A Gent from Bear Creek,* by Lawrence E. MacPhee; *On Skull-Face and Others,* by Robert Weinberg. $200.

A4   The Robert E. Howard United Press Association (REHupa). Tim C. Marion, Newport News, Virginia, 1972. An amateur press association founded in the Fall of 1972, with an initial roster of five members. Provides a bimonthly forum for membership discussion of subjects relating to the life and works of Robert E. Howard and related fantasy material. Mailings vary in volume. Membership is limited to 30 members (the age at death of Robert E. Howard), and lifetime member Glenn Lord. Annual dues are $5.00, plus a minimum balance of $3.00 in a roster account. Potential new members may join a waiting list for a minimal fee. The association has generated approximately 180 mailings since its inception. The present editor is Bill Cavalier. For membership information visit *www.rehupa.com*. $10—$75 per mailing.

A5   Cross Plains. George T. Hamilton, Yorba Linda, California, 1974. Edited by George T. Hamilton. 32 pp. Wraps. A well-designed and edited publication, containing primarily reprints of some of Howard's lesser known work. Some art by Roy G. Krenkel and Stephen Fabian. Discontinued in 1975 after the seventh issue. $25—$35 per issue.

Contents: No. 1 (1974): Editorial, by George T. Hamilton; *Amra ... A Look*

Robert E. Howard United Press Association—1972. © Robert E. Howard United Press Association.

Behind the Railway Gazette, by Wayne Warfield; *Golden Hope Christmas; Howard and Kline: Men of the Pulps,* by David Anthony Kraft; Whispers from Cross Plains (news); *The Outrage, Frustration And Righteous Indignation ... the continuing saga of Savage Tales,* by Wayne Warfield; *A Gent from Cross Plains* (REH bibliography), by George T. Hamilton; Valeria's Trading Post. No. 2 (1974): Editorial, by George T. Hamilton; *The Sign of the Snake; A Gent from Cross Plains* (REH bibliography), by George T. Hamilton; Whispers from Cross Plains (news); *Howard in the Comics,* by Wayne Warfield; Letter from E. Hoffmann Price. No. 3. (1974): Editorial, by George T. Hamilton; *A Horror in the Night; In Death As in Life,* by Joseph Payne Brennan; *A Gent from Cross Plains* (REH bibliography), by George T. Hamilton; Whispers from Cross Plains (news). No. 4 (1974): Editorial, by George T. Hamilton; *Law Shooters of Cowtown;* Book review: *The Black Star; Yellow Rider Coming* (prose poem), by John Bredon; Book review: *Worms of the Earth; An Atlas of Fantasy: A Commentary,* by William P. Hall, Jr.; Whispers from Cross Plains (news); *A Gent from Cross Plains* (REH bibliography); Valeria's Trading Post; *The Hyborean Cult* (letters); *The Last Cimmerian* (poem), by George T. Hamilton. No. 5 (1974): Editorial, by George T. Hamilton; *Under the Baobab Tree; The Vultures; Solomon Kane: Pirate,* by Fred Blosser; *Echoes From An Iron Harp,* by John Bredon; *Conan, the Barbarian Check List* (comic book index); Review: *The Oakdale Affair,* by Edgar Rice Burroughs; Whispers from Cross Plains (news); Valeria's Trading Post. No. 6 (1975): Editorial, by George T. Hamilton; *The Devil's Joker; Solomon In The Black Forest,* by Fred Blosser; Letter to Harold Preece; Letter to Farnsworth Wright; Letter to E. Hoffmann Price; *Still There* (poem), by John Bredon; *The Hyborean Cult* (letters); Whispers from Cross Plains (news). No. 7 (1975): Editorial, by George T. Hamilton; *Wild Water; The Nightmare Face,* by Joseph Payne Brennan; The Unpublished Fiction of REH; *The Road to Freedom* (poem); *Mummy* (poem), by Joseph Payne Brennan; *November Day,* by Joseph Payne Brennan.

A6 REH: Lone Star Fictioneer. Arnold Fenner and Byron L. Roark, Nemedian Chronicles, Shawnee Mission, Kansas, 1975. Edited by Byron Roark. 52 pp. Wraps. 500 copies printed. Cover price $2.50—$3.50. Specialized in unpublished Howard material. Art by several prominent artists including Roy G. Krenkel, Stephen Fabian, Howard Chaykin, and George Barr. Discontinued in 1976 after the fourth issue. $35—$40.

Contents: No. 1 (1975): *Musings*—Editorial, by Byron L. Roark and Arnie Fenner; *The Loser; The Writing Game,* by Glenn Lord; *REH: Prose to Graphic,* by Byron L. Roark; *The Characters of REH* (portfolio), by John Severin, Stan Dresser, Herb Arnold, Arnie Fenner, Stephen Fabian and Tim Conrad; *The Once and Future Kane,* by Karl Edward Wagner; *Knife River Prodigal; Death's Black Riders.* No. 2 (1975): *Sword Woman;* An Interview with Roy Thomas; An Interview with Barry Smith; *King Kull Portfolio,* by John and Marie Severin. No. 3 (1975): *Guns of Khartoum; Agonies and Ecstasies,* by Arnold Fenner; Muriela Folio. An Interview with Glenn Lord; *Vultures over Cross Plains,* by Byron L. Roark; *Wings in the Night* (folio), by Alan Weiss; *The Brazen Peacock; REH Folio,* by Alfredo Alcala, Walt Simonson and Alex Nino. No. 4 (1976): *Three-Bladed Doom; The Gods of Bal-Sagoth* (folio), by Marcus Boas; Interview with L. Sprague de Camp; Interview with John P. Severin; *My Sword is Quick* (parody), by M.M. Moamrath; *Incident At Cross Plains,* by Ben Indick; Mail; Plugs.

REH: Lone Star Fictioneer—1975. © the Nemedian Chronicles.

A7 Fantasy Crossroads. Jonathan Bacon, Stygian Isle Press, Lamoni, Iowa, 1974. Edited by Jonathan Bacon. 80 pp. Copies printed not stated. Cover price $2.00. Not limited to Howard material, but included other fantasy works. Interior illustrations by various artists. Discontinued in 1978 after issue No.14. Only Robert E. Howard related material has been included in the following list of contents. $25—$35 per issue.

Contents: No. 1 (1974): *Robert E. Howard; Recompense* (poem); *The Singer in the Mist* (poem); Conan comic book checklist; *The Hall of the Dead* (synopsis); *The Song of a Mad Minstrel* (poem); *Delenda Est.* No. 2 (1975): Letter to Harold Preece; Letter to Harold Preece; *The Curse of the Golden Skull; The Last Celt* (memoir), by Harold Preece; *Heritage* (poem); *Heritage* (another poem with the same title); *Always Comes Evening* (poem); *The Poets* (poem); Kull the Conqueror comic book checklist; *Drums of the Sunset.* No. 3 (1975): *Women and Robert E. Howard*, by Harold Preece; *The Good Knight;* Letter to Harold Preece; *The Treasures of Ali Akbar Khan* (a guide to REH hard cover books), by George T. Hamilton and Wayne Warfield; *The Ghost Kings* (poem); *Flint's Passing* (poem). No. 4/5 (1975): *Man With The Mystery Mitts; REH: MISFIT,* by Wayne Warfield; *War to the Blind* (poem); *The Abbey; Day Breaks Over Simla* (poem); *The Eyrie: An Unusual Mailbag,* by Robert Weinberg; REH Books Available in Japanese, by Masaki Abe. No. 6 (1975): *The Gondarian Man; Hope Empty of Meaning* (poem); Letter to Harold Preece. Fantasy Crossroads Special Edition (1976): *Heroes Of Swords and Sorcery,* by Jerry L. Schattenburg; *Fists of the Revolution; Visions* (poem); *More Evidence of the Innate Divinity of Man; The Miscast Barbarian in Review: The Real Robert E. Howard,* by Harold Preece; De Camp Responds. No. 7 (1976): *Madame Goose's Rhymes* (poem); Untitled fragment; Letter to Harold Preece; *College Socks.* No. 8 (1976): Letter from H.P. Lovecraft to Clark Ashton Smith with reference to Robert E. Howard; *The God in the Bowl* (art folio), by Gene Day; *Daughters of Feud; Miser's Gold* (poem). No. 9 (1976): *The Last Laugh; Of Swords & Sorcery,* by Paul C. Allen; *Red Nails* (art folio), by Gene Day; REH fanzine editors' round table discussion, part one, with Jonathan Bacon, Arnie Fenner, George T. Hamilton, Dennis McHaney; Byron L. Roark, George Scithers, Wayne Warfield and Damon C. Sasser. No. 10/11 (1977): *Genseric's Fifth-Born Son* (fragment); REH fanzine editors' round table discussion, part two, with Jonathan Bacon, Arnie Fenner, George T. Hamilton, Dennis McHaney; Byron L. Roark, George Scithers, Wayne Warfield and Damon C. Sasser; Donald M. Grant interview; *Quest for Books* (REH biography segment), by Harold Preece; *The Magic Name* (REH biography segment), by Tevis Clyde Smith; *REH Zebra Cover Blurbs vs. Reality,* by Brian Earl Brown; *Howard and the Races,* by L. Sprague de Camp; *The Night Bob Howard Died* (poem), by John Rieber; Book review: *The Devil in Iron; The Last Celt.* No. 12 (1977): Letter from L. Sprague de Camp. No. 13 (1978): *What Robert E. Howard Said One Wednesday Night* (poem), by Tevis Clyde Smith; *The Feud* (poem); *Of Swords & Sorcery,* by Paul C. Allen. No. 14 (1978): *Oh Babylon, Lost Babylon* (poem). No. 15 (1978): No Robert E. Howard Material in this issue.

A8 Fantasy Crosswinds. Jonathan Bacon, Stygian Isle Press, Lamoni, Iowa, 1977. Edited by Jonathan Bacon. Wraps. Consisted of reprints, letters and poems. Discontinued in 1977 after the third issue. Only Robert E. Howard related material has been included in the following list of contents. $25—$35 per issue.

Contents: No. 1 (1977): *The Outcast* (poem); *The Curse of Greed; The Kiowa's Tale* (poem); REH Portfolio, by Gene Day. No. 2 (1977): *Door to the Garden.* No. 3 (1977): *Roar, Silver Trumpets* (poem); *The Iron Man* reviewed by Charles Saunders; REH illustrations by Gene Day and Clyde Caldwell.

A9 The Howard Review. Dennis McHaney, Memphis, Tennessee, 1975.

Edited by Dennis McHaney. 32 pp. 204 copies printed. A second edition of issue 1, improved in quality and contents was issued later in 1975. 31 pp. About 1100 copies printed. Cover price $2.50. Reprinted some of Howard's lesser known work from *Weird Tales*. Discontinued April 1977 with issue No. 7. The Howard Review was revived again by McHaney in 1995 with issue 11. The new version is much expanded and includes complete Howard stories and color artwork. Cover price $10.95. A print-on-demand publication. For subscription information visit *www.lulu.com*. Early issues $35.

Contents: No. 1—2nd printing: Introduction, by Dennis McHaney; *The Fearsome Touch of Death; Dead Man's Hate* (poem); *A Thunder of Trumpets; Moon Mockery* (poem). No. 2 (1975): *The Riot at Bucksnort; Three Perils of Sailor Costigan;* Untitled; Untitled; Untitled; *Vikings of the Gloves*. No. 3 (1975): *The Beast from the Abyss; The Reformation of a Dream*. No. 4 (1975): *Singing in the Wind* (poem); *The TNT Punch*. No. 5 (1976): *The Noseless Horror; The Passionate Typist* (poem). No. 6 (1977): A Collection of 20 poems. No. 7 (1977): *Sailor Costigan and the Swami*. No. 11 (1995): *Thoroughbreds; Lives and Crimes of Notable Artists*. No. 12 (2004): Introduction, by Dennis McHaney; *Black Queen, Red Heart*, by Fred Blosser; *The Song of the Bats* (poem); *The Riders of Babylon* (poem); *Black Talons; Howard in Canada; In the Tradition of ...* by Charles Gramlich; *The Harp of Alfred* (poem); *Letters from Mom,* by Dennis McHaney*; The Tomb's Secret; The Gates of Nineveh* (poem); *Oriental Stories, The Magic Carpet Magazine & The Souk,* by Dennis McHaney; *Jack Dempsey's Fight Magazine Cover Gallery.* No. 13 (2004): Thirtieth Anniversary Introduction, by Dennis McHaney; *The Dark Man; The Voice of El-Lil; Voices of the Night: The Voices Waken Memory,* (poem); *Babel* (poem); *The Trouble With FAX,* by Jorge R.R. Tolkein; *Roy G. Krenkel and FAX; Breaking the First-Person Nonuse Rule* or *Through A Howard Book Darkly,* by Tom Foster; *The Fire of Asshurbanipal;* The Fantasy Magazine Howard Memorial; The Fiction of Robert E. Howard—An Illustrated Bibliography, Part One, by Dennis McHaney; Beyond *The Valley of the Worm*—A Retro Review, by Fred Blosser; Review; Howard in Print.

A10 The Conan Companion. Hall Publications, Aberdeen, Maryland, 1976. Edited by Wayne Warfield. 22 pp. Copies printed not stated. Cover price not listed. This was a one issue Conan exclusive fanzine with articles and essays about the legendary Cimmerian. Cover art by Gene Day and illustrated by other artists.

Contents: A Short Editorial Note, by Wayne Warfield; *Conan—The Hairy Hero,* by Michael Resnick; *The First Conan Comic? A revealing study,* by David and Susannah Bates; *Conan the Degraded,* by John Myer; *The Barbarian,* by L. Sprague de Camp (poem); *Conan Unarmed,* by Bill Orlikow; About the Artists. $35.

A11 REH: Two Gun Raconteur—The Definite Howard Fanzine. Black Coast Press, Houston, Texas, 1976. Edited by Damon C. Sasser. 32 to 44 pp. 300 copies printed. Cover price $1.75. Fanzine with essays, comments, letters, articles and illustrations relating to R.E. Howard and his work. Discontinued in 1977 after issue four, but revived in 2003 with issue five. Black Coast Press, Channelview, Texas, 2004. Edited by Damon C. Sasser. 36 pp.

REH: Two Gun Raconteur—1976. © **Damon C. Sasser.**

250 copies printed. Cover price $10.95. Pertinent scholarly contributions are encouraged. For subscription information visit *www.rehtwogunraconteur.com*. Early issues $35.

Contents: No. 1 (1976): Editorial, by Damon C. Sasser; *God's Angry Man,* by Damon C. Sasser; *The Annotated Solomon Kane; The Kane Glossary; The Complete Kane; The Dark Man Portfolio,* by James Bozarth; *An Astrological Look at REH,* by Elaine Kuhns; *Robert E. Howard: Retrospectively,* by Wayne Warfield; *An Experiment in Exploitation: Donald M. Grant's Conan,* by Byron L. Roark;

The Sense of Hideous Antiquity, by Bill Wallace; REH News; *Red Sonya vs. Red Sonja,* by Damon C. Sasser; Robert E. Howard's Astrological Chart cast by Elaine Kuhns. No.2 (1976): The Junto; *The Dark Lines—Editorial Noise,* by Damon C. Sasser; REH Mail; Letter From Robert E. Howard to Clark Ashton Smith; *A Fool and His Money are Sooner Strangers,* by El Diablo de Crom; *The Legendary Celts—REH and the Celtic Strain,* by Wayne Warfield; *The Pool of the Black One: A Portfolio,* by Ken Raney; *Scorpio Rising—An Astrological Look at REH: Part 2,* by Elaine Kuhns; *Collecting Howardia,* by Steve Smolins; *The Case of the Black Book,* by John Stash and Damon C. Sasser; *REH in Prose; REH in Graphics; REH News;* Billboard. No. 3 (1976): The Junto; *The Dark Lines—Editorial Nonsense,* by Damon C. Sasser; REH Mail; *The Devil's Joker; Robert E. Howard and the Ring,* Part 1, by Dennis McHaney; *The Moon of Skulls—A Portfolio,* by Gene Day; *Conan Vs. Conantics,* by Don Herron; *The Rare Ones,* by Charles Melvin; *REH in Prose; REH News;* Billboard. No. 4 (1977): The Junto; *The Dark Lines—An Attempted Editorial,* by Damon C. Sasser; REH Mail; *Golden Hope Christmas; Echoes from Bal-Sagoth,* by Damon C. Sasser; *Kings of the Night—A Portfolio,* by Don Herron; *The Stars and the Skald,* by Elaine Kuhns; *Forgotten Secrets of Bloody Pride,* by Bill Wallace; *Riding the Range with Robert E. Howard,* by Byron L. Roark; *REH in Prose; REH News.* No 5. (2003): The Junto; *The Dark Lines—The Comeback Trail—Editorial Musings,* by Damon C. Sasser; *A Horror in the Night; The Sins of Our Tastes, The Sins of Our Trade,* by Jessica Amanda Salmonson; *El Dios Diabólico de Tlasceltec,* by Damon C. Sasser; *Almuric—Folio,* by Steve Fabian; *Two Against the Post Office,* by Keith Taylor; *Fists of Cross Plains,* by Charles R. Saunders; *Was Robert E. Howard a Hack?* by Darrell Schweitzer; The REH Review; Nemedian Dispatches. No. 6 (2004): The Junto; *The Dark Lines—Welcome to the New Howard Boom*—Editorial, by Damon C. Sasser; Black Issues; *Under the Baobab Tree; The Vengeance Sword of the Norman Gael,* by Damon C. Sasser; *Red Nails—A Conan Portfolio,* by Gene Day; *Dreams Darker than Night—Reflections on Drugs and Writing,* by Karl Edward Wagner; *Sheathed in a Virgin's Skin or the Desires of Man?—Booking Passage on the Mythos Train of Thought,* by Benjamin Szumskyj; The REH Review; Nemedian Dispatches. No. 7 (2005): The Junto; *The Dark Lines—Come on in, the water's fine*—Editorial, by Damon C. Sasser; *The Haunted Hut; REH, HPL and the Cthulhu Mythos,* by Glenn Lord; *Brothers of the Night,* by Benjamin Szumskyj; *Robert E. Howard's The Four Kings—A Portfolio,* by David Burton; *A Woman Looks at Cross Plains,* by Linda Melichone; *The Dark Gray Heritage—A Collective Study of Robert E. Howard's Cimmerians, Part 1,* by Danny Street; The REH Review; Nemedian Dispatches. No. 8 (2005): The Junto; *The Dark Lines—Reflections on Centennial Eve*—Editorial, by Damon C. Sasser; Black Issues; *Black Country; Herbert Klatt: The Fourth Musketeer,* by Glenn Lord; *Robert E. Howard's Heroes and Heroines—A Portfolio,* by Stephen Fabian; *The Dark Gray Heritage—A Collective Study of Robert E. Howard's Cimmerians, Part 2,* by Danny Street; *Restless Hercules, Wild Planet,* by Morgan Holmes; Nemedian Dispatches.

A12 The Chronicler of Cross Plans. The Black Coast Press, Houston, Texas, 1978. Edited by Damon S. Sasser. Copies printed not stated. Cover price $4.00. Containing reprints of Howard's work and stories, essays and poems by other writers. Illustrated by various artists.

Contents; No. 1 (1978): Editorial: *Always Comes Dusk,* by Damon C. Sasser;

Dark Coterie; The Sign of the Snake; The Writing Game, by Glenn Lord; *Kibanda Ya Kufa,* by Charles R. Saunders; *Two Suns Setting: A Kane Portfolio,* by Ken Raney; *Skelos* (poem); *A Mouthful of Feathers,* by Charles R. Saunders; *An REH Art Folio,* by Arnold M. Fenner; *Casonettot's Last Song, Demon Clutch,* by Kenneth Huff; *R.E.H. and Cultural Trends in Literature,* by Thomas Reid. *The Night of Her Sacrifice,* by Jeffrey Goddin; Plugs. $35.

A13   Cromlech, The Journal of Robert E. Howard Criticism. Robert M. Price, Cryptic Publications, Mount Olive, North Carolina, 1985. Edited by Marc A. Cerasini. 48 pp. Wraps. Copies printed not stated. Cover price $4.50. Well-designed and edited publication, containing scholarly Howard related critical articles and essays. Discontinued in 1988 with the third issue. $25—$35.

Contents: No. 1 (1985): Editorial Comments, by Marc A. Cerasini; *Conan the Existential,* by Charles Hoffman; *Christ and Conan: Howard's View of Christianity,* by Robert M. Price; *Spectres in the Dark; Howard in the Eighties: An Overview,* by Marc A. Cerasini and Charles Hoffman; Review: *The Dark Barbarian,* by Charles Hoffman; *R.E.H.,* by Tim Prather (poem); *Cromwatch.* No. 2 (1987): Editorial Comments, by Marc A. Cerasini; *Howard's Prototypes,* by L. Sprague de Camp; *Robert E. Howard and the Southern Folk Tradition,* by Pierre Comtois; *The Shadow in the Well;* Reviews: *The Mythos and Kindred Horrors,* by Stefan R. Dziemianowicz, *Writer of the Dark,* by Daniel Gobbert, *One Who Walked Alone,* by Charles Hoffman, *One Who Walked Alone,* by C.J. Henderson; Red Mails; *Cromwatch; Guidelines for Contributors to Cromlech.* No. 3 (1988): Editorial Comments, by Robert M. Price; *The Snout in the Dark* (synopsis); *Drums of Tombalku* (synopsis); *Bran Mak Morn—A Play; Bran Mak Morn* (synopsis); *The Diablos Trail; Wolfsdung; The Vultures of Whapeton: An Alternative Ending; A Collector's Check List of Howard's Fiction,* by Robert M. Price.

A14   The Dark Man—The Journal of Robert E. Howard Studies. Necronomicon Press, West Warwick, Rhode Island, 1990. Edited by Rusty Burke. Wraps. Cover price $4.50. A journal of scholarly study, comments and literary criticism on matters relating to Robert E. Howard and his work. With issue 5 (Winter 2001), Frank Coffman became the editor and the journal was published by Mind's Eye Hyper Publishing/ Iron Harp publications, Rockford, Illinois. With issue 7 (Spring of 2004) *The Dark Man* was published by Seele Brent Publications, New Paltz, New York, in a square-bound format. Cover price $8.00. The present editor is Mark Hall. Scholarly contributions are encouraged. For subscription information visit *www.seele-brennt.com/subscribe/*

Contents: No. 1 (1990): Editorial, by Rusty Burke; *Swords at the Academy Gates; Or, Robert E. Howard Is There, Where are the Critics?* by Don Herron; *King Conan and the Aquilonian Dream,* by Steven R. Trout; *Toward Other Lands: An Approach to Robert E. Howard,* by Rusty Burke; *The Howard Complex,* by Dan Stumpf; *Herbert Klatt,* by Glenn Lord; *The Frost-Giant's Daughter; An Early Draft;* Reviews: *Echoes of Valor,* by Rusty Burke, *Post Oaks and Sand Roughs,* by Charles Hoffman; Guidelines for Submissions. No. 2 (1991): *The Horror Fiction of Robert E. Howard,* by Steven R. Trout; *Solomon and Sorcery,* by Michael Kellar; *The Old Deserted House: Images of the South in Howard's Fiction,* by Rusty

Burke; *"Come back to Valusia Ag'in, Kull Honey!":* Robert E. Howard and Mainstream American Literature, by Marc A Cerasini; *On Howardian Fairyland,* by Don Herron; *Bill Smalley and the Power of the Human Eye; Cultural Trends in Literature,* by Thomas R. Reid; *Barbarian Aftermath* by Don Herron with *A Voice from the Past,* by Paul Spencer; *The Expurgated Solomon Kane,* by Steven R. Trout with Vernon M. Clark; Reviews: *Robert E. Howard: Selected Letters 1931-1936,* by Richard L. Tierney; The Robert E. Howard Home, by Rusty Burke. No. 3 (1993): *From Cross Plains to the Stars: Robert E. Howard's Science Fiction,* by Fred Blosser; *Cosmic Filth: Howard's View of Evil,* by Charles Hoffmann; *What the Nation Owes the South; The Active Voice: Robert E. Howard's Personae,* by Rusty Burke: Reviews: *Yorick Fantasy Magazine Nos. 10/11 & 12/13,* by S.T. Joshi, *Yorick Fantasy Magazine No. 14/15,* by Vernon M. Clark, *Il segno del serpente,* by Vernon M. Clark, *Robert E. Howard's Blood and Thunder,* Number 1., by Bill Cavalier, *The Vultures of Whapeton, Songs of Bastards,* and *Blood and Thunder,* Number 1, by Vernon M. Clark. No. 4 (1996): *The Birth of Conan,* by Patrice Louinet; *The Origin of Cimmeria,* by Rusty Burke; *The Star Rover and the People of the Night,* by Fred Blosser; *Howard Publishing in Eastern Europe,* by Glenn Lord; *Conan and Robert E. Howard on the Internet,* by Edward A. Waterman; Remembrances: *Jim Neal,* by Fred Blosser; *Harold Preece,* by Rusty Burke; *Karl Edward Wagner,* by Rusty Burke; Reviews: *The Whole Wide World,* by David C. Smith, The Robert E. Howard Library, by Rusty Burke, *Tough Guys and Dangerous Dames,* by Fred Blosser, *Unaussprechlichen Kulten,* by Vernon M. Clark; Editorial Comments, by Rusty Burke. No. 5 (2001): *Editor's Welcome,* by Frank Coffman; *When Kull Rode the Range,* by Fred Blosser; *All Fled, All Done,* by Rusty Burke; *The Tower of the Elephant: A Modern Fable,* by Gary Romeo; *Escape From Eden: Genesis Subverted in "The Garden of Fear"* by Charles Hoffman; *James Allison's Incarnations,* by Joe Marek; *Soldiering for Fortune: Robert E. Howard's Kirby O'Donnell and the "Treasures of Tartary"* by Dr. Gary Hoppenstad; *Dating Wolfshead,* by Edward Waterman; Review: *Ghor, Kin-Slayer,* by Fred Blosser; *A Drawing;* The Cairn and Lock Box 313, by Frank Coffman. No. 6 (2001): *Notes on Two Versions of an Unpublished Poem by Robert E. Howard,* by Frank Coffman; *"Spartacus to the Gladiators of Capua,"* by Elijah Kellogg, Jr.; *The Lives and Death of Three Writers: A Speculative Essay on London, Howard and Hemingway,* by Dr. Charles Gramlich; Review: *Kutouru Shinwa Jiten,* by Mark Hall; *A Short History of the Kull Series,* by Patrice Louinet; A Note From the Editor, by Frank Coffman; *The Last Celt* REH Letter Citations, by Rusty Burke, Patrice Louinet and Edward Waterman; *There's a White Wolf on the Ottoman, Or, Another Revolt in the Desert,* by Steven Tompkins; The Cairn, by Leon Grin; Lock Box 313, by Karl Morris. No. 7 (2004): Editor's Corner, by Frank Coffman, Mark Hall, Charles Gramlich and Scotty Henderson; *The Robert E. Howard Collections Found in the University of California at Berkeley's Bancroft Library,* by Edward A. Waterman; *Bibliography Of the Robert E. Howard Collections held by the University of California at Berkeley Bancroft Library,* by Glenn Lord; *The Past is Dead, The Past is Deadly: Three Dragons in One Hour,* by Steven Tompkins; Call for Papers: a New Direction in Howard Studies? Comments; Reviews: *The Coming of Conan the Cimmerian,* by Fred Blosser. No. 8 (2004): Editor's Corner, by Mark Hall and Charles Gramlich; *Texas as Character in Robert E. Howard's Fiction,* by Mark Finn; *Robert E. Howard in the Gothic Tradition,* by Charles Gramlich; Two Views of *The Barbaric Triumph,* by Fred Blosser and S.T. Joshi; *Adventures—Imperial and Otherwise,* by

Mark E. Hall; Review of *Power of the Writing Mind,* by Scotty Henderson; Review of *Graveyard Rats and Others,* by Charles Hoffman; *Through a Prism, Darkly,* by David Robbins.

A15 The "New" Howard Reader. Joseph and Mona Marek, Omaha, Nebraska,1998. Edited by Joseph Marek. Associated Editor Rusty Burke. 28 to 52 pp. Wraps. First printing limited to 50 copies. Cover price not listed. Contains reprint of fiction, essays, poetry and letters by Robert E. Howard. The seventh issue was issued in 2000. Limited printing and not widely distributed. Cover art by various artists. A Howard Reader Special Edition was issued in 2000 with cover art by Richard Price. $50—$80.

Contents: No. 1 (1998): *Cimmeria* (poem); *The Devils of Dark Lake; Brachan the Kelt; Drake Sings of Yesterday* (poem); Letter to *Thrills of the Jungle Magazine; Rebellion* (poem); *Ambition in the Moonlight; The Sand-Hill's Crest* (poem); *The Last Laugh;* Letter to E. Hoffmann Price; *The Shadow of Doom; Only a Shadow on the Grass* (poem); *All Hallow's Eve* (poem); Letter to Carl Jacobi; *John L. Sullivan* (poem); Untitled; *The Sword of Mahommed* (poem); *The Shadow in the Well* (synopsis); *Flint's Passing* (poem); *The Supreme Moment;* Letter to August Derleth; Untitled; *The King and the Oak* (poem); Letter to Emil Petaja; Untitled; Letter to Novalyne Price; *Something About Eve; The Maiden of Kercheezer* (poem); Letter to R.H. Barlow; *The House of Om* (synopsis); Untitled; *Them; The Whoopansat of Humorous Kookooyam* (poem); Letter to Robert W. Gordon; *The Cuckoo's Revenge* (poem); Letter to Harold Preece; *Candles* (poem); Afterword, by Joe Marek. No. 2 (1998): *A Song of the Naked Lands* (poem); *The Touch of Death; The Tower of Time;* Letter to *The Eyrie* in *Weird Tales; Zukala's Love Song* (poem); Letter to Carl Jacobi; *Red Thunder* (poem); *The Ghost in the Doorway; For Man Was Given the Earth to Rule* (poem); *Spectres in the Dark;* Letter to August Derleth; *Golnor the Ape; Buccaneer Treasure* (poem); *The Sands of the Desert* (poem); Letter to Emil Petaja; *Custom* (poem); *A Dream; Memories* (poem); *The Heathen; A Dungeon Opens* (poem); *The Symbol* (poem); *Miss High Hat;* Letter to R.H. Barlow; *The Tale of America; The Viking of the Sky* (poem); Letter to Harold Preece; *Dreaming of Downs* (poem); Letter to Novalyne Price; *To a Man Whose Name I Never Know; An Outworn Story* (poem); Letter to Robert W. Gordon; *Aha! Or the Mystery of the Queen's Necklace; A Young Wife's Tale* (poem); *Musings; L'Envoi* (poem); Letter to Hugh G. Schonfeld; Untitled; Letter to *Argosy All-Story Weekly* Magazine; *A Man (*poem); *Mountain Man* (magazine version); Letters of Comments by Our Readers; Afterword, by Joe Marek. No. 3 (1998): *The Rhyme of the Three Slavers* (poem); Untitled; *Serpent Vines;* Letter to *The Eyrie* in *Weird Tales; Zukala's Jest* (poem); Letter to Clark Ashton Smith; *Dance Macabre* (poem); *Bran Mak Morn* (synopsis); *The Chant Demoniac* (poem); *Etched in Ebony;* Letter to *Ft. Worth Star Telegram; The Jade God; Miser's Gold* (poem); *These Things Are Gods* (poem); Letter to August Derleth; *War to the Blind* (poem); *The Return of the Sorcerer; Seven Kings* (poem); *Empire's Destiny* (poem); *The Devil in His Brain;* Letter to Emil Petaja; *The Hand of Obeah; L'Envoi* (poem); Letter to R.H. Barlow; *Drowned* (poem); Postcard to Novalyne Price; *Hashish Land; Girls* (poem); Letter to August Lenninger; *Dagon Manor; The Galveston Affair;* Letter to Robert W. Gordon; Untitled; Letter to Harold Preece; *Up, John Kane!* (poem); *Guns of the Mountains* (magazine version); *The Ghost of Camp Colorado* (facsimile); Letters of Comments by Our Readers; Afterword, by Joe

Marek. No. 4 (1999): *The Return of the Sea-Farer* (poem); *Under the Baobab Tree; The Gondarian Man;* Letter to *The Eyrie* in *Weird Tales; Drum Gods* (poem); Letter to August Derleth; *The Coming of Bast* (poem); *Guests of the Hoodoo Room; The Gods Remember* (poem); *The Voice of the Mob;* Letter to E. Hoffmann Price; *She-Cats of Samarcand* (synopsis); *A Pledge* (poem); *The Road to Freedom* (poem); Letter to R.H. Barlow; *Mad Meg Gill* (poem); *Stones of Destiny; The Phases of Life* (poem); *The Haunted Hut; A Dying Pirate Speaks of Treasures* (poem); *The Thessalians;* Letter to August Lenninger; *The Spell of Damballah; The Weakling* (poem); Letter to Robert W. Gordon; *L'Envoi* (poem); Postcard to Novalyne Price; *With a Set of Rattlesnake Rattles;* Letter to Harold Preece; *Golden Hope Christmas; My Sentiments, Set to Jazz* (poem); *The Celtica Notes of Robert E. Howard; The Zulu Lord* (poem); Letter to Tevis Clyde Smith; Untitled; *The Song of Yar Ali Khan* (poem); *A Gent from Bear Creek* (magazine version); Letters of Comments by Our Readers; Afterword, by Joe Marek. No. 5 (1999): *The Dance with Death* (poem); *Redflame;* Letter to *The Eyrie* in *Weird Tales; When Death Drops Her Veil* (poem); Letter to E. Hoffmann Price; *Heritage* (poem); *Black Country; Nocturne* (poem); *Intrigue in Kurdistan;* Letter to August Derleth; *The Doom Chant of Than-Kul* (poem); *Counterspells* (poem); Letter to Kirk Mashburn; *A Song of the Werewolf Folk* (poem); *Halt! Who Goes There; Dreams* (poem); *The People of the Serpent;* Letter to Robert W. Gordon; *Wolfsdung; Universe* (poem); Letter to R.H. Barlow; *The Feud* (poem); Letter to Novalyne Price; *The Strange Case of Josiah Wilbarger; Madame Goose's Rhymes* (poem); Letter to Robert W. Gordon; *The Fear-Master; What is Love?* (poem); Letter to Carl Jacobi; *The Vicar of Wakefield; Rules of Etiquette* (poem); Letter to *The Ring Magazine; Tides* (poem); Untitled; Letter to Tevis Clyde Smith; *The Feud Buster* (magazine version); *Verses in Ebony* (facsimile); Letters of Comments by Our Readers; Afterword, by Joe Marek. No. 6 (1999): *The Ballad of King Geraint* (poem); *Genseric; Black Eons;* Letter to *The Eyrie* in *Weird Tales;* Letter to *Adventure* magazine; *Musings of a Moron; The Spirit of Brian Boru; The Vultures of Wahpeton* (both endings); *Harvest* (poem); Letter to August Derleth; *Unhand Me, Villain; Le Gentil Homme le Diable; A Matter of Age; The Weaker Sex;* Letter to Novalyne Price; *More Evidence of the Innate Divinity of Man; On with the Play* (poem); *The Ideal Girl; Eighttoes Makes a Play* (alternate ending); *The Road to Bear Creek* (magazine version); Letters of Comments by Our Readers; Afterword, by Joe Marek. No. 7 (2000): *Always Comes Evening; Three-Bladed Doom; Spanish Gold on Devil Horse;* Letter to *The Eyrie* in *Weird Tales;* Letter to *Adventure* magazine; *Sunday in a Small Town; Age Lasting Love; Roads* (poem); *The Fire of Asshurbanipal;* Letter to Charles D. Hornig; *The Sheik; Midnight; The Curse of Greed; Pictures in the Fire;* Letter to Novalyne Price; *Sentiment; West is West; Destiny* (poem); *Surrender—Your Money or Your Vice; The Last White Man; A Stranger in Grizzly Claw* (magazine version); Letters of Comments by Our Readers; Afterword, by Joe Marek. The Howard Reader Special Edition (2000): *A Legend of Faring Town* (poem); *Tigers of the Sea; The Adventurer's Mistress* (poem); *The Slave Princess; The Ballad of Bucksnort Roberts* (poem); Letter to *The Eyrie* in *Weird Tales; Men Build Them Houses* (poem); Letter to the *California Magazine; A Hairy-Chested Idealist Sings* (poem); *Taverel Manor; The Isle of Hy-Brasil* (poem); *Blades of the Brotherhood* (Malachi Grim version); *To All Sophisticates* (poem); Letter to P. Schuyler Miller; *Two Men* (poem); *Nekht Semerkeht; The Adventurer* (poem); *The Tomb of the Dragon; To a Woman* (poem); Letter to Novalyne Price; *The Night Winds* (poem); *An Autobiography; The Grim*

Land (poem); *Mistress of Death; To An Earthbound Soul* (poem); *The House; Shadows from Yesterday* (poem); Letter to Dennis Archer; *Shadow Thing* (poem); *The Frost-King's Daughter; The Gods of the Jungle Drums* (poem); *The Mystery of Tannernoe Lodge; The Gates of Babylon* (poem); Letter to Novalyne Price; *Nectar* (poem); *Some People Who Have Had Influence Over Me; Today* (poem); *The Isle of the Eons; The Outgoing of Sigurd the Jerusalem-Farer* (poem); *The Door to the World; A Pirate Remembers* (poem); Letter to Emil Petaja; *De Ol' River Ox* (poem); *The Devil's Woodchopper; To All the Lords of Commerce* (poem); *The Guardian of the Idol; Man Am* I(poem); Letter to Novalyne Price; *memories of Alfred* (poem); *The Wandering Years; Alien* (poem); *The Abbey; Revolt Pagan* (poem); *Black Canaan; The Road to Yesterday* (poem); *Ring-Tailed Tornado* (Buckner J. Grimes); *Never Beyond the Beast* (poem); *While Smoke Rolled* (Pike Bearfield); *The Ghost Ocean* (poem); *Sailor Dorgan and the Turkish Menace; To All Evangelists* (poem); *A Touch of Trivia; The End of the Glory Trail* (poem); Authorship uncertain: *For the Honor of the School, Rivals, His War Medals, From Tea to Tee; The Outcast* (poem); *When the Glaciers Rumbled South* (poem); *Cupid from Bear Creek* (magazine version); *The Haunted Mountain* (magazine version); *War on Bear Creek* (magazine version); The Complete Howard Collection; Index to *The "New" Howard Reader* and *The Howard Reader Special Edition;* Afterword, by Joe Marek.

A16 Glenn Lord's Ultimate Thule. Joseph Marek, Omaha, Nebraska, 2000. Edited by Joseph Marek. 52 pp. Facsimile reproduction. Copies printed not stated. Cover price $12.00. Cover art by Rafael Kayanan. The Hyperborean League was an amateur press association dedicated to the serious discussion and study of Robert E. Howard and Clark Ashton Smith. In the late 1970s, the Hyperborean League merged with the Robert E. Howard United Press Association. *Ultima Thule* was Glenn Lord's contributing apa zine to the mailings of the Hyperborean League and contained many little known particulars about Robert E. Howard's life and work. In this volume, Joe Marek has collected all Glenn Lord's *Ultimate Thule* as they appeared in the Hyperborean League's apa mailings.

Contents: No. 1 (1975): Recounts Robert E. Howard's first effort to sell "The Hour of the Dragon," to the British publisher Denis Archer. No. 2 (1976): Examples of personal rejection letters received by Robert E. Howard. No. 3 (1976): An exchange of letters between Oscar J. Friend and Dr. P.M. Kuykendall, with regards to the possible sale of all rights to Robert E. Howard's work to Oscar J. Friend. No. 4 (1976): A list of total sales of stories and poems made by Howard in his lifetime and earnings made from these sales. No. 5 (1977): More personal rejection letters and letter requests for rewrites, and an attempt by Glenn Lord at updating the "Translations" section of "The Last Celt" (D.M. Grant 1976). No. 6 (1978): Further "Translations" updates of "The Last Celt," some publishing news and a final batch of personal rejection letters. In the Hyperborean League's mailing No. 12 in July, 1978, Glenn Lord featured a proposed catalogue of the books from Robert E. Howard's personal library, which had been donated to the Memorial Collection at the Howard Payne College Library in Brownwood, Texas. This was the last *Ultima Thule* contribution by Glenn Lord to the Hyperborean League's apa mailings. Soon thereafter the League merged with REHupa. $15.

A17 The Robert E. Howard Companion. Joseph Marek, Omaha, Nebraska, 2004. Edited by Joseph Marek. 48 pp. Wraps. Copies printed not stated. Cover price $12.00. Contains critical articles and essays on Robert E. Howard. Illustrated by various artists.

Contents: No. 1 (2004): *"The Voice of El-Lil" and the Lost Race Tradition,* by Morgan Holmes; *The Trouble With Swords,* by Fred Blosser; *North by Southwest—by chaos out of dream in "The Marchers of Valhalla,"* by Steve Tompkins; *Travels with Robert E. Howard,* by Rusty Burke; *Pike Bearfield: An Appreciation,* by Joe Marek; *King Kull of Lost Atlantis—a Portfolio,* by Brian Laub; News; Reviews; Editorial by Joe Marek. $15.

A18 The Cimmerian. Playa del Rey, California, 2004. Edited by Leo Grin. 40 pp. Wraps. Printed in two editions; a deluxe edition, numbered 1 to 75 and a limited edition, numbered 76 to 225. Cover price deluxe $15.00; limited $10.00. A scholarly journal dedicated to the study of Robert E. Howard. Published bimonthly. Illustrations by Jason Castagna, Jae Woo Kim and other artists. Pertinent scholarly contributions are encouraged. For subscription information visit *www.thecimmerian.com.*

Contents: Vol. 1—No. 1 (2004): Editorial: *It's Morning Again in Howardia,* by Leo Grin; The Robert E. Howard Library of Classics—Symposium: *Conan the Expensive,* by Don Herron; *The One and Authentic Cimmerian,* by Darrell Schweitzer; *Napoleon's Triumph?* by Gary Romeo; *Hell Needs a New Devil,* by Leo Grin; Announcements; *The Stain of Victory* (poem), by Richard L. Tierney; Howard History: *A Few Hours From Death,* by R.C. "Bob" Baker; Contributors. Vol. 1—No. 2 (2004): Editorial: *The Old and the New,* by Leo Grin; *The Great Game,* by David A. Hardy; *The Runyonesque Raconteur,* by Mark Finn; *Dog in the Manger—A Review of The Barbaric Triumph,* by Richard A. Lupoff; *Small Poets Sing—Two reviews of The Barbaric Triumph* by Robert Weinberg; Announcements; *Near the End of the Epic* (poem), by Darrell Schweitzer; Howard History: *Cross Plains Journal,* by Richard L Tierney; The Lion's Den; Contributors. Vol. 1—No. 3 (2004): Editorial: *Cross Plains Or Bust,* by Leo Grin; *Cross Plains Memories,* by Leo Grin; *Sacred Ground:* The keynote address from the Howard Days 2004 banquet, by Robert Weinberg; Announcements; *A Spirit on the Wind* (poem), by Frank Coffman; Howard History: *He Was Deadly,* by Don Herron; The Lion's Den; Contributors. Vol. 1—No. 4 (2004): Editorial: *Honoring the Past,* by Leo Grin; *Reverend Bob on Two-Gun Bob—A Conversation with Robert M. Price,* by Benjamin Szumskyj; *The Last Temptation of Conan,* by Robert M. Price; Announcements; *Heart's Blood,* by Leo Grin; *Vengeance Quest* (poem), by Richard L. Tierney; Howard History: *The Ghosts of Fort McKavett,* by Leo Grin; The Lion's Den; *Requiescat in Pace: Joe Howser 1926—2004;* Contributors. Vol. 1—No. 5 (2004): Editorial: *One Book to Rule Them All...; After Twenty Years, A Landmark,* by Darrell Schweitzer; *Hard-Boiled Heroic Critic,* by Charles Hoffman; *Thirty Years as a Howard Critic (in Twenty Minutes or Less),* by Don Herron; Howard History: *TDB Reviews: 1984—85,* various writers; *To A Dead City—Cartagena de las Indias 1532—1583—1697* (poem), translated from the French of José-Maria de Heredia by Donald Sidney-Fryer; The Lion's Den; Contributors. Vol. 2—No. 1 (2005): Editorial: *Momentum,* by Leo Grin; *Howard's Run,* by Rob Roehm; *Inspirations From Life,* by Gary Romeo; *Conquistadors of Doom,* by David A. Hardy;

Announcements; *The Companion's Tale* (poem) by Darrell Schweitzer; The Lion's Den; Contributors. Vol. 2—No. 2 (2005): The Robert E. Howard Bison Books, Symposium, Part 1; Editorial: *The Origin of Species*; *How the West Was Wondered*, by Steve Tompkins; *A Gent Up Bear Creek*, by David Gentzel; *A More Sincere Form of Flattery*, by Rick McCollum; Howard History: *Old Pickets Find New Homes*, by Era Lee Hanke; *The Blades of Hell* (poem), by Don Herron; The Lion's Den; Contributors. Vol. 2—No. 3 (2005): The Robert E. Howard Bison Books, Symposium, Part 2; Editorial: *The Most Wonderful Time of the Year*, by Leo Grin; *Born to Edit Boxing Stories*, by Chris Gruber; *Frontiers of Imagination*, by Rusty Burke; *Fight Stories Feeding Frenzy*, by Mark Finn; *Demeure Exotique* (poem), by Donald Sidney-Fryer; The Lion's Den; Contributors. Vol. 2—No. 4 (2005): Editorial: *The British Invasion of Texas; Crazy Son* (poem), by Frank Coffman; *When you Wish Upon a (Wandering) Star*, by Leo Grin; *The Mystery of the Treasure Room*, by Rob Roehm; *Bundling Inscribed*, by Joseph Linzalone; The Lion's Den; Contributors. Vol. 2—No. 5 (2005): Editorial: *Swordplay and Spice and Everything Nice; Bloodlust*, by Charles Hoffman; *Asgard, Vanaheim, and Cimmeria*, by Leon Nielsen; Announcements; *Trail of the Veiled Prophet*, by David A. Hardy; *Small World*, by James Reasoner; *That Bed Beneath the Stars* (poem), by Anthony Avacato; The Lion's Den; Contributors. Vol. 2—6 (2005): Editorial: *Christmas with the Kooks; Robert E. Howard in the Necronomicon Press*, by John D. Haefele; *In Defense of "Little Boys,"* by Donald Sidney-Fryer; *At the Mammaries of Madness*, by Rick McCollum; *The Unseen Gods of Ancient Egypt* (poem), by Stanley C. Sargent; The Lion's Den; Contributors.

A19   Sword & Fantasy. James Van Hise, Yucca Valley, California, 2005. Edited by James Van Hise. 82 pages. Side-stapled wraps. Copies printed not stated. Cover price $12.00. Not an entirely Howard-oriented fanzine, but a general forum for sword and sorcery writings. Contains reprinted items from REHupa mailings and some new material. Color cover art and interior illustrations in b/w by various artists. For subscription information contact *jimvanhise@aol.com*.

Contents: No. 1 (2005): Editorial: *Mission Statement*, by James Van Hise; *In Memoriam: Robert Ervin Howard*, by H.P. Lovecraft, Otis Adelbert Kline, E. Hoffmann Price and Jack Byrne; *The 2002 San Diego Comicon Wandering Star/ Robert E. Howard Panel*, by James Van Hise; *A Robert E, Howard Fanzine Rises from the Grave: R.E.H.: Two-Gun Raconteur; The R.E.H. Fanzines: Cross Plains; REH: Lone Star Fictioneer; A Guide to the Robert E. Howard Related Material in Fantasy Crossroad*, by James Van Hise; *Karl Edward Wagner's Kane;* by James Van Hise; *The Valley of the Worm(s)*, by James Van Hise; *Gil Kane's Blackmark: The First Sword & Sorcery Graphic Novel*, by James Van Hise; *An Explanation for Censorship from Donald M. Grant*, by James Van Hise: Letter from Donald M. Grant to James Van Hise. No. 2 (2005): Editorial: *Sword and Fantasy: Back for More*, by James Van Hise; *The Adventures of Two-Gun Bob—An Interview with Jim and Ruth Keegan*, by James Van Hise; *Sword & Sorcery or Thud & Blunder? It's All in How it's Done*, by James Van Hise; *The Modern Revival of Robert E. Howard Fandom*, by James Van Hise; *Selling the Fantasy Story*, by Henry Kuttner; *Stories We Reject—*, by Charles D. Horning; *Superman on a Psychotic Bender*, by H.R. Hays; Book Reviews: A Howard Anthology *Skull-Face and Others (1947)*, by Arthur Hillman; *Robert E. Howard*, by Charles Dumbleton; Robert E.

Howard Bio Excerpt by Harold Preece; *Swords and Sorcery in the Warren Magazines,* by James Van Hise; *A Look at "The Scarlet Citadel,"* by James Van Hise; Collecting Robert E. Howard Material, by James Van Hise; *A Robert E. Howard Weird Tales Folio,* by various artists. No. 3 (2005): Editorial: *History and Histrionics,* by James Van Hise; *R.E.H.,* by R.H. Barlow; *Kull: The Road to Kull Was Paved With Good Intentions,* by James Van Hise; *Kull the Conqueror: As Bad As We Feared,* film review by James Van Hise; *A Biographical Sketch of E. Hoffmann Price,* by Alvin Earl Perry; *Men Who Make the Argosy,* by E. Hoffman Price; Letter from E. Hoffmann Price to August Derleth (1945); *Author, Author,* by L. Sprague de Camp; Review: *The Humor of de Camp,* by John K. Aiken; *Shadows in the Moonlight,* by James Van Hise; *Hannes Bok Looks at Fantasy, Art and Illustration,* by Hannes Bok; Book Reviews: *Forward Into the Past,* by James Van Hise; *A Weird Tales Cover Folio.* No. 4 (2005): Editorial, *Forward, Into the Past!* by James Van Hise; The *Weird Tales* Panel, August 13, 1998, by James Van Hise; *The Challenge from Beyond,* by C.L. Moore, A. Merritt, H.P. Lovecraft, Robert E. Howard & Frank Belknap Long, Jr.; *An Interview with Karl Edward Wagner,* by Cart T. Ford; *Modern Sword and Sorcery in Comics,* by James Van Hise; *The Legend of the Water Horse,* by Jim & Ruth Keegan; *An Interlude in Cross Plains,* by Rick McCollum; *The Elak Stories of Henry Kuttner,* by Richard Toogood; Henry Kuttner Obituary, by Forrest J. Ackerman; *The People Who Write Science Stories,* by Virgil Finlay; *Dragonheart: The Chuck Pogue Interview,* by James Van Hise; *Robert E. Howard in Paperback,* by James Van Hise; *The Krenkel and Frazetta Question,* by Stephen J. Cassinelli.

A20 **The Cimmerian Library.** Playa del Rey, California, 2005. Edited by Leo Grin. 8vo. 40 pp. Wraps. 100 numbered copies printed. Cover price $8.00. A scholarly reference journal intended to form a database of indexes, articles, essays and other published references on the study of Robert E. Howard and his work. For subscription information visit *www.thecimmerian.com.*

Contents: Vol. 1 (2005): *Introduction,* by Rob Roehm; Index to *Cromlech 1–3;* Index to *The Dark Man 1–6. Author and Subject Index; Title Index;* Acknowledgments.

Addendum

Hyborian Times, George R. Heap, New York 1967. Number 1, August 1967. Edited by George R. Heap. 4to. 8 pp. Type-written, side-stapled sheets. Small printing for distribution with the amateur press publication SCIENCE FICTION TIMES. Cover price $.25. Appears to be a supplementary publication with writings and reviews by Lin Carter, George Heap and others, focusing on Howard's Sword and Sorcery work. Half of the last page is blank with return address, so the issue could be folded, stapled and used as a mailing piece. An uncommon item. $50.

6
Most Collectible Titles

How collectible a Robert E. Howard title may be, depends largely on its scarcity and demand, not necessarily on its literary merits. If a title is available in limited numbers and have a high demand, its value as a collectible increases. Since value is prompted by the relationship between scarcity and demand, its price may often be an indicator of how collectible a title is at the time.

Which titles of Robert E. Howard's work are the most collectible, has been widely debated among collectors and will most likely change with time and trends. Each collector have personal preferences and reaching a general consensus would be difficult. The following listing is based on my personal experience as a Howard collector and book seller.

Pulps and other magazines have not been included. Magazines from the 1920s and 1930s which carry stories or poems by Robert E. Howard are especially collectible, as indicated by their high value. Key numbers and issues which illustrate the Howard contribution on the cover are particularly sought after by collectors and demand premium prices. For more information, the reader is referred to the magazine section of the bibliography to find these issues and suggested value. Amateur press journals (with one exception), titles which are still in print or titles available as print-on-demand publications are not included. The following titles are listed in the chronological order of publication.

1. *A Gent from Bear Creek* (Herbert Jenkins, 1937)
2. *The Hyborean Age* (LANY Cooperative Publishers, 1938)
3. *Skull-Face and Others* (Arkham House, 1946)
4. *Conan the Conqueror* (Gnome Press, 1950)
5. *The Sword of Conan* (Gnome Press, 1952)
6. *King Conan* (Gnome Press, 1953)
7. *The Coming of Conan* (Gnome Press, 1953)
8. *Conan the Barbarian* (Gnome Press, 1954)
9. *Always Comes Evening* (Arkham House, 1957)
10. *The Dark Man and Others* (Arkham House, 1963)

11. *The Pride of Bear Creek* (D.M. Grant, 1966)
12. *Conan the Adventurer* (Lancer Books, 1966)
13. *Conan the Warrior* (Lancer Books, 1967)
14. *King Kull* (Lancer Books, 1967)
15. *The Howard Collector.* (1 to 18. Glenn Lord, 1961 to 1973)
16. *Conan* (Lancer Books, 1968)
17. *Wolfshead* (Lancer Books, 1968)
18. *Etchings in Ivory* (Glenn Lord, 1968)
19. *Red Shadows* (D.M. Grant, 1968)
20. *Bran Mak Morn* (Dell Books, 1969)
21. *Singers in the Shadows* (D.M. Grant, 1970)
22. *Red Blades of Black Cathay* (D.M. Grant, 1971)
23. *Black Dawn* (Roy Squires, 1972)
24. *Echoes from an Iron Harp* (D.M. Grant, 1972)
25. *Marchers of Valhalla* (D.M. Grant, 1972)
26. *The Sowers of the Thunder* (D.M. Grant, 1973)
27. *A Song of the Naked Land* (Roy Squires, 1973)
28. *The Vultures* (Fictioneer Books, 1973)
29. *The Gold and the Grey* (Roy Squires, 1974)
30. *Altars and Jesters* (Roy Squires, 1974)
31. *Verses in Ebony* (George T. Hamilton, 1974 and 1975)
32. *The Incredible Adventures of Dennis Dorgan* (Fax, 1974)
33. *The Lost Valley of Iskander* (Fax, 1974)
34. *Blades for France* (George T. Hamilton, 1975)
35. *Shadow of the Hun* (George T. Hamilton, 1975)
36. *The Tower of the Elephant* (D.M. Grant, 1975)
37. *A Witch Shall Be Born* (D.M. Grant, 1975)
38. *The Iron Man* (D.M. Grant, 1976)
39. *Swords of Shahrazar* (Fax, 1976)
40. *Black Vulmea's Vengeance* (D.M. Grant, 1976)
41. *Pigeons from Hell* (Zebra Books, 1976)
42. *The Grim Land and Others* (Jonathan Bacon, 1976)
43. *The Kings Service* (George T. Hamilton, 1976)
44. *Bicentennial Tribute to Robert E. Howard*, (George T. Hamilton, 1976)
45. *The Sword Woman* (Zebra Books, 1977)
46. *Three-Bladed Doom* (Zebra Books, 1977)
47. *The People of the Black Circle* (Berkley/Putnam, 1977)
48. *Red Nails* (Berkley/Putnam, 1977)
49. *The Hour of the Dragon* (Berkley/Putnam, 1977)
50. *The Shadow of the Beast* (George T. Hamilton, 1977)
51. *Up, John Kane! and Other Poems* (Roy Squires, 1977)
52. *Queen of the Black Coast* (D.M. Grant, 1978)

Three-Bladed Doom. Zebra Books 1977. Cover art by Enrich. © 1977 Glenn Lord.

The People of the Black Circle. Berkley Books 1977. Cover art by Ken Kelly. © 1977 Glenn Lord.

The Hour of the Dragon. Berkley Books 1977. Cover art by Ken Kelly. © 1977 Glenn Lord.

53. *Black Canaan* (Berkley Books, 1978)
54. *The Last Ride* (Berkley Books, 1978)
55. *Spears of Clontarf* (George T. Hamilton, 1978)
56. *The Road of Azrael* (D.M. Grant, 1979)
57. *Hawks of Outremer* (D.M. Grant, 1979)
58. *The Howard Collector* (Ace Books, 1979)
59. *Lord of the Dead* (D.M. Grant, 1981)
60. *The Ghost Ocean* (Gibbelins Gazette, 1982)
61. *Two-Fisted Detective Stories* (Cryptic Publications, 1984)
62. *Kull* (D.M. Grant, 1985)
63. *The Adventures of Lal-Singh* (Cryptic Publications, 1985)
64. *Writer of the Dark* (Dark Carneval, Zurich, 1986)
65. *North of Khyber* (Cryptic Publications, 1987)
66. *Shadows of Dreams* (D.M. Grant, 1989)
67. *A Man-Eating Jeopard* (Alla Ray Morris, 1994)
68. *The Savage Tales of Solomon Kane* (Wandering Star, 1998)
69. *The Ultimate Triumph* (Wandering Star, 2000)
70. *The Black Stranger* (Wandering Star, 2002)

7
A REPRESENTATIVE ROBERT E. HOWARD COLLECTION

For his relatively brief career as a writer, Robert E. Howard produced an unprecedented amount of diversified material, including, stories, novelettes, novels, poems, essays, and articles. He also wrote in several different genres, including heroic fantasy, sword and sorcery, weird tales, boxing stories, historical fiction, action adventure stories, detective stories and horror stories. A representative collection of Howard's work should preferably cover all of these genres, perhaps not of equal representation for the best of Howard's writings is not comparably distributed.

The works of many writers published in the early part of the 20th century are difficult to find today. Not so with Robert E. Howard. Most of what he wrote has been reprinted again and again, so it is not difficult to find very recent copies of his work. As mentioned previously, many of the modern printings have also been textually corrected and are true to the original text as written by Howard. Thanks to publishers such as the University of Nebraska, Wildside Press and Wandering Star it is possible to obtain new printings of the greater body of Howard's works today for a reasonable price.

As for most other writers, not everything that Howard wrote was superb or better than average. Not every sentence that emanated from his typewriter was golden or the work of a genius. Howard wrote for money, he wrote volumes and he wrote fast. Among the many great pieces he produced, there are also plot-redundant, cliche-ridden writings or story lines and poems that do not work as intended. Much of this lesser material, however, has been rediscovered, acclaimed by Howard enthusiasts or enterprising editors and, regardless of its literary merits or lack thereof, reprinted in various publications. Robert E. Howard was a man of opposites. When he was inspired and wrote well, the result was remarkably good, but when he was uninspired and just put words on paper, the outcome could be equally unremarkable.

For the general collector of fantasy, adventure, science fiction, and sword and sorcery literature, a representative sample of Howard's works need not be especially voluminous. For the collector who only wants a few, quintessential volumes, I would suggest the following titles, listed in order of publication:

> *Skull-Face and Other Stories* (Arkham House, 1946)
> *Always Comes Evening* (Arkham House, 1957)
> *The Dark Man and Others* (Arkham House, 1964)
> *A Gent From Bear Creek* (D. M. Grant, 1965)
> *Red Shadows* (D.M. Grant, 1968)
> *The Sowers of the Thunder* (D. M. Grant, 1973)
> *Worms of the Earth* (D. M. Grant, 1974)
> *The Incredible Adventures of Dennis Dorgan* (Fax, 1974)
> *The Swords of Shahrazar* (Fax, 1976)
> *Kull* (D.M. Grant, 1985)
> *The Conan Chronicles* (Gollancz, 2000)

For the more discerning Howard collector the list is considerably longer and there are inevitably some repetition of stories and poems. Again one should keep in mind that many of the earlier works mentioned in the following have been edited for political correctness, revised and at times entirely rewritten by various editors and writers. To characterize these altered texts as being truly 'representative' of Robert E. Howard would be a misnomer. The following are listed in order of publication:

> *Skull-Face and Others* (Arkham House, 1946)
> *Conan the Conqueror* (Gnome Press, 1950)
> *The Sword of Conan* (Gnome Press, 1952)
> *King Conan* (Gnome Press, 1953)
> *The Coming of Conan* (Gnome Press, 1953)
> *Conan the Barbarian* (Gnome Press, 1954)
> *Always Comes Evening* (Arkham House, 1957)
> *The Dark Man and Others* (Arkham House, 1963)
> *A Gent From Bear Creek* (D.M. Grant, 1965)
> *The Pride of Bear Creek* (D.M. Grant, 1966)
> *King Kull* (Lancer Books, 1967)
> *Wolfshead* (Lancer Books, 1968)
> *Etchings in Ivory* (Glenn Lord, 1968)
> *Red Shadows* (D.M. Grant, 1968)
> *Bran Mak Morn* (Dell Books, 1969)

7—A Representative Robert E. Howard Collection

Singers in the Shadows (D.M. Grant, 1970)
Red Blades of Black Cathay (D.M. Grant, 1971)
Echoes from an Iron Harp (D.M. Grant, 1972)
Marchers of Valhalla (D.M. Grant, 1972)
The Sowers of the Thunder (D.M. Grant, 1973)
The Vultures (Fictioneer Books, 1973)
Verses in Ebony (George T. Hamilton, 1975)
The Incredible Adventures of Dennis Dorgan (Fax, 1974)
The Lost Valley of Iskander (Fax, 1974)
Shadow of the Hun (George T. Hamilton, 1975)
The Tower of the Elephant (D.M. Grant, 1975)
A Witch Shall Be Born (D.M. Grant, 1975)
The Iron Man (D.M. Grant, 1976)
Swords of Shahrazar (Fax, 1976)
Black Vulmea's Vengeance (D.M. Grant, 1976)
Pigeons from Hell (Zebra Books, 1976)
The Grim Land and Others (Jonathan Bacon, 1976)
Night Images (Morning Star, 1976)
The Sword Woman (Zebra Books, 1977)
Three-Bladed Doom (Zebra Books, 1977)
The People of the Black Circle (Berkley/Putnam, 1977)
Red Nails (Berkley/Putnam, 1977)
The Hour of the Dragon (Berkley/Putnam, 1977)
The Shadow of the Beast (George T. Hamilton, 1977
Queen of the Black Coast (D.M. Grant, 1978)
Black Canaan (Berkley Books, 1978)
The Last Ride (Berkley Books, 1978)
Spears of Clontarf (George T. Hamilton, 1978)
The Road of Azrael (D.M. Grant, 1979)
Hawks of Outremer (D.M. Grant, 1979)
Mayhem at Bear Creek (D.M. Grant, 1979)
The Howard Collector (Ace Books, 1979)
Lord of the Dead (D.M. Grant, 1981)
Kull (D.M. Grant, 1985)
Writer of the Dark (Dark Carneval, Zurich, 1986)
Shadows of Dreams (D.M. Grant, 1989)
The Savage Tales of Solomon Kane (Wandering Star, 1998)
The Ultimate Triumph (Wandering Star, 2000)
Bran Mak Morn (Wandering Star, 2001)
Nameless Cults (Chaosium, 2001)
The Black Stranger (Wandering Star, 2002)
The Complete Action Stories (Wildside Press, 2003)

Marchers of Valhalla. Berkley Books 1978. Cover art by Ken Kelly. © 1978 Glenn Lord.

7—*A Representative Robert E. Howard Collection* 257

The Sword Woman. Zebra Books 1977. Cover art by Stephen Fabian. © 1977 Glenn Lord.

Spears of Clontarf. George T. Hamilton 1978. Cover art by Stephen Fabian. © 1978 Glenn Lord and George T. Hamilton.

Conan of Cimmeria, Vol. 1 (Wandering Star, 2002)
Graveyard Rats and Others (Wildside Press, 2003)
Conan of Cimmeria, Vol. 2 (Wandering Star, 2003)
Shadow Kingdoms (Wildside Press, 2004)
Moon of Skulls (Wildside Press, 2005)
People of the Dark (Wildside Press, 2005)

The last category of collectors are the completists who wants to acquire a sample of everything written by or about Robert E. Howard and published in every format and in various media. Such collection would include all pulp magazines, hardcover books, paperbacks, special printings, amateur press publications, newspaper articles, letters, typescripts and miscellaneous memorabilia. Few such complete collections exists and the acquisition of this amount of material in collectible condition may be a high-priced and lifetime endeavor. For these collectors, I hope that the bibliography in this book may provide some guidance and assistance in their arduous, but worthy pursuit of the perfectly all-inclusive Robert E. Howard collection.

8
Reference Bibliography

The following sources were consulted during the research and preparation for this book. All of the listed titles are highly recommended for more in-depth information on Robert E. Howard, his life and works, and on relevant literary studies and criticism, and book collecting in general.

Ahearn, Allen and P. Ahearn (2001). *Book Collecting 2000.* New York: G.P. Putnam's Sons. 536 pp.
____. (2001). *Collected Books—The Guide to Values 2002 Edition.* New York: G.P. Putnam's Sons. 788 pp.
Burke, Rusty (1998). *The Robert E. Howard Bookshelf.* New York: A Celtic Weirdness Production. www.rehupa.com.
____. (1999). *REH: A Short Biography of Robert E. Howard.* New York: Cross Plains Comics. 64 pp.
____. (2000). *Robert E. Howard, Bran Mak Morn, and the Picts. Worms of the Earth.* New York: Cross Plains Comics, and London, England: Wandering Star. 58–61.
____. (2001). *Robert E. Howard in Cross Plains.* (Revised edition 2004), Houston, Texas: A Celtic Weirdness Production. 30 pp.
____. (2001). *"All Fled , All Done."* Rockford, Illinois: *The Dark Man. The Journal of Robert E. Howard Studies.* Vol. 1, Number 5; 15–17.
____. (2002). *Bob Howard and the Bullies.* Houston, Texas: A Celtic Weirdness Production: The Iron Harp # 3, Vol. 2, Number 1. www.robert-e-howard.org.
Canja, Jeff (2002). *Collectable Paperback Books.* East Lansing, Michigan: Glenmoor Publishing. 377 pp.
Cottrill, Tim (2001). *Bookery's Ultimate Guide to the Pulps and Related Magazines.* Fairborn, Ohio: Bookery Press. 540 pp.
De Camp, L. Sprague (1968). *The Conan Reader.* Baltimore, Maryland: The Mirage Press. 148 pp.
____. (ed.) (1979). *The Blade of Conan.* New York: Ace Books. 310 pp.
____. (ed.) (1980). *The Spell of Conan.* New York: Ace Books. 244 pp.
De Camp, L. Sprague and G.H. Scithers (ed.) (1969) *The Conan Sword Book.* Baltimore, Maryland: The Mirage Press. 255 pp.
____ and ____ (eds.) (1972). *The Conan Grimoire.* Baltimore, Maryland: The Mirage Press. 261 pp.
De Camp, L. Sprague, C.C. de Camp, and J.W. Griffin (1983). *Dark Valley Destiny, The Life of Robert E. Howard, The Creator of Conan.* New York: Bluejay Books, Inc. 402 pp.
Elliot, G.F. Scott (1909). *The Romance of Early British Life.* London, England: Seeley and Co., Limited. 358 pp.

Eng, Stephen (1984). *Appendix A—Robert E. Howard's Library.* In Don Herron *The Dark Barbarian.* Westport, Connecticut: Greenwood Press. 183–200.

Greenfield, Jane (1983). *Books Their Care & Repair.* New York: The H.W. Wilson Company. 204 pp.

Hancer, Kevin (1990). *Hancer's Price Guide to Paperback Books—Third Edition.* Radnor, Pennsylvania: Wallace-Homestead Book Company. 353 pp.

Herron, Don (1984). *The Dark Barbarian.* Westport, Connecticut: Greenwood Press. 242 pp.

_____. (2000). *Collecting Robert E. Howard.* Tucson, Arizona: *Firsts, The Book Collector's Magazine.* Vol. 10, Number 7/8; 26–41.

_____. (2000). *The Best Barbarian.* Tucson, Arizona: *Firsts, The Book Collector's Magazine.* Vol. 10, Number 7/8; 34–35.

_____. (2000). *A Robert E. Howard Check List.* Tucson, Arizona: *Firsts, The Book Collector's Magazine.* Vol. 10, Number 7/8; 36–37.

_____. (2004). *The Barbarian Triumph.* Holicong, Pennsylvania: Wildside Press. 200 pp.

_____. (2004). *Conan the Expensive.* Downey, California: *The Cimmerian,* Vol. 1, Number 1; 5–13.

Howard, Robert E. (1990). *Post Oaks & Sand Roughs.* West Kingston, Rhode Island: Donald M. Grant, Publisher, Inc. 176 pp.

Howlett-West, Stephanie (ed.) (1999). *The Inter-Galactic Price Guide to Science Fiction, Fantasy & Horror 1999.* Peoria, Illinois: Spoon River Press. 253 pp.

Lord, Glenn (ed.) (1970). *Letter: Dr. I.M. Howard to H.P. Lovecraft, dated June 29, 1936.* Pasadena, Texas: The Howard Collector. Vol. 3, Number 1; 9–13.

_____. (1976). *The Last Celt.* West Kingston, Rhode Island: Donald M. Grant, Publisher. 416 pp.

_____. (1976) *ULTIMA THULE, Number 3.* In *Bicentennial Tribute to Robert E. Howard.* Yorba Linda, California: George T. Hamilton. 26–29.

_____. (ed.) (1989). *Robert E. Howard, Selected Letters 1923–1930.* West Warwick, Rhode Island: Necronomicon Press. 84 pp.

_____. (ed.) (1991). *Robert E. Howard, Selected Letters 1931–1936.* West Warwick, Rhode Island: Necronomicon Press. 80 pp.

McHaney, Dennis and Glenn Lord (1975). *The Fiction of Robert E. Howard.* Memphis, Tennessee: D.M. McHaney and Tom Foster. 24 pp.

Nielsen, Leon (2004). *Arkham House Books—A Collector's Guide.* Jefferson, North Carolina: McFarland & Company, Inc., Publishers. 194 pp.

_____. (2005). *Asgard, Vanaheim, and Cimmeria.* Playa del Rey, California: *The Cimmerian,* Vol. 2. Number 5; 15–19.

Price, E. Hoffmann (2001). *Book of the Dead. Friends of Yesteryear. Fictioneers and Others.* Sauk City, Wisconsin: Arkham House Publishers, Inc. 423 pp.

Price Ellis, Novalyne (1986). *One Who Walked Alone.* West Kingston, Rhode Island: Donald M. Grant, Publishers, Inc. 317 pp.

_____. (1989). *The Day of the Stranger.* West Warwick, Rhode Island: Necronomicon Press. 47 pp.

Rippke, Dale E. (2004). *The Hyborian Heresies.* Wildcat Books, Lulu Enterprises, Inc. 99 pp.

Roehm, Rob (2005). *The Mystery of the Treasure Room.* Playa del Rey, California: *The Cimmerian,* Vol. 2, Number 4; 19–26.

Romeo, Gary (2004). *In Search of Cimmeria.* The Cimmerian Press. 40 pp.

Ruber, Peter (ed.) (1999). *Arkham's Masters of Horror.* Sauk City, Wisconsin: Arkham House Publishers, Inc. 443 pp.

Schweitzer, Darrell (2004). *The One and Authentic Cimmerian.* Downey, California: *The Cimmerian,* Vol. 1, Number 1; 14–19.

Smith, Tevis Clyde, Jr. (1991). *Report on a Writing Man and Other Reminiscences of Robert E. Howard.* West Warwick, Rhode Island: Necronomicon Press. 48 pp.

Szumskyj, Ben (ed.) (2003). *Robert E. Howard, The Power of the Writing Mind.* Poplar Bluff, Missouri: Mythos Books, LLC. 76 pp.

Van Hise, James (ed.) (1997). *The Fantastic Worlds of Robert E. Howard.* Yucca Valley, California: James Van Hise. 190 pp.

———. (2001). *The History of the Robert E. Howard APA #1–175.* Yucca Valley, California: James Van Hise. 110 pp.

Warfield, Wayne (ed.) (1976). *The Ultimate Guide to Howardia 1925–1975.* Cross Plains, Texas: Wayne Warfield. 32 pp.

Weinberg, Robert (1976). *The Annotated Guide to Robert E. Howard's Sword & Sorcery.* West Linn, Oregon: Starmont House. 152 pp.

———. (1999). *The Weird Tales Story.* Berkeley Heights, New Jersey: Wildside Press. 134 pp.

Index to Poems and Prose Poems

References are to bibliography serial numbers. This index includes Robert E. Howard poems or prose poems published in magazines, hardcover and softcover books, mass market paperbacks or in special, limited printings. Reprints are listed in categorical/chronological order.

The bibliography serial numbers are identified as follows: Magazines with the prefix letter M. Books with the letter B. Mass market paperbacks with the letter P. Special printings with the letter S. Amateur press journals with the letter A.

Abe Lincoln B50
Adventure B35
The Adventurer S21, A15/SE
The Adventurer's Mistress S28, A15/SE
Age B35, A2/14
Age Comes to Rabelais B15, A2/8
Alien S11, A15/SE
Altars and Jesters B35, S9
Always Comes Evening M32(2/41), B9, B35, S23, A7/2, A15/7
Ancient Englishe Ballad S36
And Beowulf Rides Again B35
Arkham M39(8/32), B9, B76, P58, S14
Attila Rides No More B13
Autumn M39(4/33), B9, B76

Babel B9, A9/13
Babylon B9
A Ballad of Beer B50
The Ballad of Bucksnort Roberts B70, S14, A15/SE
The Ballad of King Geraint S41, A15/6
The Ballad of Singapore Nell S42
Ballade B50
The Bar by the Side of the Road P27, P52, A2/17
Bastards All (play) S36
Belshazzar B15, A2/5

Black Chant Imperial M39(9/30), B9, B67
Black Dawn B35, S5, S10
Black Harps in the Hills B35
Black Seas B50, S51
The Black Stone B15
The Blood of Belshazzar B15
Bloodstones and Ebony P27, S4
The Bride of Cuchulain B13
A Buccaneer Speaks B35
Buccaneer Treasure A15/2
But the Hills Were Ancient Then B15

The Call of Pan B50, S51
The Campus at Midnight B35
Candles S28, A15/1
Castaway B50
The Cats of Anubis B35
A Challenge to Bast B50
The Champ S46
The Chant Demoniac A15/3
Chant of the White Beard B9
Cimmeria B15, B56, B60, P27, A2/7, A15/1
The Coming of Bast A15/4
The Cooling of Spike McRue S34
Counterspells A15/5
Crete M39(2/29), B9, B66
A Crown for a King B9b

263

The Cuckoo's Revenge A15/1
Custom A15/2

Dance Macabre A15/3
The Dance with Death A15/5
Daughter of Evil S42
A Dawn in Flanders B15, A2/5
The Day Breaks Over Simla B35, A7/4–5
The Day That I Die B15, P27, A2/9
Days of Glory B35
De Ole River Ox S21, A15/SE
Dead Man's Hate M39(1/30), B9, B67, A9/1
The Dead Slaver's Tale B35
Death's Black Riders B15, P17b
Desert Dawn M39(3/39), B9
Desire S42
Destination M20(Win/66), B13
Destiny B50, S51, A15/7
The Doom Chant of Than-Kul A15/5
Drake Sings of Yesterday A15/1
The Dream and the Shadow M39(9/37), B9
Dreaming in Israel B50
Dreaming of Downs A15/2
Dreams S25, A15/5
The Dreams of Men B50
Dreams of Nineveh B15
Drowned A15/3
Drum Gods A15/4
The Drums of Pictdom B19, P14, P21
A Dungeon Opens A15/2
The Dust Dance (Version 1) B15, B50, P27, S42, A2/7
The Dust Dance (Version 2) B15, A2/10
The Dweller in Dark Valley M20(11/65), B15
A Dying Pirate Speaks of Treasure S25, A15/4

Earth-Born B15
Easter Island M39(12/28), B9, B66
Echoes from an Anvil B35, S11
Ecstasy S14
The Ecstasy of Desolation B50
Egypt B35
Emancipation B9, S14
Empire B35, P27, S11, S51
Empire's Destiny A15/3
The End of the Glory Trail S14, A15/SE
Etchings in Ivory P27

A Fable for Critics B50
Fables for Little Folks B15

A Far Country B50, S51
"Feach Air Muir Lionadhi Gealach Buidhe Mar Or" B15
The Fear That Follows B13
The Fearsome Touch of Death B15
The Feud A7/13, A15/5
Flaming Marble B50, P27, S4, S51
Flight B35, S49
Flint's Passing S49, A7/3, A15/1
The Flood S28
For Man Was Given the Earth to Rule A15/2
Forbidden Magic M39(7/29), B9, B66
Fragment M39(12/37), B9, S14
Futility M39(11/37), B9, B15, S14, A2/4

The Gates of Babylon S28, A15/SE
The Gates of Nineveh M39(7/28), B9, B66, A9/12
Ghost Dancers S34
The Ghost Kings M39(12/38), B9, B35, A7/3
The Ghost Ocean S28, A15/SE
Girls A15/3
The Gladiator and the Lady B50
The Gods of Easter Island B9
The Gods of the Jungle Drums S21, A15/SE
The Gods Remember A15/4
The Gods That Men Forget P27, S4
The Gold and the Grey B35, P27, S8, S10
Good Mistress Brown S42
The Grey God Passes B15
The Grim Land B68, S21, A15/SE
The Guise of Youth P28

Hadrian's Wall B13
A Hairy Chested Idealist Sings S14, A15/SE
The Harlot S42
The Harp of Alfred M39(9/28), B9, B66, A9/12
Harvest P52, A2/17, A15/6
Haunting Columns M39(2/38), B9, B35
The Heart of the Sea's Desire B9, B35
Heritage B15, A2/10, A7/2, A15/5
Heritage (another poem) A7/2
The Hills of Kandahar M39(6/39), B9
Hope Empty of Meaning B35, P52, A2/15, A7/6
Hopes of Dreams B35
The Hour of the Dragon B15, A2/11
Hymn of Hatred B9

I Praise My Nativity B50
The Ideal Girl A15/6

Illusion B15
In the Ring B69, S52
Invective B9
The Isle of Hy-Brasil S28, A15/SE

The Jackal B35
John Brown B50
John L. Sullivan A15/1
John Ringold B15, B70, A2/5

Kelly the Conjure-Man B15
Keresa, Keresa B50
Kid Lavigne Is Dead B15, B61, B69
The King and the Mallet B35
The King and the Oak M39(2/39), B6, B9, B35, B47, P7, A15/1
The King of the Ages Comes B35
Kings of the Night B9, B35
The Kiowa's Tale B35, A8/1
The Kissing of Sal Snooboo B15

A Lady's Chamber B15
The Last Day M39(3/32), B15, B74
The Last Hour M39(6/38), B9
The Last Words He Heard B50
Laughter in the Gulfs B9
The Legacy of Tubal-Cain B35, P52, A2/18
A Legend S34
A Legend of Faring Town S11, A15/SE
L'Envoi A15/2, A15/3, A15/4
Lesbia S42
Let the Gods Die S34
Life P28, P52, A2/18
Lilith S28, S42
Lines Written in the Realization That I Must Die M39(8/38), B2, B9, B24, P28, P33
The Lion of Tiberias B15
Long Ago S34
Lost Altars B15
Lost Babylon B35
The Lost Galley B13
Love B50, S51
Love's Young Dream B50

Mad Meg Gill S25, A15/4
Madame Goose's Rhymes A7/7, A15/5
The Maiden of Kercheezer A15/1
A Man A15/2
Man Am I S28, A15/SE
Marching Song of Connacht B35, P52, A2/16
Mark of the Beast B35
The Master Drum B35
Medallions in the Moon P27, S4

Memories B15, A15/2
Memories of Alfred S28, A15/SE
Men Build Them Houses S11, A15/SE
Men of the Shadows B9, P14
The Men That Walk with Satan B13
Miser's Gold A7/8, A15/3
A Moment B15, A2/13
Moon Mockery M39(4/29), B9, B66, A9/1
Moon Shame B9
Moonlight on a Skull M39(5/33), B15, B76
The Moor Ghost M39(9/29), B9, B66
Musings B35, B50, P28, S51, A15/2
My Sentiments, Set to Jazz A15/4
The Myth S42

Nectar S21, A15/SE
A Negro Girl S42
Neolithic Love Song S39
Never Beyond the Beast S28, A15/SE
Niflheim B9, S14
Night Mood B13
The Night Winds S11, A15/SE
Nights to Both of Us Known B50
Nisapur B9
No More the Serpent Prow B35, A2/14
Nocturne A15/5
Not Only in Death They Die M20(7/69), B15

The Odyssey of Israel B50
Oh Babylon, Lost Babylon B35, A7/14
On with the Play P52, A2/17, A15/6
The One Black Stain B12, B53, P17b, P47, S28, A2/2
One Who Comes at Eventide B9
Only a Shadow on the Grass A15/1
An Open Window M39(9/32), B9, P58, B76, S14
The Outcast S21, A8/1, A15/SE
The Outgoing of Sigurd the Jerusalem-Farer S11, A15/SE
An Outworn Story A15/2

The Palace of Bast S42
The Passionate Typist A9/5
The Path of the Strange Wanderers B50
The Phases of Life A15/4
The Phoenix on the Sword B9, B35
A Pirate Remembers S21, A15/SE
A Pledge A2/14, A15/4
The Poets M39(3/38), B9, A7/2
A Poet's Skull B50
The Pool of the Black One B9

Prelude S42
Prince and Beggar B9
Private Magrath of the A.E.F. B15, S54
Proem S4

Queen of the Black Coast B9

Rebel B13
Rebellion A15/1
Recompense M39(11/38), B9, P27, A7/1
Reuben's Brethren B15, P28, A2/11
Red Blades of Black Cathay B9
Red Thunder B66, A15/2
Remembrance M39(4/28), B9, B66
Retribution B9
The Return of Sir Richard Grenville B12, B53, P17, P48
The Return of the Sea-Farer A15/4
Revolt Pagan S11, A15/SE
The Rhyme of the Three Slavers S30, A15/3
The Ride of Falume M39(10/27), B9, B66
The Riders of Babylon M39(1/28), B9, B66, A9/12
A Riding Song B50
The Road of Azrael B9
The Road to Babel B50
The Road to Freedom A5/7, A15/4
The Road to Hell B13
The Road to Rome B35, S6, S10
The Road to Yesterday S21, A15/SE
Roads P52, A2/17, A15/7
Roar, Silver Trumpets B35, A8/3
Romany Road B50
Roundelay of the Roughneck B15, A2/8
Rules of Etiquette A15/5
Rune B9

Sacrifice B13
Samson's Broodings B50
The Sand-Hill's Crest B70, A15/1
The Sands of the Desert A15/2
The Sands of Time B15, A2/1
The Scarlet Citadel B9
The Sea B15
Sea Girl B35
The Sea Woman B13
Sentiment P52, A2/9, A15/7
Seven Kings A15/3
Shadow Thing S28, A15/SE
Shadows B13
Shadows from Yesterday S28, A15/SE
Shadows of Dreams B50
Shadows on the Road M39(5/30), B9, B67

Ships M39(7/38), B9
Silence Falls on Mecca's Walls B50, P58
The Singer in the Mist M39(4/38), B9, A7/1
Singing Hemp B35, S11
Singing in the Wind A2/14, A9/4
The Skull in the Clouds B15, A2/2
Skulls S34
Skulls and Dust B15, A2/4
Skulls and Orchids P27, S4
Skulls Over Judah B15, A2/9
Slugger's Wow S52
Slumber M20(12/69), B15
Solomon Kane's Homecoming B9, B12, B35, B53, P17, P48, P52, A2/15
Solomon Kane's Homecoming (variant) B53, P52
Something About Eve B15, A15/1
Song at Midnight B9, S23
Song Before Clontarf B35, S34
A Song for All Women S42
A Song for Men That Laugh M20(Sum/67), B15
Song from an Ebony Heart B50
Song of a Fugitive Bard B50
The Song of a Mad Minstrel M39(2/31), B9, B74, P28, A7/1
A Song of Defeat M20(Fal/70), B15
The Song of Horsa's Galley B15, P28, A2/13
A Song of the Anchor Chain B50
The Song of the Bats M39(5/27), B9, B66, A9/12
A Song of the Don Cossacks B9
The Song of the Gallows Tree S34
The Song of the Jackal B35
The Song of the Last Briton S28
A Song of the Legions B15, A2/12
A Song of the Naked Lands S7, S10, A15/2
Song of the Pict B9, S28
A Song of the Race B19, B57, P14, P21
A Song of the Werewolf Folk A15/5
The Song of Yar Ali Khan A15/4
A Song Out of East B35
A Song Out of Midian M39(4/30), B9, B67, P27
Songs of Bastards (play) S36
A Sonnet of Good Cheer B15, P27, A2/9
Sonora to Del Rio B15, A2/1
The Soul-Eater M39(8/37), B9
The Sowers of the Thunder B15
Stay Not from Me B50
A Stirring of Green Leaves B50
Strange Passion S42

Index to Poems and Prose Poems

The Stranger B13
Surrender B15, B50, P28, A2/3
Swamp Murder B35, S11, S34
The Sword of Mahommed A15/1
The Symbol A15/2
Symbols B50, S51

Tarantella B15
The Tavern B13
The Tempter B9, S14
These Things Are Gods A15/3
The Thing on the Roof B15
Thor's Son B15, P27, A2/11
A Thousand Years Ago B35
Thus Spake Sven the Fool B13
The Tide B35
Tides A15/5
Tiger Girl B35, S34
Timur-lang B15, B71, A2/5
To a Friend B35, S11
To a Nameless Woman B50
To a Woman B9, S28, A15/SE
To All Evangelists A15/SE
To All Sophisticates S28, A15/SE
To All the Lords of Commerce S11, A15/SE
To an Earthbound Soul S21, A15/SE
To Certain Orthodox Brethren B15, A2/12
To Harry the Oliad Men B35
To Lyle Saxon B50
Today S21, A15/SE
Twilight on Stonehenge B50
The Twin Gates B13
Two Men S28, A15/SE

Universe A15/5
Up, John Kane! S25, A15/3

Victory B35
The Viking of the Sky A15/2
Viking's Trail B35, S11

Viking's Vision S28
A Vision M30 (Fal/67), B15
Visions B35, P52, A2/16, A7 (Special edition)
Voices of the Night S23
The Voices Waken Memory B9, A9/13

War to the Blind A7/4–5, A15/3
A Warning B15, A2/5
A Warning to Orthodoxy B50
The Weakling A15/4
A Weird Ballad B50
What Is Love? A15/5
When Death Drops Her Veil S25, A15/5
When the Glaciers Rumbled South S28, A15/SE
When the Gods were Kings B35
When You Were a Set-up and I Was a Ham B69, S46
Where Are Your Knights, Donn Othna? B15, A2/11
Which Will Scarcely Be Understood M39,(10/37), B2, B9, B24, P28, P31, P32, P33, S14
Whispers B50
Whispers on the Nightwinds B50
White Thunder B13
Who Is Grandpa Theobold? B15, A2/6
The Whoopansat of Humorous Kookooyam A15/1
The Witch B13
A Word from the Outer Dark B35, P28

The Years Are as a Knife M20(1/68), B15
A Young Wife's Tale A15/2

Zukala's Hour B13
Zukala's Jest A15/3
Zukala's Love Song A15/2
The Zulu Lord A15/4

Index to Story Titles

References are to bibliography serial numbers. This index includes Robert E. Howard stories published in magazines, hardcover and soft cover books, mass market paperbacks or in special, limited printings. Reprints are listed in categorical/chronological order.

The bibliography serial numbers are identified as follows: Magazines with the prefix letter M. Books with the letter B. Mass market paperbacks with the letter P. Special printings with the letter S. Amateur press journals with the letter A.

The Abbey B59, A7/4–5, A15/SE
After the Game S54
Age Lasting Love A15/7
Aha! Or the Mystery of the Queen's Necklace A2/4, A15/2
Alleys of Darkness M24(1/34), B61
Alleys of Peril M14(1/31), B61, S46
The Alleys of Singapore B20, P24, P26b
Alleys of Treachery A2/8
Almuric M39(5/6/8/39), B25, P2
The Altar and the Scorpion B47, P7
Ambition in the Moonlight A15/1
The Apache Mountain War M1(12/35), B11, B58, P56
The Apparition in the Prize Ring M15(4/29), B61
An Autobiography P40, A15/SE

The Beast from the Abyss P52, A2/15, A9/3
Beyond the Black River M39(5/6/35), B5, B28b, B52, B54, B56, B75, B77, P4, P39
Beyond the Brazos River B70
Bill Smalley and the Power of the Human Eye A14/2
Billy the Kid and the Lincoln County War B70
Black Abyss P7
The Black Bear Bites B59, P29b
Black Canaan M39(6/36), B2, B24, B68, P28, P31, P45, P62, S56, A15/SE
The Black City B47, P7c

Black Colossus M39(6/33), B7, B41, B55, B60, P11
Black Country A11/8, A15/5
Black Eons B59, A15/6
The Black Hound of Death M39(11/36), P62
The Black Moon S29
The Black Reaper S51
The Black Stone M39(11/31), M39(11/53), B2, B24, B59, B74, P9, P31, P58
The Black Stranger M13(3/53), B56, B68, B75, P64, S55
Black Talons M33(12/33), B62, P27, A9/12
Black Vulmea's Vengeance M16(11/38), B33, B65, B68, P34, P41
Black Wind Blowing M37(6/36), B62, P27
Blades for France P35, S16
Blades of the Brotherhood B12, P17, P47, A15/SE
The Block S33
The Blonde Goddess of Bal-Sagoth M4(12/50)
The Blood of Bellshazzar M23(Fal/31), B44, B64, B71
Blood of the Gods M38(7/35), B38, B73, P44
The Blood-Stained God M11(4/56), B8, P13
Bloodstar B30
Blow the Chinks Down M1(10/31), B58
The Blue Flame of Vengeance B53
Boot Hill Payoff M40(10/35), B65

Index to Story Titles

Brachan the Kelt A15/1
Bran Mak Morn B57, A13/3, A15/3
Bran Mak Morn—A Play S29, A13/3
The Brazen Peacock P29b, A6/3
Breed of Battle M1(11/31), B58
Brotherly Advice S40
The Bull Dog Breed M14(2/30), B61, B69, S45
By the Law of the Shark S52
By This Axe I Rule B47, P7

The Cairn on the Headland M4(7/48), M34(1/33), B2, B24, B76, P9, P31, P63, S56
Cannibal Fists M14(Win/38)
Casonetto's Last Song P51, P63, A12/1
The Castle of the Devil B12, B53, P17, P47
The Challenge from Beyond B59, S3
Champ of the Seven Seas M14(6/38)
Champion of the Forecastle M14(11/30), B61, B69, S46
The Children of Asshur B12, B53, P16, P48
The Children of the Night M39(4/31), B10, B57, B59, B74, P18, P30, P50, P63
Circus Fists M14(12/31), B61, S47
"The Classic Tale of the Southwest" B68
The Cobra in the Dream P45, P63
College Socks M29(9/31), A7/7
The Coming of El Borak S38
Conan, Man of Destiny M11(12/55)
Conan the Conqueror B3, P1, P5
The Conquerin' Hero of the Humbolts M1(10/36), B11, B58, B72, P56
Costigan vs. Kid Camera M14(Spr/38)
Country of the Knife M5(8/36), B38, B73, P44
Crowd-Horror M2(7/29), B69
Cultured Cauliflowers B69
Cupid from Bear Creek M1(8/35), B1, B58, P22, P56, A15/SE
Cupid vs. Pollux P52, S54, A2/7
The Curly Wolf of Sawtooth M31(9/36)
The Curse of Greed S35, A8/1, A15/7
The Curse of the Crimson God B31, P29
The Curse of the Golden Skull P7d, P27, P51, P52, A2/9, A7/2

Dagon Manor A15/3
The Dark Man M39(12/31), M39(9/54), B10, B19, B57, B74, P14, P18, P21, P49, A9/13
Dark Shanghai M1(1/32), B58

The Daughter of Erlik Khan M38(12/34), B21, B73, P25, P59
Daughters of Feud P57, A7/8
The Dead Remember M3(8/36), M10(12/61), B10, B70, P18, P30, P50, P62
Death's Black Riders B53, P52, A2/10, A6/1
Delcarde's Cat B47, P7
Delenda Est P45, P61, A7/1
Dermod's Bane M20(Fal/67), P41, P45, P63
Desert Blood M28(6/36), P57
Desert Rendezvous S40
The Destiny Gorilla B20, P24, P26b
The Devil in His Brain S35, A15/3
The Devil in Iron M39(8/34), B7, B22b, B32, B52, B55, B60, B77, P12, P38
The Devil's Joker B70, P46, A5/6, A11/3
The Devils of Dark Lake A15/1
The Devil's Woodchopper S21, A15/SE
The Diablos Trail S29, A13/3
Dig Me No Grave M39(2/37), B10, B59, P18, P30, P50, P58, P63
Diogenes of Today B14
Door to the Garden A8/2
The Door to the World B59, A15/SE
Double Cross S29
The Dragon of Kao Tsu M28(9/36), P57
A Dream A2/14, A15/2
The Dream Snake M39(2/28), B10, B66, P18, P30, P50, P63
Drums of the Sunset B70, P23, P41, A7/2
Drums of Tombalku B48, B55, P3, A13/3
Dula Due to Be Champion B61
The Dwellers under the Tombs P45

Educate or Bust B1, P22, P56
Eighttoes Makes a Play B14, A2/15
Eighttoes Makes a Play (alternate ending) A15/6
El Borak S37, S38
A Elkins Never Surrender B40, P56
Etched in Ebony A15/3
Evil Deeds at Red Cougar M1(6/36), B40, B58, P56
Exile of Atlantis B47, P7
The Extermination of Yellow Donory M41(6/70), B70, P46

Fangs of Gold M33(2/34), B62
The Fear-Master A15/5
The Fearsome Touch of Death M39(2/30), B67, S56, A9/1

The Feud Buster M1(6/35), B1, B58, B72, P22, P56, A15/5
The Fightin'est Pair B69, S46
The Fire of Asshurbanipal M39(12/36), B2, B24, B59, P9, P32, P58, P63, A2/16, A9/13, A15/7
Fist and Fang M14(5/30), B61, S45
Fists of the Desert B34, B69, P26
Fists of the Revolution A7(Special edition)
The Flame-Knife B8, P12, P55
Flying Knuckles S52
The Footfalls Within M39(9/31), B12, B53, B74, B77, P15, P28, P41, P48
"For the Love of Barbara Allen" M19(8/66), P28, P42, P62
The Frost-Giant's Daughter M12(8/53), B6, B29, B55, B60, P13, A14/1, A15/SE
The Further Adventures of Lal Singh S32

The Galveston Affair A15/3
The Garden of Fear M10(5/61), B10, P18, P30, P50, P61, S2, S56
Gates of Empire M16(1/39), B43, B64, B71, P41, P53
General Ironfist M18(6/34), B61, S47
Genseric A15/6
Genseric's Fifth-Born Son A7/10–11
A Gent from Bear Creek M1(10/34), B1, B58, P22, P56, A15/4
A Gent from the Pecos M3(10/36), B72, S34
Le Gentil Homme le Diable A15/6
Gents on the Lynch M3(10/36), B72, P27
Ghor, Kin-Slayer S53
The Ghost Camp of Colorado B70, S20, A15/3
The Ghost in the Doorway A2/11, A15/2
The Ghost with the Silk Hat S34
The God in the Bowl M26(9/52), B6, B26, B55, B60, P8
The Gods of Bal-Sagoth M39(10/31), B10, B59, B68, B74, P14b, P18, P30, P49, P51, P59
Gods of the North M11(12/56), S26, S56
"Golden Hope" Christmas B70, A5/1, A11/4, A15/4
Golnor the Ape A15/2
The Gondarian Man A7/6, A15/4
The Good Knight M29(12/31), P28, P41, A7/3
Graveyard Rats M37(2/36), B62, S34
The Grey God Passes B16, P41, P42, S13
The Grisly Horror M20(4/71), M39(2/35)
The Guardian of the Idol A15/SE

Guests of the Hoodoo Room A15/4
Gunman's Debt B70, P46
Guns of Khartum P28, P57, A6/3
Guns of the Mountain M1(5/34), B1, B58, B72, P22, P56, A15/3

The Hall of the Dead M19(2/67), B55, P8, P40, A7/1
Halt, Who Goes There! S54, A15/5
The Hand of Nergal B55, P8
The Hand of Obeah A15/3
Hand of the Black Goddess S29
Hard-Fisted Sentiment B69, S52
Hashish Land A15/3
The Haunted Hut A11/7, A15/4
The Haunted Mountain M1(2/35), B1, B58, B72, P22, P56, A15/SE
The Haunter of the Ring M30(Win/68), M39(6/34), P45, P63
Hawk of Basti B12, B53, P16, P17b, P48
Hawk of the Hills M38(6/35), B21, B73, P25
Hawks of Outremer M23(4/31), B44, B64, B71, P41, P59
Hawks over Egypt B43, B71, P53
Hawks over Shem M11(10/55), B8, P11
"He knew de Brazy..." B71
The Heathen P52, A2/13, A15/2
High Horse Rampage M1(8/36), B11, B58, P56
The Hills of the Dead M39(8/30), B2, B12, B24, B53, B67, B77, P16, P17b, P32, P48
The Honor of the Ship S52
The Hoofed Thing B59, P62
The Horror from the Mound M39(5/32), B2, B24, B68, B74, P9, P31, P62
A Horror in the Night S33, A5/3, A11/5
The Hour of the Dragon M39(12/35–1/2/3/4/36), B36, B52, B56, B63, P37, A16/1
The House A15/SE
The House in the Oaks B59, P45
The House of Arabu B54, P9, P41, P61
The House of Om A15/1
The House of Suspicion P28
The Hyborian Age B2, B6, B24, B28b, B52, B55, P8, P10, P33, P39, S1
The Hyena M39(3/28), B10, B66, P18, P30, P50, P63

In High Society B20, P24, P26b
In the Forest of Villefére M39(8/25), B10, B66, P18, P30, P49, P61
"...Includin' the Scandinavian" M14(Fal/40)

Index to Story Titles

Intrigue in Kurdistan A15/5
Iron Jaw M7(4/36)
The Iron Man M14(6/30), B34, B61, P26
Iron Men B69
Iron Shadows in the Moon B60, P40
The Iron Terror S38
The Isle of Pirate's Doom B33, P34, S18
The Isle of the Eons P51, A15/SE

The Jade God A15/3
The Jade Monkey B20, P24, P26b
Jewels of Gwahlur M39(3/35), B5, B22, B42, B52, B56, B77, P4, P38, P59
The Judgment of the Desert B70

Kelly, the Conjure-Man B68, P28, P52, P62, A2/5
Khoda Khan's Tale S38
Kid Galahad B69
King of the Forgotten People P51, P63
Kings of the Night M20(5/68), M39(11/30), B2, B19, B57, B74, P14, P21, P32, P59
The King's Service P35, S19
Knife, Bullet and Noose B70, P27, P46, P52, A2/6
Knife River Prodigal M6(7/37), B72, P28, P41, A6/1
A Knight of the Round Table B20, P24, P26b

Lal Singh, Oriental Gentleman S32
The Land of Mystery S37
The Last Cat Book B46
The Last Celt P40
The Last Laugh A7/9, A15/1
The Last Ride B70, P46
The Last White Man A2/5, A15/7
Law-Shooters of Cowtown B70, P46, A5/4
Leather Lightning M14(Win/40)
The Lion of Tiberias M24(7/33), B17, B64, B71, P19
The Little People B57, B59
Lives and Crimes of Notable Artists A9/11
Lord of Samarcand M23(Spr/32), B17, B54, B64, B71, P19
The Lord of the Dead B45, P43
The Loser S33, A6/1
The Lost Race M39(1/27), B19, B57, B66, P14, P21
The Lost Valley of Iskander B21, P25

The Mandarin Ruby B20, P24, P26b
The Man-Eaters of Zamboula B75
A Man-Eating Jeopard M6(6/36), B2, B24, B72, P32, S50
The Man on the Ground M39(7/33), M39(Fal/73), B10, B70, P18, P30, P49, P62
Man with the Mystery Mitts M29(10/31), A7/4-5
Manila Manslaughter M14(Fal/37)
Marchers of Valhalla B16, B68, P42, P61
The Mark of the Bloody Hand S34
A Matter of Age S35, A15/6
Mayhem and Taxes B40, P56
Meet Cap'n Kid B1, B72, P22, P56
Men of Iron B34, P26
Men of the Shadows B19, B57, P14, P21
Midnight P52, A2/1, A15/7
The Mirrors of Tuzun Thune M4(2/47), M39(9/29), B2, B6, B24, B47, B66, P7, P33
Miss High Hat A15/2
Mistress of Death P35, A15/SE
The Moon of Skulls M39(6/7/30), B12, B53, B67, B77, P15, P17b, P47
Moon of Zambebwei P45, P62
More Evidence of the Innate Divinity of Man A7(Special edition), A15/6
Mountain Man M1(3/34), B1, B58, B72, P22, P56, A15/2
Murderer's Grog M28(1/37), P57
Musings A15/2
Musings of a Moron P52, A2/10, A15/6
The Mystery of Tannernoe Lodge B45, A15/SE

Names in the Black Book M35(5/34), B45, B62, P43
Nekht Semerkeht B68, P51, A15/SE
Nerve S33
A New Game for Costigan B69
Night of Battle M14(3/32), B61, S47
Night of the Wolf B23, B54, P14, P20, P60
"No Cowherders Wanted" M1(9/36), B40, B58, B72, P56
North of Khyber S37
The Noseless Horror M20(2/70), P45, A9/5
Nothing to Lose M28(10/42)
The Nut's Shell S33

Old Garfield's Heart M39(12/33), B10, B68, P18, P30, P50, P58
On Reading—and Writing P40

Out of the Deep M20(11/67), P42, P61
Outlaw Working M28(11/42)

Pay Day S33
The Peaceful Pilgrim B40, B72, P56
The People of the Black Circle M10(1/67), M39(9/10/11/34), B4, B22, B52, B55, B63, P3, P38
People of the Black Coast M27(9/69), P45, P63
People of the Dark M34(6/32), B10, B59, B74, P18, P30, P50, P58, S56
The People of the Serpent A15/5
The Persians had all fled . . ." B71
The Phoenix on the Sword M39(12/32), B2, B5, B24, B56, B60, B76, P6, P33
Pictures in the Fire A15/7, P40
Pigeons from Hell M39(5/38), M39(11/51), B10, B49, B68, B77, P18, P27, P30, P49, P58
Pilgrims to the Pecos M1(2/36), B11, B58, P56
Pistol Politics M1(4/36), B11, B58, B72, P56
The Pit of the Serpent M14(7/29), B61, B69, P27, S45
Playing Journalist B20, P24, P26b
Playing Santa Claus B20, P24, P26b
The Pool of the Black One M39(10/33), B4, B48, B55, B60, P3, P41
Post Oaks and Sand Roughs B51
A Power Among the Islands S37
Prolog (The Hyborean Age) B47, P7
The Purple Heart of Erlik M28(11/36), P57

Queen of the Black Coast M4(8/48), M39(5/34), B6, B39, B55, B60, P13

Rattle of Bones M20(11/65), M39(6/29), B2, B12, B24, B53, B66, P17, P32, P47
Recap of Harold Lamb's "The Wolf Chaser." B71
Red Blades of Black Cathay M23(2/31), B14, B64, B71, P27
Red Curls and Bobbed Hair S40
Red Nails M39(7/8/10/36), B4, B28, B52, B56, B75, P4, P39
Red Shadows M39(8/28), B12, B53, B66, P17, P47
Redflame A15/5
The Reformation of a Dream S54, A9/3
Res Adventura P35
Restless Waters P51
The Return of Skull-Face B37

The Return of the Sorcerer S22, A15/3
Revenge by Proxy M28(9/42)
Riders Beyond the Sunrise P7
The Right Hand of Doom B12, B53, P17, P47
A Ring-Tailed Tornado B11, P56, A15/SE
The Riot at Bucksnort M3(10/36), B72, A9/2
The Riot at Cougar Paw M1(10/35), B11, B58, B72, P56
The Road of Azrael B43, B71, P53
The Road of the Eagles B8, B71, P11
The Road to Bear Creek M1(12/34), B1, B58, P22, P56, A15/6
Rogues in the House M39(1/34), B2, B6, B24, B29, B55, B60, B77, P8, P33

Sailor Costigan and the Swami S52, A9/7
Sailor Dorgan and the Jade Monkey A2/14
Sailor Dorgan and the Turkish Menace A15/SE
Sailor's Grudge M14(3/30), B61, S45
Sampson Had a Soft Spot M14(Spr/42)
The Scalp Hunter M1(8/34), B1, B58, P22, P56
The Scarlet Citadel M39(1/33), B2, B5, B24, B56, B60, B76, P6, P33
Sea Curse M39(5/28), M39(Win/73), B66, P42, P52, P61, A2/4
Secret of the Lost Valley M30(Spr/67), P41
Serpent Vines A15/3
The Servants of Bit-Yakin B75
The Shadow in the Well A13/2, A15/1
The Shadow Kingdom M39(8/29), B2, B6, B24, B47, B59, B66, P7, P33, P59
The Shadow of Doom A2/8, A15/1
The Shadow of the Beast P51, P58, S24
The Shadow of the Hun B71, P35, S17
The Shadow of the Vulture M24(1/34), B17, B64, B71, P19
Shadows in the Moonlight M39(4/34), B41, B55, P11
Shadows in Zamboula M39(11/35), B2, B7, B24, B28b, B32, B52, B55, B77, P12, P33, P39
Shanghaied Mitts M14(Sum/39)
Sharp's Gun Serenade M1(1/37), B40, B58, P56
Shave That Hawg! M22(1/50)
She-Cats of Samarcand A15/4
She Devil M28(4/36), P27, P57
The Shiek A15/7
Ship in Mutiny P57, S29

Index to Story Titles

Shore Leave for a Slugger M14(Fal/42)
Showdown at Hell's Canyon B18, P23
The Shunned Castle S37
The Sign of the Snake M1(6/31), B58, A5/2, A12/1
The Silver Heel S31
Skull-Face M9(12/52), M39(10/11/12/29), B2, B24, B59, B67, P31, P43
The Skull of Silence B47, P7
Skulls in the Stars M20(6/65), M39(1/29), B2, B12, B24, B53, B66, B77, P15, P17b, P32, P47
The Slave-Princess B44, B71, A15/SE
Sleeping Beauty S54
The Slithering Shadow M39(9/33), B4, B55, P3
Slugger Bait M14(Sum/42)
The Slugger's Game M18(5/34), B61, S47
Sluggers of the Beach M18(8/34), B61, S47
The Snout in the Dark B42, B55, P13, A13/3
Some People Who Have Had Influence Over Me A15/SE
Something About Eve A15/1
Son of the White Wolf M36(12/36), B38, B65, P44
The Sonora Kid-Cowhand S40
The Sonora Kid's Winning Hand S40
Sons of Hate S31
The Sophisticate S33
The Sowers of the Thunder M23(Win/32), B17, B64, B71, P19
Spanish Gold on Devil Horse P52, A2/17–18, A15/7
Spear and Fang M39(7/25), M39(Sum/73), B54, B66, P61, A2/7
Spears of Clontarf B54, S27, S34
Spectres in the Dark A13/1, A15/2
The Spell of Damballah A15/4
The Spirit of Brian Boru A15/6
The Spirit of Tom Molyneaux B69
Stand Up and Slug M14(Sum/40)
Stones of Destiny A15/4
The Story Thus Far... B63
A Stranger in Grizzly Claw A15/7
The Strange Case of Josiah Wilbarger B68, B70, A15/5
The Striking of the Gong B47, P7, P28
Striped Shirts and Busted Hearts B1, P22, P56
Sucker M14(Win/39)
Sunday in a Small Town P52, A2/11, A15/7
The Supreme Moment A15/1

Surrender—Your Money or Your Vice A15/7
Sword Woman P28, A6/2
Swords of Shahrazar M38(10/34), B31, B73, P29, P59
Swords of the Northern Sea B23, P20, P60
Swords of the Purple Kingdom B47, P7
Swords of the Red Brotherhood B33, P34

The Tale of America A15/2
The Tale of the Rajah's Ring S32
Taverel Manor P43, A15/SE
Teeth of Doom S34
The Temple of Abomination B23, P20, P60
The Temptress of the Tower of Torture and Sin M4(14/50)
Texas Fists M14(5/31), B61, B69, S46
Texas John Alden M17(Fal/50), M21(5/44), B1e
Them A15/1
The Thessalians P52, S54, A2/6, A15/4
They Always Come Back B34, B69, P26
The Thing on the Roof M39(2/32), B10, B59, B74, P18, P50, P58
Thoroughbreds A9/11
Three-Bladed Doom P36, A6/4, A15/7
Three Perils of Sailor Costigan A9/2
A Thunder of Trumpets M39(9/38), P42, S56, A9/1
The Thunder-Rider B16, B68, P42
Tigers of the Sea B23, P20, P60, A15/SE
The TNT Punch M1(1/31), B58, A9/4
To a Man Whose Name I Never Knew A15/2
The Tomb of the Dragon S24, A15/SE
The Tomb's Secret M33(2/34), B62, A9/12
A Touch of Color S33
The Touch of Death A15/2
A Touch of Trivia P40, A15/SE
The Tower of the Elephant M39(3/33), B2, B6, B24, B26, B55, B60, B76, P8, P33
The Tower of Time A15/2
The Track of Bohemund B43, B71, P53
The Treasure of Shaibar Khan B31
The Treasure of Tranicos B5, P6, P54
The Treasures of Tartary M36(1/35), B31, B65, P29
The Turkish Menace B20, P24, P26b
The Twilight of the Grey Gods P61
Two Against Tyre B71, P28, P52, S15, A2/12

Under the Baobab Tree A5/5, A11/6, A15/4
Unhand Me, Villain A15/6
Usurp the Night P51

The Vale of Lost Women M20(Spr/67), B39, B55, B60, P13
The Valley of the Lost M20(Sum/66), B68, P42, P62, S12
The Valley of the Worm M39(2/34), B2, B24, B30, B54, B77, P9, P32, P58, P59
The Vicar of Wakefield A15/5
Vikings of the Gloves M14(2/32), B61, B69, S47, A9/2
The Voice of Death S31
The Voice of El-Lil M23(10/30), B10, B67, P18, P27, P30, P49, P63, S56, A9/13
The Voice of the Mob S35, A15/4
The Vultures B18, A5/5
Vultures of Wahpeton B70, A15/6
Vultures of Wahpeton (Alternate ending) B70, A13/3, A15/6
The Vultures of Whapeton M25(12/36), B65, P23
Vultures' Sanctuary M3(11/36), M22(6/50), B70, P46

The Wandering Years P40, A15/SE
War on Bear Creek M1(4/35), B1, B58, B72, P22, P56, A15/SE
Waterfront Fists M14(9/30), B61, S45
Waterfront Law B69, S46
The Waterfront Wallop M14(Fal/41)
The Way of the Swords B43, P53
The Weaker Sex A15/6
Weekly Short Story S54
West Is West P52, A2/3, A15/7

The West Tower S40
What the Nation Owes the South A14/3
When Bear Creek came to Chawed Ear B1, P22, P56
While Smoke Rolled M8(12/56), B1e, B40, P56, A15/SE
Wild Water P23, A5/7
"The Wind from the Mediterranean..." B71
Wings in the Night M39(7/32), B2, B12, B24, B53, B76, B77, P16, P17b, P32, P48, P59
Winner Take All M14(7/30), B61, S45
The Witch from Hell's Kitchen M4(18/52)
A Witch Shall Be Born M4(10/49), M39(12/34), B7, B22, B27, B52, B55, B63, P11, P38
With a Set of Rattlesnake Rattles P52, A2/1, A15/4
Wizard and Warrior P7
Wolfsdung A13/3, A15/5
Wolfshead M39(4/26), B2, B24, B66, P9, P31, P61
Wolves Beyond the Border B56, B75, P6
Worms of the Earth M9(6/53), M20 (7/68), M39(11/32), M39(10/39), B2, B19, B24, B57, B59, B76, P14, P21, P32, P58, P59

Xuthal of the Dusk B60

Ye College Days P52, S54, A2/11
The Yellow Cobra B20, P24, P26b
You Got to Kill a Bulldog M14(Win/37)

Index to Book Titles

References are to bibliography serial numbers. This index includes Robert E. Howard book titles published commercially in hardcover or soft cover books, mass market paperbacks or in special, limited printings. Reprints are listed in categorical/chronological order.

The bibliography serial numbers are identified as follows: Books with the letter B. Mass market paperbacks with the letter P. Special printings with the letter S.

The Adventures of Lal Singh S32
Almuric B25, P2
Altars and Jesters S9
Always Comes Evening B9

The Ballad of King Geraint S41
Beyond the Borders P63
Bicentennial Tribute to Robert E. Howard S22
Black Canaan P45
Black Colossus B41
Black Dawn S5
The Black Reaper S51
The Black Stranger S55
The Black Stranger and Other American Tales B68
Black Vulmea's Vengeance B33, P34
Blades for France S16
Blood of the Gods and Other Stories B73
Bloodstar B30
The Bloody Crown of Conan B63
The Book of Robert E. Howard P27
Boxing Stories B69
Bran Mak Morn P14
Bran Mak Morn A Play and Others S29
Bran Mak Morn The Last King B57

The Challenge from Beyond S3
The Coming of Conan B6
The Coming of Conan the Cimmerian B60
The Coming of El Borak S38

The Complete Action Stories B58
The Complete Yellow Jacket S54
Conan P8
The Conan Chronicles. Vol. 1. B55
The Conan Chronicles. Vol. 2. B56
Conan of Cimmeria P13
Conan of Cimmeria. Vol. 1. B60
Conan of Cimmeria. Vol. 2. B63
Conan the Adventurer P3
Conan the Avenger P10
Conan the Barbarian B7
Conan the Conqueror B3, P1, P5
Conan the Freebooter P11
Conan the Usurper P6
Conan the Wanderer P12
Conan the Warrior P4
The Conquering Sword of Conan B75
Cormac Mac Art P60
Cthulhu—The Mythos and Kindred Horrors P58

The Dark Man and Others B10, P18
The Dark Man Omnibus Vol 1. P49
The Dark Man Omnibus Vol. 2. The Dead Remember P50
Desire and Other Erotic Poems S42
The Devil in Iron B32

Echoes from an Iron Harp B15
Echoes of Valor P64
The End of the Trail B70
Eons of the Night P61

The Essential Conan B52
Etchings in Ivory S4

The Flame Knife P55
Flight S49

The Garden of Fear S2
Gates of Empire B64
A Gent from Bear Creek B1, P22
Ghor, Kin-Slayer S53
The Ghost Ocean S28
The Gods of Bal-Sagoth P51
The Gold and the Grey S8
Graveyard Rats and Others B62
The Grey God Passes S13
The Grim Land S21

The Hand of Kane P16
Hawks of Outremer B44
Heroes of Bear Creek P56
The Hour of the Dragon B36, P37
The Howard Collector P52
The Hyborian Age S1

The Illustrated Gods of the North S26
The Incredible Adventures of Dennis Dorgan B20, P24
The Iron Man B34, P26
The Iron Man with the Adventures of Dennis Dorgan P26
Isle of Pirates' Doom S18

Jewels of Gwahlur B42

King Conan B5
King Kull P7
The King's Service S19
Kull B47, P7

The Last Cat Book B46
The Last Celt P40
The Last Ride P46
Lewd Tales S36
Lord of Samarkand and Other Adventure Tales ... B71
Lord of the Dead B45
The Lost Valley of Iskander B21, P25
Lurid Confession #1 S35

A Man-Eating Jeopard S50
Marchers of Valhalla B16, P42
Mayhem at Bear Creek B40
Moon of Skulls B67
The Moon of Skulls P15

Nameless Cults B59
Neolithic Love Song S39
Night Images B35
No Refuge S43
North of Khyber S37

Pay Day S33
The People of the Black Circle B22, P38
People of the Dark B74
Pigeons from Hell B49, P30
The Pool of the Black One B48
Post Oaks and Sand Roughs B51
The Pride of Bear Creek B11

Queen of the Black Coast B39

Red Blades of Black Cathay B14
Red Nails B28, P39
Red Shadows B12
The Return of Skull-Face B37
The Rhyme of the Three Slavers S30
Rhymes of Death S14
The Riot at Bucksnort and Other Western Tales B72
The Road of Azrael B43, P53
The Road to Rome S6
Robert E. Howard Omnibus P41
Robert E. Howard's Fight Magazine No. 1 S45
Robert E. Howard's Fight Magazine No. 2 S46
Robert E. Howard's Fight Magazine No. 3 S47
Robert E. Howard's Fight Magazine No. 4 S52
Robert E. Howard's Strange Tales S56
Robert E. Howard's World of Heroes P59
Rogues in the House B29
Runes of Ahrh-Eih-Eche S20

Savage Adventures B77
The Savage Tales of Solomon Kane B53
The Second Book of Robert E. Howard P28
Selected Letters 1923–30 S44
Selected Letters 1931–36 S48
Shadow Kingdoms B66
The Shadow of the Beast S24
The Shadow of the Hun S17
Shadows of Dreams B50
The She Devil P57
Singers in the Shadows B13
Skull-Face P43
Skull-Face and Others B2
Skull-Face Omnibus B24

Skull-Face Omnibus Vol. 1 Skull-Face and Others P31
Skull-Face Omnibus Vol. 2 The Valley of the Worm P32
Skull-Face Omnibus Vol. 3 The Shadow Kingdom P33
Solomon Kane P17
Solomon Kane—The Hills of the Dead P48
Solomon Kane—Skulls in the Stars P47
Son of the White Wolf B38, P44
A Song of the Naked Lands S7
The Sonora Kid S40
The Sowers of the Thunder B17, P19
Spears of Clontarf S27
The Sword of Conan B4
The Swords of Shahrazar B31, P29
The Sword Woman P35

Tales of Conan B8
Three-Bladed Doom P36
Tigers of the Sea B23, P20
The Tower of the Elephant B26
Trails in Darkness P62
The Treasure of Tranicos P54
Treasures of Tartary B65
Two Against Tyre S15
Two-Fisted Detective Stories S31

The Ultimate Triumph B54
Up John Kane! and Other Poems S25

Valley of the Lost S12
Verses in Ebony S10, S11
Voices of the Night and Other Poems S23
The Vultures B18
The Vultures of Whapeton P23

Waterfront Fists and Others B61
Wings in the Night B76
A Witch Shall Be Born B27
Wolfshead P9
Worms of the Earth B19, P21
Writer of the Dark S34

www.ingramcontent.com/pod-product-compliance
Lightning Source LLC
Chambersburg PA
CBHW030104170426
43198CB00009B/485